"Latah," the Malayan hyperstartle pattern, has fascinated Western observers since the late nineteenth century, and is widely regarded as a "culture-bound syndrome." Dr. Winzeler critically reviews the literature on the subject, and presents new ethnographic information based on his own fieldwork in Malaya and Borneo. He considers the biological and psychological hypotheses that have been proposed to account for "latah," and explain the ways in which local people understand it. Arguing that "latah" has specific social uses, he concludes that it is not generally appropriate to regard it as an "illness" or "syndrome."

T0381757

Publications of the Society for Psychological Anthropology

Editors
Robert A. Paul, Graduate Institute of the Liberal Arts,
Emory University, Atlanta

Richard A. Shweder, Committee on Human Development,
The University of Chicago

Publications of the Society for Psychological Anthropology is a joint initiative of Cambridge University Press and the Society for Psychological Anthropology, a unit of the American Anthropological Association. The series has been established to publish books in psychological anthropology and related fields of cognitive anthropology, ethnopsychology and cultural psychology. It will include works of original theory, empirical research, and edited collections that address current issues. The creation of this series reflects a renewed interest among culture theorists in ideas about the self, mind–body interaction, social cognition, mental models, processes of cultural acquisition, motivation and agency, gender and emotion. The books will appeal to an international readership of scholars, students and professionals in the social sciences.

Publications of the Society for Psychological Anthropology 7

Latah in Southeast Asia

Latah in Southeast Asia:

The history and ethnography of a culture-bound syndrome

Robert L. Winzeler

University of Nevada, Reno

CAMBRIDGE
UNIVERSITY PRESS

CAMBRIDGE UNIVERSITY PRESS
Cambridge, New York, Melbourne, Madrid, Cape Town, Singapore, São Paulo, Delhi

Cambridge University Press
The Edinburgh Building, Cambridge CB2 8RU, UK

Published in the United States of America by Cambridge University Press, New York

www.cambridge.org
Information on this title: www.cambridge.org/9780521472197

First published 1995
This digitally printed version 2008

A catalogue record for this publication is available from the British Library

Library of Congress Cataloguing in Publication data
Winzeler, Robert L.
    Latah in Southeast Asia : the history and ethnography of a culture-bound
syndrome / Robert L. Winzeler.
        p.   cm. – (Publications of the Society for Psychological
Anthropology; 7).
    Includes bibliographical references and index.
    ISBN 0 521 47219 9 (hardback)
    1. Ethnopsychology – Malaysia – Pasir Mas (Kelantan)
2. Ethnopsychology – Malaysia – Sarawak.   3. Latah (Disease) –
Malaysia – History.   4. Malays (Asian people) – Psychology.
5. Malays (Asian people) – Social life and customs.   6. Pasir Mas
(Kelantan) – Social life and customs.   7. Sarawak – Social life and
customs.   I. Title.   II. Series.
GN635.M4W56   1995
155.8′4992–dc20   94-14427
                                                                    CIP

ISBN 978-0-521-47219-7 hardback
ISBN 978-0-521-03137-0 paperback

latah (lah'tah) [Malay, ticklish]. A nervous affection characterized by an exaggerated physical response to being startled or to unexpected suggestion, the subjects involuntarily uttering cries or executing movements in response to command or in imitation of what they hear or see in others. See also jumper *disease*.

Steadman's Medical Dictionary, 25th edition (1990)

Contents

Maps and tables

Tables

Maps

Preface

While I have been fascinated by *latah* – the "hyperstartle" pattern of the Malays, Javanese, and other Malayan peoples – since my first stay in Kelantan in 1966–7, it was not until I had systematically worked through the many published accounts (Winzeler 1984) that I decided to do field research on the topic. The current project began in 1984 and continued in 1985–6 and involved a region of Kelantan with which I was very familiar. After completing work in Kelantan I shifted to Sarawak, Malaysian Borneo, for comparative purposes. I remained in Sarawak until the end of the summer of that year and then returned for further research in 1987, 1988, 1989, and 1990, first regarding latah and then concerning another project.

Further information about what I did where, and why, is included at various points throughout the book. In particular, as I later discuss in some detail, previous first-hand descriptions of the pattern are flawed by inadequate consideration of the range of individuals who are regarded by themselves and others as *latah*, and who are hardly "abnormal" in the usual sense of this term. In addition to obtaining new information on the meaning and social uses of latah in local settings, I needed to get in touch with a fairly large and diverse number of latah persons. My fieldwork thus consisted of four types of inquiry: (1) "participant-observation" and informal discussions with friends and acquaintances in and around Pasir Mas and in several areas of Sarawak, especially rural Lundu in the far west; (2) lengthy interviews with a hundred latah persons, about half of them Malays and half other ethnic inhabitants of Kelantan and Sarawak; (3) surveys of about six hundred and fifty households in Malay and other ethnic villages in Kelantan and Sarawak which yielded (among other things) further information on a hundred and fifty latah persons, some of whom were among those interviewed at length; (4) a broader ethnographic survey of the occurrence of latah among the principal ethnic populations in western and central Sarawak. I had intended to conduct a survey of the latter sort among the aboriginal peoples of the interior of peninsular Malaysia. However, after an initial effort in far-southern Kelantan I gave this up, because of difficulties in obtaining government permission and moving from one region to another, in favor of more substantial work in Sarawak where official policies were much more open and where travel, mainly by river, to many different villages was relatively easy.

Each of the various lines of investigation that I pursued has its strengths and weaknesses but together they provided a considerably larger and more diverse body of information about latah than, in so far as I am aware, has been previously obtained. With local assistants I did all of the research myself, using Malay. For reasons which I hope will become clear later on, I decided at the beginning of the project that I was not going to provoke latah myself or encourage others to do so on my behalf. Doubtless doing so would have provided interesting results in some instances but aside from ethical considerations, it would have probably also restricted my inquiries in other respects. Of the hundreds of persons I approached and asked for help I was flatly turned down and thereafter avoided by only one person, a latah Malay man in Pasir Mas. Some individuals were at first puzzled about my motives but, after these were explained, were willing to talk, some more fully than others, but most very forthrightly. However, the fact of my not deliberately instigating it not withstanding, I saw a fair amount of latah, several instances of which I have described in later chapters. In a few cases the interviews produced what I took to be nervous latah reactions that could not be helped; in many others the mere mention of latah led, before (or in spite of) my explanation of my purposes, to the assumption that if I was interested in latah then I wanted to see it. The attitude in such instances seemed to be "oh, so you are interested in latah, well watch this." In one incident I was nearly knocked down. Ronald Simons (1983c) has produced a valuable documentary film about latah and latah interaction, to which the interested reader is referred.

Finally, it has seemed to me that an adequate consideration of latah must include a reasonably detailed treatment of previous accounts of both latah and other patterns in the world with which it has frequently been compared. In particular, one of the main issues in the literature has involved the degree of similarity of the various instances. For some this is doubtless a sterile matter but for others – myself included – it goes to the heart of anthropology. In any case, this book is about the study of latah as well as about latah itself. Here I make no claim to have exhausted all sources. In particular I suspect that there is more to be found in the older literature on Indonesia than has so far been brought to light. And as far as the various non-Malayan instances are concerned, if I had to satisfy myself that all lines of inquiry had been pursued this book would never be finished. I have, however, attempted to provide a considerably fuller account of the study of latah and other such patterns than has yet appeared.

Acknowledgments

Financial support for this study in 1985–6 was generously provided by a research grant from the National Science Foundation (BNS8507584) and a Southeast Asian Studies Research Grant from the Fulbright Program. Research in 1984 was sponsored by a Faculty Research Award from the Graduate School of the University of Nevada, Reno. A supplemental grant from the Australian–American Educational Foundation in 1986 made possible lecture-visits to a series of Australian universities and, hence, valuable opportunities to discuss latah with Australian colleagues. Much of the writing of this book was accomplished during a sabbatical leave during the 1990–1 academic year.

My other debts in this project are also multiple. I am first of all grateful to the large numbers of latah persons and others in Kelantan and Sarawak who talked to me about latah and answered my many questions. I am also very grateful to the national government of Malaysia and the state government of Sarawak for permission to visit and do research in Kelantan and Sarawak. I also wish to thank the Sarawak Museum in Kuching for supporting my research, providing valuable letters of introduction, advice, and other assistance at the beginning of my study, and for providing an extremely pleasant and stimulating base to which I have had frequent recourse throughout all of my stays in Kuching. In Malaysia I was also helped by many individuals. I wish to thank especially Professor Wazir Jahan Karim for hospitality at the University Sains in Penang, Encik Hasan Sulong of Pasir Mas and the Kelantan Civil Service, Encik Mohammed Dollah of Pasir Mas, Dr. Peter Kedit and Mr. Tuton Kaboy of the Sarawak Museum, Encik Leo Janek of Lundu, Temenggung Anthony Sedei of Dalat, and Graman Suat of Kapit. For help in Australia I am grateful to Derek Freeman for information regarding the Iban, to David Chandler, James Warren, and the late William Geddes for information regarding the Bidayuh and for hospitality. I am also indebted to Esteban Sarmiento for translations of the Italian studies of "latah" in north Africa and Yemen, and to Ken Smith for help with the several maps used in the present work.

Many other persons have also provided valuable information or assistance, including a number who replied to my queries about the occurrence of latah among particular groups or regions: Anne Schiller regarding the Ngaju of Borneo, Bob Dentan regarding the Semai, and Karl Heider regarding the Minangkabau. I have also benefited from information and discussion regarding latah in Borneo provided by many other colleagues including Vinson Sutlive, Laura and George Appell, Allen Maxwell, Peter Metcalf, Peter Brosius, and Antonio Guerreiro. Of the many other friends and colleagues who have shared my interests in the topics dealt with in this book and with whom I have stimulating discussions, I want to acknowledge especially Ron Provencher, Bob McKinley, Susan Ackerman, and Raymond Lee. While Ronald Simons and I disagree in certain respects in our interpretations of latah, I greatly appreciate his help in formulating my own study, his hospitality, and the very stimulating exchanges we have had on several occasions.

The book itself has also had the benefit of the excellent comments and advice of several readers of various drafts of the manuscript. My colleague Marie Boutté read an early version and discussed it with me from the perspective of medical anthropology. The several readers for Cambridge University Press have been very helpful. James Peacock and Carol Laderman read an early draft and provided much useful criticism and support. Kirk Endicott similarly read a later draft with great care and offered many detailed comments and suggestions. I am also grateful for the interest, advice, and help Bobby Paul provided as an editor of the monograph series in psychological anthropology of which this book is a part. My daughter Elizabeth Winzeler provided the fine drawing which forms the frontispiece. My wife and colleague Judy Winzeler has been a part of the project from the beginning, from the fieldwork through the editing and proofreading, and it is to her I owe my deepest thanks.

Parts of chapters 1 and 2 were first published in different form in *Indonesia*, vol. 37, 1984, while different versions of chapters 7 and 8 first appeared respectively in the *Sarawak Museum Journal*, vol. 41(62), 1990, and in *Female and Male in Borneo*, edited by Vinson Sutlive and published by the Borneo Research Council.

Introduction: the problem of latah

My first encounter with *latah* was in 1966 while I was living in Pasir Mas, Kelantan, early in my initial period of fieldwork (Map 1). It was a minor incident but it impressed me and led to further inquiries. I was walking across what was then an open field in the center of town. Several women were in front, one of whom slipped on some loose gravel at the side of the railroad track running through the field. This woman quickly exclaimed a sexual obscenity and repeated *"mati"* (dead/death/die) rapidly several times. The outburst lasted only a second or two. Others in the vicinity looked around but did not pay much attention. The woman who had slipped regained her balance and proceeded on.

Having read the older literature on the Malays I was familiar with latah and later mentioned the incident to Pak Tengah, one of my friends who lived in a nearby village and who was for me a major repository of information (and whose own wife became slightly latah many years later). He told me about other persons in the vicinity who were also latah, and he and other villagers told me about things that some latah persons had done. One of the incidents he described was especially interesting because it was reminiscent of an episode recounted by Hugh Clifford (1898) in a famous early article on latah. Clifford's account focused on an episode he reported as involving two Malay men that took place in his house in rural Pahang. His cook, Sat, and a visitor were seated on a mat facing one another and chewing *sirih* (betel). A malicious boy who knew that both men were latah suddenly came up and struck the *sirih* box that was sitting on the mat between them with a piece of rattan. The men both jumped and began to shout obscenities and to repeat and imitate each another. This continued for a half an hour until both fell over in exhaustion "foaming horribly at the mouth." Clifford went on to say that he was unaware of what was happening until it was over, at which point he intruded and nursed the men back to consciousness. He asked the men what had happened but they claimed to remember nothing except sitting and eating *sirih*.

The incident recounted to me by Pak Tengah was reminiscent of Clifford's tale in that it also involved two latah men who continued to

1

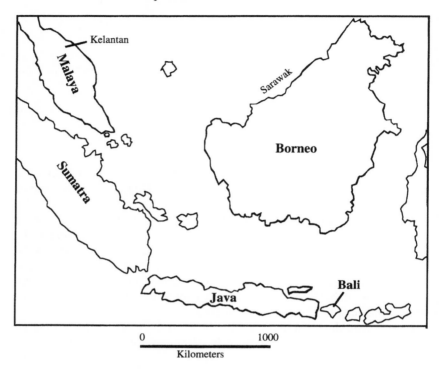

Map 1. Malaya, Java, Borneo

provoke one another in a continuing manner. In this instance one latah man was preparing *laksa*, a fresh rice noodle used in a favorite Malay festive dish of the same name. Another man, who was also latah, came up to watch and talk. Then a third man, who had been standing around with some friends and who knew that the men conversing over the *laksa* were both latah, came up and suddenly shouted *"ramas laksa!"* (knead the laksa!). Both of the latah men were badly startled (*kejut*) and began to repeat *"ramas laksa"* and to knead the dough in imitation of one another. Pak Tengah described the incident as a "story" (*cerita*) which he knew rather than an occurrence which he himself had witnessed. I have sometimes wondered if this story somehow had its origins in Clifford's written account or, alternatively, if the incident that Clifford described derived in whole or part from Malay oral tradition.

In the mid-1980s I returned to work systematically on latah. My decision to do so was due partly to my previous interest and partly to the emergence of renewed discussion and controversy about latah and about what has come to be known as the "culture-bound syndromes." Latah itself has been an important topic of Western discourse about Malayan peoples for a long period of time. By the middle of the nineteenth century or soon after, European observers in Malaya and Java began to note that certain persons upon provocation, usually by a startle, would behave in the manner noted above – shout an obscene utterance, or in some instances imitate words, gestures or actions, or automatically obey commands that would not normally be followed. They also noted that it affected certain individuals slightly and others very strongly, that the pattern was well known to the Malays and Javanese themselves, and that it apparently occurred among other Malayan peoples as well, though this was less certain. In the last decades of the nineteenth century and the early decades of the twentieth, numerous accounts of latah in both Malaya and Java were published which offered further instances or new interpretations.[1] From these latah soon made its way into the second- and third-hand literature of manuals of tropical medicine and psychiatric handbooks as a recognizable (if apparently incurable) mental disease of uncertain nature, where it tended to remain.[2] Eventually also on the basis of this existing literature latah became a standard textbook case of an exotic psychosis or neurosis in studies in culture and personality, then in psychological anthropology[3] and more recently in medical anthropology.[4]

Beginning in the late 1970s latah was taken up again as a theoretical problem by anthropologists and transcultural psychiatrists in a series of articles (Drush 1984; Kenny 1978; Murphy 1972, 1976; Simons 1980) and in a documentary film (Simons 1983c), followed by further exchanges (Kenny 1983; Murphy 1983; Simons 1983a, 1983b). These discussions have focused on various issues but especially on the "latah paradox," an idea set out by Hildred Geertz in 1968. The paradox, in brief, is the proposition that while latah can only be understood in highly specific cultural terms, unique to the Javanese (or to the Javanese and other Malayan peoples) it occurs also among various distant peoples as well.

It has been noted concerning Malayan studies that writing about latah as well as *amok* and other favorite colonialist topics created and perpetuated images of mental deficiency of the Malayan Other, which justified and encouraged European domination (Alatas 1977: 48, 177). No one who has read the older accounts of latah would likely deny that they would contribute to such Orientalist notions, which is not to say that the observers who wrote them intended to do so. Such accounts do typically contain general observations about Malayan character which might both indicate inferiority and suggest the possibility of improvement under European influence. Orientalism everywhere involved certain assumptions about the psychological nature of the Oriental Other – about such matters as stability, sensuality, femininity, and masculinity. In Malayanist versions of Orientalism, sensuality and femininity (focal points of Indological Orientalist concern [Inden 1990: 115–116]) were seldom raised, but instability was given great emphasis. It was axiomatic that Malays, Javanese, and other Malayan peoples were by nature "nervous," "sensitive to the slightest insult," "volatile," preoccupied with maintaining balance and composure, and so forth. Such psychological tendencies were held to be in part a matter of inherent character and in part a consequence of despotic political rule and a rigidly hierarchical social order that was to be changed through the creation of a new way of life under European guidance.

The accounts of latah written in the second half of this century are less subject to such criticism. Westerners have been responsible for the bulk of the more recent work on latah but Asian scholars have also produced both descriptive and interpretative studies. In particular, the findings and ideas of P. M. Yap will be referred to throughout this book. A brilliant Chinese psychiatrist who was born in Malaya and educated at Cambridge and the University of London, Yap is responsible for both one of the most important accounts of latah and the development of the notion of "culture-bound syndrome" (Yap 1952, 1966, 1967, 1974). There are also more specific studies of Thai and Malay latah by the Thai psychiatrist Sangun Suwanalert (1972, 1984) and of Javanese latah by the Javanese psychiatrist R. Kusumanto Setyonegoro (1971). Nor are the culture-bound syndromes – the category of psychic afflictions into which latah is (rightly or wrongly) generally put – still regarded, as theỹ formerly were, only as exotic patterns found among non-Western peoples. As will be noted below, one of the main applications of the concept in recent years has been to the interpretation of various conditions and afflictions in post-industrial Western (and Japanese) society.

Whatever colonialist associations the study of latah may continue to have, the topic is also a matter of interest and importance to contemporary Malays. It continues to figure in national consciousness as a symbol of traditional Malay culture in various ways. During the mid-1980s latah was shown on Malaysian television in two different contexts. One of these was a humorous government commercial in which a person was startled and then repeatedly said "buy shares." The other was a serial drama about an urban Malay family in which the kindly but old-fashioned and perplexed grandmother Opah, for whom the drama was named, was latah. The use of latah in an advertisement and in a popular drama as a characteristic of a sympathetic figure strongly indicates that it continues to be viewed with curiosity and amusement by the mass Malay audiences to which such material is directed, and that it continues to be regarded as a part of Malay life.

Another incident involving latah which also received national publicity was of a tragic rather than an amusing nature. It took place in the bitter and divisive aftermath of the "Memali" incident in 1985 in which the police used force to arrest a dissident religious leader and his followers in Kedah, resulting in the deaths of eighteen persons. Among those reported killed was an elderly woman. The critics of the police action and of its justification by the ruling Malay political party cited the killing of a harmless woman as pointless brutality. The government response was that the woman had not been harmless for she was killed while waving a knife and acting like she was attempting to attack. This, however, drew the retort that the woman had been behaving that way simply because she was latah. She had, it was said, become startled by the noise and confusion and was simply imitating what she had seen around her. However pathetic, this incident also suggests that latah comes readily to the minds of contemporary Malays.

Latah and the culture-bound syndromes

The resurgence of interest in latah over the past several decades has been closely associated with the emergence of the culture-bound syndromes as a central focus of discussion in transcultural psychiatry and in medical and psychological anthropology. As originally formulated by Yap (1966) and first applied to latah, *amok*, *koro* (all initially linked with Malayan peoples), and a few other instances, the concept of culture-bound syndrome meant a class of abnormal and pathological patterns found in non-Western societies which could not be readily explained in Western psychiatric terms. Given the acknowledged complexity of understanding Western, let alone non-Western, mental health, and the existence of competing theoretical systems in psychiatry and psychology, there was room for disagreement and reinterpretation. But there appeared to be consensus among a community of scholars that culture-bound syndromes existed and that they should be explained through a synthesis of ethnographic and psychiatric or psychological knowledge. Conferences were held, proceedings were published, and further instances were discovered and described (Caudill and Lin 1969; Pfeiffer 1968, 1971, 1982; Lebra 1976).

By the 1980s the culture-bound syndromes had become a matter of controversy. In the case of one of the classic instances (Windigo psychosis, the cannibal compulsion complex) the actual existence of the pattern itself had been disputed (Marano 1982). While this has not been so of most of the others, questions have begun to be raised about the general field of inquiry. Some scholars who have conducted research or read the literature on one or another reported syndrome, or who have examined the general logic of the concept, have either expressed basic doubts about its meaning or utility, or have advocated its abandonment altogether (Hahn 1985; Hughes 1985a; Jilek and Jilek Aall 1985; Karp 1985).[5]

The problems have concerned both the "culture-bound" and the "syndrome" parts of the concept. In regard to the former, the problem (well illustrated by latah) is how restricted a "syndrome" must be in order to be regarded as "culture-bound" rather than "universal," or at least "transcultural." Nor does the assumption of complete cultural relativism solve the problem. For if all syndromes (or at least all those with a mental or behavioral basis) are said to be culture-bound, then the phrase "culture-bound syndrome" is redundant. In regard to the latter (also well illustrated by latah) the problem is in determining how pathological (and how frequently so) a pattern of behavior must be to be considered a "syndrome" rather than something else. Yap originally meant the notion to refer to a psychosis, the severest form of mental disturbance, although he acknowledged that this would not fit in the case of all the persons said to be suffering from one or another syndrome. Yet it soon became apparent that such use was often inappropriate, that it was often difficult to tell how dysfunctional an exotic pattern of behavior was, and that in some instances it might not be dysfunctional at all.

But if the culture-bound syndromes have become controversial they have also increased in importance as a field of inquiry. Over the past decade the scope of the concept has continued to be expanded and more and more new examples have been noted. A glossary published in 1985 includes more than 180 instances, though some are different ethnic versions of the same pattern (Hughes 1985b). Most notably, however, the notion has been increasingly applied to a variety of conditions and maladies occurring in modern post-industrial society as well. Examples coming from the United States and Great Britain include *para suicide* (overdosing of medical drugs), *agoraphobia* (inability to go into public places alone), *anorexia nervosa*, shoplifting (by affluent persons), flashing (Littlewood and Lipsedge 1987), and even obesity (Ritenbaugh 1982) and "adolescence" (Hill and Fortenberry 1992). In Japan such syndromes include the "childrearing neurosis," the "high-rise apartment neurosis," the "kitchen syndrome," and the "school-refusal syndrome," all of which are recognized by Japanese psychiatrists and the public as "diseases of civilization" and "medicalized" (Lock 1992). Roland Littlewood and Maurice Lipsedge (1985, 1987) have sought to generalize about a wide range of both old/non-Western and new/Western culture-bound syndromes. They attempt to use the older culture-bound syndromes as a model for analyzing the newer ones, and they seek to show what all of them have in common with other ritualistic, expressive, dramatic modes of behavior.

The present study

With the exception of spirit-possession, few of the culture-bound syndromes have been the focus of extended, ethnographically and historically contextualized treatment.[6] For the most part the literature has been one of notes and articles, book-chapters and anthologies, rather than of monographs and books on particular instances.

Latah is particularly appropriate for more detailed consideration. As two recent analysts point out, it has been the most frequently discussed and most important of the culture-bound syndromes (Prince and Tcheng-Laroche 1987: 11). It has also been the most controversial. The status of latah both as "culture-bound" and as a "syndrome" have been sharply disputed. Further, as with the literature on the older culture-bound syndromes generally, much of the discussion of latah has had a strong armchair character. The reader who is familiar with the recent discussions of latah will know that, overall, they are considerably longer on interpretation and argument than on new information. Several of the most important and stimulating modern accounts have been written by scholars who have not claimed to have seen a latah person at first-hand, or in one instance to have been near the Malayan world, let alone latah.

The organization of the book and the use of the term "latah"

In the remainder of this book I develop more fully the background to my own inquiries and discuss the results of my own fieldwork. The book is organized into four parts, the first of which concerns the historical and comparative background of the problem of latah. I begin in the following chapter with the history of European discourse about latah in Malaya and Java from the nineteenth century to the present, including the recent arguments with which I am most concerned. In Chapter 2 I deal with the specific question of whether the existing evidence indicates a pattern of demographic change in the occurrence of latah over time, and in Chapter 3 I examine the controversy regarding the comparability of the non-Malay and non-Javanese cases and then evaluate the information which has played a greater or lesser role in theories about latah, including that from Africa and the Arabian peninsula, northern Eurasia and North America, as well as the broader region of Southeast Asia.

In Part II I present my own information and develop an interpretation of the pattern in more general terms. Chapter 4 deals with latah in present-day Kelantan, first and principally among Malays and then among several non-Malay populations. After this I take up in Chapter 5 the question of the nature of the relationship of latah to Malay (and Malayan) culture, initially with regard to notions about metaphysical transformation and magic and then regarding altered states of consciousness. In Chapter 6 I continue this line of inquiry and discuss the social uses and context of latah.

In Part III I shift to Borneo. Here I first discuss in Chapter 7 the occurrence of latah in Sarawak and attempt to show that its spread from

Malays to various Dayak groups is based upon its compatibility with indigenous Bornean ideas, sentiments, and social practices. I follow this in Chapter 8 with a more specific analysis of latah among the Iban, the largest of the Dayak peoples of northwestern Borneo. Following these eight chapters I conclude in Part IV with a more general discussion of the problem of latah and the culture-bound syndromes.

My own use of the word latah itself presents a problem that requires some initial comment. As noted earlier, once the Malayan term *latah* became well known it was often applied to other apparently similar patterns noted elsewhere. The result is that the term has achieved a general usage in the comparative literature of psychological anthropology and transcultural psychiatry approaching that of "mana" and "taboo" in ethnology and comparative religion. The use of "latah" to refer to startle reactions in different parts of the world which have certain notable family resemblances to it is perfectly reasonable. However it creates a problem when one of the points of contention is the extent to which the Malayan pattern is the same as those found elsewhere.

There are various possible ways of distinguishing references to Malayan latah from those concerning "generic" latah. One would be to italicize or capitalize the latter (Simons's [1980] solution). I prefer to set off generic latah with quotation marks, as "latah," in part because I have concluded that some of the patterns so labelled are much more similar to the Malayan one than others. Admittedly this or another means of distinguishing generic from Malayan latah is open to objection in the sense that not all forms of Malayan latah are necessarily the same. Nor is Malayan latah referred to everywhere in the same way. I am aware of three other local words for latah in different areas of Borneo, and there may be others. However, the term latah is extremely widespread among Malaysian and Indonesian peoples, including all of those among whom I gathered information in both Kelantan and Sarawak.

Part I

The problem of latah

1 The study of latah

The earliest European account to be cited as an actual or possible reference to latah (by Yap 1952: 516; Murphy 1972: 43) is contained in J. R. Logan's journal of his trip from Melaka into Naning, published in 1849. A visit to the house of a villager had been arranged. Upon arrival Logan was met at the gate by his host whose character and behavior struck him as peculiar. It is his description of what occurred next that has been cited, though not quoted:

At first his manner was embarrassed and apparently dry, and his efforts to break through the restraint under which he laboured were abrupt and highly grotesque. When we ascended into the veranda he blurted out his welcome again, jerked his head about and bent his body forward, and shifted his position every second. He was most delighted, he said, highly honoured, but oppressed with shame. His house was such a miserable hut, and he was such a poor, ignorant, vile person, mere dung in fact! "*Sáyá oráng méskín tuán, – oráng bodo – tái,*" and so he continued vilifying himself, and accompanying each new expression of humility by a sudden and antic alteration of his attitude and position. (Logan 1849: 29)

Little about this episode is latah-like.[1] There is no mention of the blurting out of any obscenities, of any verbal or gestured mimicry. It is, of course, possible that the man did say something obscene which Logan chose not to mention in his account. Even so, Logan, while finding it extraordinary, did not identify it as latah or latah-like. Nor evidently did his Malay companions. As an ethnologist with a well-developed interest in Malay culture and language Logan should have been familiar with latah, if it existed in its later characteristic form and had come to the attention of European observers. However, while such a description would suggest that Europeans were by that time still unaware of latah it would not prove it.

Whether or not Logan had witnessed an instance of latah, the pattern had entered European cognizance by the 1860s when it was clearly identified in both Malaya (by Thomson [1984: 170] in 1864) and Java (by F. J. van Leent [1867: 172–173]). By the mid-1870s it was included in at least one European Malay dictionary (Favre 1875(2): 501) and by the 1880s references and detailed descriptions of latah in both places were common.

For Java, for example, the naturalist Henry Forbes provided descriptive and analytical notes on "that curious cerebral affection called by the natives latah." He reported that it was confined chiefly to women, but that he had also seen a man affected, that it was caused by startle or excitement, and that latah was fairly common, at least among the Javanese with which he had contact: his own male servant became latah at the sight of a caterpillar, as did his host's maid when she unexpectedly met a large lizard (Forbes 1885: 69). As was typical in regard to latah for the next several decades, Forbes provided anecdotal material on latah attacks which he instigated and which suggest that the line between science and mischief was sometimes thin. He described one incident in which he provoked a servant into eating a piece of soap and another in which he caused this same person to tear off her clothes by flicking a caterpillar on to her dress (Forbes 1885: 70).

For Malaya, H. A. O'Brien's notes (1883, 1884) are the most comprehensive for this period, and the most extensively cited in later writings on the topic. Although modest (as a "non-scientist") about his own abilities to interpret what he found, O'Brien identified many of the basic features of latah and attempted a classification of sub-types, an enduring preoccupation of latah scholars. He also sought to relate the condition to Malay character and briefly explored the etymology of the term. Latah, he noted, was essentially a Malay malady, weakly exhibited in Bengalis, Sikhs, and Tamils, but never in Chinese – a claim that was contested at the time by other observers. More women were latah than men; and it was rare among younger women but common among mature women. O'Brien supposed further that latah was related to *amok* in that both were a manifestation of an intensified nervous sensibility (O'Brien 1883) and suggested that he had evidence to support this.[2] Finally, if the early non-medical accounts of latah were clearly influenced by late nineteenth-century European psychological ideas, they were also constrained by late nineteenth-century standards of propriety. Because of the "popular nature of the journal" O'Brien thus noted that he was unable to report fully the sexual obscenity which he took to be an important but puzzling dimension of latah.

However circumscribed, common knowledge of latah among Europeans with an interest in Malayanist topics continued to develop in the closing years of the century. The British proconsuls Frank Swettenham and Hugh Clifford both published influential accounts at this time. These were popular rather than technical or theoretical and appeared in books of "tales and sketches" of Malaya, a literary form in which both men were prolific and successful. As with the other sorts of topics on which the two wrote, their approach to latah was anecdotal, based upon actual events and persons, but embellished with the style of the essayist or writer of short stories. Their material was drawn from their own career experiences in

Malaya which extended from the establishment of British protection in the Peninsula in the 1870s. The focus was on individuals they had known who were colorful or in one way or another interesting. They claimed with considerable justification to have been familiar with Malays in all walks of life and in a range of locations in Malaya. But judging from both the nature of the work they did and the content of their writings, they were especially familiar with two sectors of Malay society. The first were the royalty and nobility, whom they first had to pacify and then work closely with in developing and administering indirect rule; the second were their own personal retainers including household servants, bearers, boatmen, and police. In their writings on latah this latter category was especially significant. Swettenham's study thus focused upon the cases of two men who were both members of his personal police force, while Clifford's dealt with latah among his household servants, especially his cook.

Of these two individuals, Swettenham (1900[1896]: 82) made little claim to offer an explanation of latah, except to say he imagined that it was a nervous disease "affecting the brain but not the body." Clifford, on the other hand, was more confident in this regard. Like O'Brien and most of the other non-medical observers of the period, he was inclined to explain latah simply by reference to the Malay racial character, specifically by a tendency to nervousness. All Malays, he stressed, were to some extent latah, and capable of developing into a typical case if sufficiently teased, persecuted or harassed. Here he also introduced another favorite European causal notion into the discussion. This was that the nervousness to which all Malays were prone and which underlay latah was probably due to the climate. It was, he asserted, within the experience of every European who spent time in Malaya that his nerves were affected by the climate. And if a European became jumpy and nervous after a few years in Malaya then it was no surprise that a race which had spent many generations there had become morbidly so (Clifford 1898: 198).

In noting that overt latah was induced through repeated teasing and harassment Clifford came close to offering a sociological thesis. He departed from such an interpretation when he asserted – perhaps incorrectly – that it equally affected all sectors of Malay society. However, he made an additional brief observation about latah among his servants that is interesting in this regard, though it was not followed up. This was that latah appeared to be contagious: "It was about this time that a number of other people in my household began to develop signs of the affliction" (Clifford 1898: 192). He went on to say that what he meant by this was not that latah in his household had been spread by "infection," for he learned that those who had newly begun to display latah had already been previously subject to occasional episodes. However, once in his household, where they were exposed to the severe attacks of his poor bedeviled cook, Sat, they began to lose the control that they had previously exercised over their condition.

Both Clifford and Swettenham also offered observations about the pattern of occurrence of latah that have frequently been cited by later scholars. Clifford asserted that it was to be seen among all classes of Malays – "the well-fed and gently nurtured, as often as among the poor and indigent" – though among women more than men, and always among adults rather than children (Clifford 1898: 195). In fact, however, as with Swettenham, the instances he discussed were all among his male servants. Swettenham suggested that it appeared to him to be common, but much more so in some regions and among some Malay ethnic sectors than others. "Thus while there is generally one or more *orang-latah* to be found in every kampong in Krian, where the Malays are mostly from Kedah, in other parts of Perak it is rare to ever meet a latah person" (Swettenham 1900[1896]: 65–66). Otherwise he held it to be more common among the people of Amboina (in the Moluccan Islands of present-day Eastern Indonesia) than among the people of Java, Sumatra, or the Malay peninsula. How he knew this to be so, except that the two latah men in his police force were both Ambonese, he did not say.

Beyond the fact that it provided vivid case material – of which by then, however, there was certainly no lack – Clifford's discussion of latah opened an argument between what may be called medical and anthropological interpretations. His account was written in reaction to the existing medical reports of the period. He considered these to be lacking in compassion and humane understanding: "It is doubtless difficult for a medical man to always bear in mind that a patient is a human being, in the first instance, and a 'case' purely incidently" (Clifford 1898: 187). In contrast to the doctors who described a latah case as if it were a bug on a pin, he presented himself as a "mere untrained observer" who had gained his knowledge "from living among Malays, often in constant daily intercourse with latah folk," rather than being carefully educated in some school of pathology. In this same vein he was also caustic about European license in experimenting upon Malays by provoking latah reactions in the name of science (Clifford 1898: 197). While Clifford did not name names he probably had recently-published reports by Gilmore Ellis and John Gimlette especially in mind. However, his sarcastic reference to the practice of provoking latah reactions does not appear to have discouraged further medical experimentation. This in fact continued, but in new directions.

Early medical reports

By the 1890s latah had thus attracted considerable interest among colonial doctors in both Java and Malaya. Their reports do show greater effort to fully describe latah clinically and to explain it in positivistic, scientific terms. For Java C. L. van der Burg and P. C. van Brero both produced accounts. The former argued that the locus of the problem of latah was in the central nervous system. Akin to hysteria, it thus consisted of an increased irritability of the brain, which gave rise to peculiar functional disorders (van der Burg 1887). The account of van Brero, who was then serving as a physician at the asylum in Buitzenzorg (now Bogor), was similar. He suggested latah, which he held to be very common, involved an "increased excitability of the nervous system which must extend to the cortex," and a "paralysis of the will" (van Brero 1895: 537). Having a physiological basis the condition was thus presumed to be hereditary. However, it also represented in acute form traits which were general among the Javanese, namely a "mental feebleness which prevents them from becoming independent in thought and action, so that there is always a weak development of individuality" (van Brero 1895: 537). He also felt that since the disorder warranted serious medical interest it needed a scientific designation rather than the vulgar "latah." He thus proposed the phrase "provoked imitative impulsive myospasia" (van Brero 1895: 538). This did not, however, catch on and does not appear in the later primary literature, except when Yap (1952: 517) held it up to ridicule many years later as an "astounding name."

For Malaya, on the other hand, Gilmore Ellis (1897: 32–37), then the medical superintendent of the government asylum in Singapore, defined latah more or less along the same line as a "transitory nervous condition that was difficult to classify" and provided the first of a number of technical terms for latah symptoms, in this instance "coprolalia" for what had been previously referred to as verbal "obscenity." It was to be followed by "echopraxia" for verbal mimicry and "echolalia" for bodily mimicry. He also raised or commented upon several issues that were to continue to interest analysts (Ellis 1897: 33). One of these was the similarity of the mimetic form of latah to hypnosis, and another was the much-asked question of a possible connection between latah and amok – though here he observed that latah episodes were of much shorter duration, and that there was no evidence that latah persons were prone to amok, or that those who had run amok had been especially subject to latah. Ellis (1897: 40) further supposed that latah was hereditary in that it attacked a large portion of the members of a family. He also noted that women were more frequently affected than men, and older women more frequently than younger (Ellis 1897: 40).

The bulk of Ellis's treatment of the topic consisted of a discussion of a series of latah cases which were used to illustrate his two types of latah – paroxysmal and imitative. Several of these were redundant with ones discussed by O'Brien (1883) or were taken from his article. One, however, which contained new information, concerned a latah man who, when startled, would shout "puki" (vagina), and throw whatever he had in his hand at the nearest person (Ellis 1897: 36). Here we learn for the first time that among the words commonly expressed in latah reactions, which had before been referred to only as "obscenities," are slang terms for genitalia. We are also provided with a specific example of a latah person who is Eurasian rather than Malay or Javanese.

John Gimlette also published an important medical report from another part of Malaya at this time. Gimlette, who was then serving in the interior of Pahang, provided a clinical description of two latah women which included information on the results of physical examinations (neither of which yielded any particular clues about the pattern). One woman was a midwife, both were married and middle aged. Gimlette does not appear to have found the latah behavior of either woman amusing. Indeed, he referred to one as a "pitiable exhibition" and his descriptions of both are among the starkest to be found in the latah literature:

... the patient was gradually robbed of her power of self consciousness and command. She invariably repeated aloud the suggestions offered to her, and not only imitated grimaces, however absurd, but mimicked different qualities of voice, and repeated strange English words with remarkable accuracy. On being handed a box of matches and told to eat it, the operator at the same time pretending to masticate, she had no hesitation in commencing and declaring it delicious; but on the suggestion of another person that it was pork, she readily threw the box away with an expression of great disgust. (Gimlette 1897: 456)

Gimlette's explanation of latah was positivistic but eclectic. He described it in neurological terms as "... having its origin perchance with both hysteria and hypnotism in a neurosis which lowers nerve force and brings about an abnormal reflex discharge of it" (Gimlette 1897: 457). He also thought that heredity played a great role in the development of latah while neither social position "nor hygiene" was involved. No increase in latah could be seen among boys educated under newly imposed government supervision. While latah was usually common among the poor inhabitants of obscure villages, cases were also encountered in Singapore and in the larger Malay towns. Gimlette also thought that the condition might have links with the "mixture of religion and superstition with the fearful belief in devils, familiars, and ghosts so common among Malays ..." (Gimlette 1897: 456). On the popular question of a possible link between latah and amok, he suggested that both reflected a pattern of "morbid impulses," a matter which he viewed in a sort of Dr.-Jekyll-and-Mr.-Hyde perspective:

In both cases – self-control being lost for the time being – the attention is occupied mainly by a single idea – in the latah woman by an uncontrollable desire to imitate, in which the servile portion of human nature is unconsciously displayed; in the amok man, by a reckless idea to persist in killing, in which the wild beast part of a man comes uppermost. (Gimlette 1897: 457)

Finally, Gimlette suggested that while latah might be prevented through "the gradual removal of ignorant superstition by means of lucid education," a cure was impossible without a more precise knowledge of the physiological pathology involved, which would have to be verified by post mortem examination. However, he also suggested that experimentation upon monkeys, which are by nature highly mimetic, might prove useful (Gimlette 1897: 457).

While neither of these suggestions appears to have been taken up or, if so, reported, further medical experimentation was pursued in several directions. In one instance Percy Gerrard, a surgeon posted in Pahang, published a brief article in 1904 in which he described a single, advanced case of latah that he had attempted to treat with hypnosis. He reported that by putting the woman into a hypnotic state he was able to relieve a severe attack:

Having ordered her to lie down the order was promptly obeyed, while she repeated it to herself. I then told her to go to sleep, and closing her eyes with my hand, I made some direct contact passes over her, the forehead and temples, suggesting at the same time, sleep. . . . I then suggested, "You are now quite well again, and you must wake up." She opened her eyes and sat up, uttered a long sigh, and when asked what she had done, declared that she had done nothing. (Gerrard: 1904: 16)

Another effort at experimentation at this time concerned crime. If latah behavior bore some resemblance to a hypnotic state, as several observers had suggested (though Bramwell [1903: 356–357], an authority on hypnosis, argued against this), then the possibility existed that a latah person would obey a command to assault or even kill another person. This possibility, which had been raised by several writers, was pursued by William Fletcher, a surgeon at the mental hospital in Kuala Lumpur. Fletcher (1908: 254–255) reported several instances – one told to him by Wilkinson – in which a Malay had maimed others during a latah episode and posed the question of whether a latah person would follow a command to attack another person. He thus performed an experiment with a latah female patient in which a large amputating knife was suddenly thrust into her hands and a command was shouted at her, "Kill that woman and steal her jewelry." As a result, the patient "rushed at the bed and with great force drove the knife into the blanket and the raincoat underneath. Hardly had she struck before she uttered a cry of remorse and threw herself back with a look of horror on her face." Fletcher than shouted the command "kill" (*potong* [actually "cut"]) at her again and she fell to hacking the raincoat with her knife (Fletcher 1908: 255).

While experimentation appears to have ceased with this effort, occasional new contributions continued to be published by local medical authorities about the possible causes of latah. At one point it was suggested that one of these might be the chewing of betel nut (Abraham 1911: 249) though the author of this observation took it back a year later in a subsequent publication, noting shrewdly that he had been informed that there were places where betel was chewed but which had no latah. The same author also raised and then dismissed, for a similar reason, the possibility that latah was caused by the effects of tropical climate – Clifford's argument – and concluded that the causes of latah remained unknown (Abraham 1912: 439). More generally, local medical interest in latah was beginning to be played out by the second decade of the century. Descriptions of Malay latah continued to appear in secondary works of both a popular and technical medical nature but published evidence of primary investigations waned.

Freudian and other psychiatric interpretations of latah and personality

Beginning in the 1920s, a new series of accounts appeared. These differ from the earlier ones in a number of respects. The early non-medical accounts treated latah as a manifestation of racial character traits ("nervousness," "sensitivity") found among Malays in general – traits which, it was supposed, might in turn be explained by the influence of the tropical climate (Clifford 1898). And while early medical interpreters presumed that latah had an organic neurological basis – if a poorly understood and largely unexplained one – the colonial psychiatrists returned to psychological factors and their context. One such study was by David Galloway (1922: 140–150). While he offered little that was new in the way of substantive information, Galloway referred to Freud and Yung (sic), drew upon psychodynamic concepts at some points, and prefaced his interpretation with an attempt to develop a profile of the Malay personality in relation to the setting of traditional village life. He observed that Malay villagers traditionally had abundant time on their hands (a major theme in the colonial-Malayanist literature) and that much of this leisure was

... spent in daydreaming or abstraction, really a subconscious state. It is difficult to conceive more favorable conditions for such a state than in a quiet village, with its warmth, its stillness and the absence of any disturbing element. So long as these moods of abstraction are intermittent and occasional, they are quite within the normal limit but when they are prolonged, as in the "fakir," they pass that limit and may be looked on as an auto-hypnosis, or in any case, a hypnoidal state. (Galloway 1922: 143)

And since the Malay tended to operate so much in the realm of the subconscious he was readily influenced by suggestions or stimuli which would be rejected by the conscious mind. The language that was used by the latah when provoked reflected a breakthrough of repressed materials (Galloway 1922: 143), a notion that has remained a central thesis of psychodynamic interpretations.

In Java medical thought about latah appears to have been on the same track. F. H. G. van Loon, a lecturer in neurology and psychiatry in the Medical School in Batavia (now Jakarta), published a series of papers on latah, amok, and Malayan personality that introduced new data as well as new ideas into latah studies (van Loon 1927: 439–444). In regard to latah, he offered a psychodynamic interpretation based on the role of dreams. These (he did not say how many he collected or how many latah persons were involved) were always basically the same. They specifically concerned "one or more naked men, or penes in erection, wriggling like worms, trying to attack the dreamster, etc." (van Loon 1927: 440). He argued that they indicated sexual repression because the dreamer always awoke with a start. He also held that repression explained why women were more prone to latah than men: Javanese men did not, he felt, suffer any check on their sexual needs. Moreover, the greater sexual repression that Malay women experienced was combined with a greater degree of "infantile primitiveness" that was characteristic of women in general. This combination provided the basis for the hyper-suggestivity and loss of will that occurred with latah (van Loon 1927: 440).

Following the studies of van Loon (and the later ones of van Wulfften Palthe [1933, 1936], also a professor at Batavia), psychiatric interest in Malayan and Indonesian latah appears to have lapsed until the early 1950s when P. M. Yap turned his attention to it. In a long article Yap – a British-trained Chinese psychiatrist – reviewed the development of Malayan latah studies and discussed the state of psychiatric knowledge regarding hysteria and other possibly related forms of psychopathology (Yap 1952: 515–564). He also presented the results of his own field investigations in Malaya, which included interviews with seven latah persons, and offered an interpretation of nosological status of the syndrome. Latah, he argued, was essentially a "primitive fear reaction" or neurosis. Those affected react with fright "because of an overwhelming sense of hazard ... they are unable to develop adequately their own biological apparatus of mastery, and react to fear-stimuli by a disorganization of the ego ... a dissolution of the body-ego ..." (Yap 1952: 557–558). Yap did not stress the breakthrough of subconscious material, though he did clearly link latah to psychosexual factors.

Yap also attempted to explain latah in relation to personality, as had often been done in the past, asserting that it is associated with passivity, submissiveness, and a "weakly integrated personality":

The untutored person in Malay society, especially in the case of females, is a shy, retiring, nonaggressive, self-effacing, changeable and colorless person, with little individuality, in so much as her whole life is spent within the confines of her family, and molded by the monotonous demands of infancy, childhood, wedlock, and motherhood in a simple and static rural environment. (1952: 553)

Not all Malays exhibit such personalities, he cautions, but those who are latah do.

Such assertions either imply or claim that latah individuals have personalities which in these respects are distinguished from those of others.[3] Yet little of the specific biographical information provided by earlier observers supports such notions. In some instances Europeans reported discovering that a Malay was latah by accident after having known the individual for a long period of time. Rathbone (1898: 57) thus wrote that

unless you happen by chance to hit upon the subject upon which they are *latah*, you may never discover that there is anything wrong with them. On one occasion I accidentally found it out in a man whom I had known for years, often travelled with, and never suspected to be at all afflicted with any sort of nervous complaint, for several times to my knowledge he had behaved in a very plucky way.

In other instances the personality of the latah individual was described in terms quite different from those said to characterize latah persons in general. In well-known accounts, both O'Brien and Clifford made this point about latah men that they had known: O'Brien said of one of his workmen that while the man would become latah at the mention of the word "tiger," he was in the habit of spending nights alone in the jungle, by which he presumably meant that the man was not otherwise fearful or timid. Similarly Clifford (1898: 189–190) wrote that his cook Sat, "who was the most typical case of *latah* within my experience ... [was] ... the last person in the world, one would have thought, to be the victim of any nervous disorder"; and that Sat "had been an inmate in my hut for nearly a year before any one discovered that he was *latah*." Nor was Sat unique in this respect, for Clifford (1898: 192) went on to say that at one point others in his household also began to develop signs of latah which, he subsequently learned, they had – unbeknownst to him – previously had.

Dreams and consciousness

Dreams have received considerable but sporadic attention in latah studies over a long period of time. In 1897 the psychiatrist Ellis reported that Malays had on more than one occasion told him that latah was caused by dreams. He dismissed this suggestion as of little interest by noting that the Malays were simply great believers in dreams, ghosts, and the like (Ellis: 1897: 40). A few years later Gerrard (1904: 14), a medical doctor who experimented with hypnosis in relation to the latah of a Javanese woman in Malaya, did mention a specific dream. "During the post-latah sleeps [*sic*] she dreams invariably that she is flying amongst white ladies and men, all winged, and some of them riding on winged horses." Gerrard did not, however, attempt to explain or comment on the significance of the dream.

Subsequent accounts of latah have in some instances mentioned dreams or included information on them and in other cases not. In his report on latah in Java, the Dutch colonial psychiatrist van Loon (1927: 440) reported that the natives commonly attributed latah to dreams, that such dreams were of an explicitly erotic character, and that they indicated sexual repression. Fifty years later the psychiatrist W. Pfeiffer (1968) found the same sort of erotic dreams of male organs recounted by the latah women he interviewed in East Java as van Loon had earlier described. Hildred Geertz (1968), on the other hand, makes no mention of dreams, sexual or otherwise, in her account of latah in Central Java. As for Malaya, the psychiatrist P. M. Yap, while undoubtedly aware of van Loon's accounts of erotic dreams among latah persons in Java, did not deal with them in his review of the literature or in his interpretation of latah; nor did he report dreams in his case studies of latah persons in Melaka, except to say that in one of these instances there were "anxiety dreams" (Yap 1952: 537). Nor does Ronald Simons (1980, 1983a, 1983b) mention dreams either in his comments on his own field material (also from Melaka) or in his interpretation of latah.

It is tempting to suppose that the pattern of report and omission of mention of dreams in Western accounts of latah reflects factors relating to the investigator and the investigation – the investigator's own scholarly if not personal predispositions and the conditions under which information was gathered. This is likely to be in part the case, but it may also be possible that dreams, erotic or otherwise, are subject to variation, occurring and being attributed much significance regarding latah in some places and not in others. As we have seen, the woman described by Gerrard (1904) who associated her latah with a dream of flying among winged-white ladies and gentlemen was actually said to have been a Javanese. Of the existing accounts of latah in Malaya, Java, and Borneo, those noting erotic dreams all concern the latter two places, and then only in some reports.[4]

As with dreams, attention to alterations in consciousness as a characteristic of latah have been inconsistent. A problem here is that what is involved are both observations of apparent behavior during latah – that is more or less radical changes in consciousness – and explanations of how or why the activities of imitation and automatic obedience occur. Further, there is no commonly used vocabulary by which to describe what an observer thinks may or may not occur during latah. The early reports, which show less reticence than later ones, offered differing opinions about the extent to which persons were able to recall what had occurred at the time of latah. Ellis (1897: 34) described one person during an episode as "conscious," and noted that while "Consciousness is certainly sometimes lost during a paroxysm, ... in those cases I have seen it is not the rule." Gerrard (1904:

16) on the other hand reported that the woman upon whom he experimented with hypnosis was in a state of mental giddiness, as not recognizing people, being absolutely unaware of what had occurred, having no recollection of anything later, and of requiring a full half-hour to return to normal following latah. Quite apart from the matter of conscious awareness and memory, early observers frequently referred to latah in terms of hypnosis – as "very like hypnosis" (Ellis 1897: 33), as "self-hypnosis" (Gimlette 1897: 457), a form of "autohypnosis" or a "hypnoidal state" (Galloway 1922: 143), and so forth.

Later observers of latah became more guarded about making assertions about states of consciousness and memory, or of offering interpretations referring to autohypnosis and the like. Yap (1952: 544) thus refers to "clouded consciousness" and "reduced consciousness" and suggests that while knowledge of hypnosis may offer certain insights about how imitation and automatic obedience may occur in latah, comparisons are otherwise false (Yap 1952: 543). Of the recent theorists of latah, only Murphy (1976) makes the alteration of consciousness a central part of the explanation of latah and its relation to the Malayan ethos; he also refers to certain analogies with hypnosis in Western societies.[5] Further, absent in both recent and earlier European reports is any reference to Malay or Javanese ideas about alterations in awareness, consciousness or memory in regard to latah.

Epidemiology

The "epidemiology" of latah is a matter that most writers have addressed in one way or another from the late nineteenth century onward. At one point the Dutch psychiatrist van Loon had attempted to survey the occurrence of latah by sending a questionnaire to some six hundred physicians throughout the Netherlands Indies. Of these, one hundred and six replied, of whom eighty-six had witnessed latah and were able to provide satisfactory information on one hundred and sixty-nine cases. The questionnaire asked for information on the number of latah persons observed and on the age, sex, and ethnic group of each.

P. M. Yap also took a particular interest in this matter. His own information on the occurrence of latah was based on interviews with seven latah women in the Melaka area. From these data and from a review of the literature he concluded that latah was characteristic of unsophisticated rural persons, above all women, and that it was unlikely to exist in urban areas.

But while such a generalization may have fit with existing reports of latah in Malaya, it did so less well with those concerning Java. In his earlier survey, van Loon had been interested in the question of whether latah was especially common among natives in contact with European society, as well as whether they were urban or rural. He thus asked whether latah persons were *orang udik* ("jungle people") – that is, villagers living away from Europeans – or whether they were people who had considerable contact with European society (van Loon 1924: 309). The responses that he got indicated that latah was less common among villagers than among natives living among Europeans, presumably in towns and cities. These also showed that latah was especially common among servants. These formed a large portion of those identified in the survey, followed by artisans. Ordinary village farmers, who would presumably most fully typify Yap's general category of "unsophisticated rural person" were not present at all.

The "epidemiology" of latah thus appears to be confused. Van Loon's survey was subject to fundamental bias. European doctors, and probably also Indonesian or Eurasian ones, would have been concentrated in the towns and in the regions of the Indies where there were larger European populations, above all in Java. They were thus certainly more likely to observe those natives in contact with European society than the "jungle people." And of course latah among servants in Dutch colonial households would have been most often noticed. Van Loon himself noted that whereas European doctors did not tend to report latah cases from among the ranks of the *orang udik* the native doctors did.

However, more recent reports also present an uncertain picture of the occurrence and milieu of latah in Java. Two studies published in 1968, one by a German psychiatrist and one by an American cultural anthropologist, give seemingly contradictory results. In her study based on research in the Central Javanese town of "Modjokuto" (Pari) in the early 1950s, Hildred Geertz reports that latah was especially common among lower-class townsmen, and that extensive inquiries showed that it was lacking among villagers in the rural environment surrounding the town. She thus suggests that latah was associated not with "tradition" but with "marginality" and noted that the proletariat to which all of her latah cases belonged was a modern development. Such individuals lacked the "support of a firm tradition which might provide such a lower class status with intangible satisfactions, or at least the conviction that membership in it is a part of the natural order of things" (Geertz 1968: 103). The fact that so many latah women had been servants of Dutch families was further indication of the importance of marginality. One woman Geertz learned of was reported to have become latah upon beginning employment as a servant, and two others, who were also from the servant class, had been mistresses of Dutchmen.

Wolfgang Pfeiffer, on the other hand, found some twenty-two latah persons in eastern Java, all of whom were villagers. They were mainly either lower-status workers at the hospital, petty traders or agricultural laborers. He also noted that, contrary to earlier reports, none of his cases included servants or former servants of Europeans; all were from traditional village backgrounds (Pfeiffer 1968: 34–35; 1971: 89). Finally, in an even more recent study, James Siegel (1986: 30–31, 285, 314) reports that as a result of frequent questioning of people of various social ranks and neighborhoods he found no latah at all among the inhabitants – lower class or other – of Solo in Central Java.

2 Latah, history, and gender

It is possible that the apparent ambiguity and contradictions regarding the occurrence and milieu of latah may be explained as a matter of change. This is one of the major revisionist interpretations. The transcultural psychiatrist H. B. M. Murphy seeks to show that what seems to be a muddled epidemiological picture actually reflects a pattern of development over time. He takes bits and pieces from the accounts of various observers and attempts to arrange them into a coherent picture showing a pattern of development from the latter part of the nineteenth century to the recent period. Murphy's (1976: 11–12) general model is that of an infectious disease:

Some of these changes [that latah has undergone] might be interpreted as the result of an infection – a mild encephalitis, for instance – brought in by Europeans and spreading outward like the wave in a pond from a dropped stone, leaving immune populations in its wake.

Latah thus began, he suggests, among natives in contact with Europeans in cosmopolitan centers of the Malayan world and then spread among Malays, Javanese and, eventually, other ethnic groups. It initially affected adults in general – that is men and women, the more and the less intelligent, and persons of all social strata. Then, however, as well as moving outward and disappearing from the regions in which it had begun, it came to affect mainly rural persons, those of lower social strata, those older in age, and women.

The beginning of what Murphy calls the story of latah is, of course, its origins. He asserts that there is little evidence of latah in the Malayan world before the latter part of the nineteenth century. Murphy thus assumes that the development of latah had to do with the political and cultural changes which were beginning to affect Malayan societies deeply at this time. Since Europeans did not have latah, they could not have introduced it in the way they did various infectious diseases, into newly penetrated areas of the world. Latah was rather a native reaction to the evolving European presence, in which case it had more in common with nativistic or millennial movements than with a communicable organically based affliction:

... it seems preferable, therefore, to think of the Europeans not as bearing some infection but as creating or precipitating a new social problem, and when one approaches the problem from this angle the obvious key is rapid social change. (Murphy 1976: 12)

But how would this produce latah? It is Murphy's contention that latah was an overreaction based on indigenous attitudes toward authority and learning. Malays and Javanese lived in hierarchical societies in which persons were especially inclined to look to those in powerful positions as guides for correct conduct. And since culture was for the most part transmitted orally there was an emphasis on learning by rote and example. Around 1850 Europeans came to be increasingly seen as powerful figures worthy of copying. But since Europeans were also very different, efforts to do so were inherently problematic and frustrating, which led to extremes, that is to latah. And once latah had developed among those natives in contact with Europeans it developed a life of its own and spread to other sections of Malayan societies:

the condition is moving away from the centers of European influence and into the countryside. According to Fletcher's account (1908), it is now quite frequent in such locations as Pahang and upper Perak, with cases encountered every day in the streets and courtrooms there, whereas anecdotal sketches and medical reports from Singapore, Batavia, Penang and Melaka almost cease to mention it. (Murphy 1972: 45)

For the modern scholar this is certainly an attractive argument, not in the least for its ironic conclusion that a pathological condition which earlier colonial scholars had taken to be a manifestation of traditional Malayan mentality had, in actuality, developed as a response to European domination. There are, however, several questions. For one thing, how certain can we be that latah is such a "history-bound" syndrome, that it appeared and developed when it is suggested it did? The facts of Murphy's claim about the earliest European awareness of latah have not so far been shown to be incorrect. Logan probably did not describe an incident of latah in Naning, Melaka in 1845. Nor (in so far as I have been able to determine) did any of the other leading British Malayanists of the early and mid-nineteenth century who prided themselves on their expertise – Raffles, Marsden, or Crawfurd – ever take note of it.[1]

The significance of the time of the first European reports of latah is another matter. The evidence regarding the temporal point of origin is mainly of a negative sort so far as European accounts are concerned. Murphy's assertions about the development of latah in the Malay world assume that European accounts more or less accurately indicate its onset. But it has been suggested in another recent, revisionist account (Kenny 1978) – one that seeks to interpret latah as very much a part of traditional

Malayan culture and, therefore, not only present but more important in the past than in the more recent period – that latah was there all along, and the fact that Europeans did not record anything about it may only mean that they did not bother to do so, or that they did not know what to make of it.

It is true that the British Malayanists, at least, thought about Malayans as persons in different ways in the first and second parts of the nineteenth century (Maier 1988: 30–61). In the latter part of the eighteenth and the first part of the nineteenth centuries British ethnology remained essentially non-racial. The Malays and other Malayans were thought of as a "nation" which shared a common human nature with other peoples (including Europeans) although they were lower on the scale of cultural-evolutionary development, that is civilization. By the latter part of the nineteenth century the British had largely abandoned such notions about the commonalities of human nature in favor of racial thought in their interpretations. The differences between Malayans and other peoples, especially white Europeans, were thus assumed to be not only great but inherent.

It is also possible (as Kenny [1978: 213] notes) that the emergence of psychology and psychiatry as modes of discourse about human behavior made it more likely Europeans would take note of latah in the latter part of the nineteenth century than before this time. As we have already seen, European awareness of latah and similar patterns elsewhere first crystallized at the same time – the mid-1880s. But while significant, are such differences in earlier and later thought about Malays really adequate to explain how latah could have been as common in Malaya and Java (as it was held to be later in the nineteenth century) and not have been noted and described by Europeans in earlier periods – if only as an inscrutable curiosity? While amok was not treated in psychiatric terms until the middle of the nineteenth century (Oxley 1849) it had been frequently noted by Europeans for several centuries before this time. It is of course true that interest in latah was not as deeply rooted in the sort of utilitarian considerations that partially accounted for the attention paid to amok. At times amok was regarded as a significant threat to public safety, and when it was not, it was still thought necessary to convey this information to readers of accounts of the Malay lands (Winzeler 1990a). However, pragmatic interest in latah was not entirely lacking. At one point it was suggested that persons may have occasionally injured or even killed others while latah, resulting in court cases to determine guilt. As we have seen, Dr. Fletcher (1908) was sufficiently taken with such possibilities to concoct a wild experiment to see if a latah person could be made to commit a violent assault upon another. And as his account showed, there was at some points considerable interest in a possible connection between latah and amok. It was supposed that an accidental attack of the former might lead to the latter or, more commonly, that latah and amok were different manifestations of common underlying tendencies in racial character.

However, if Murphy's assertions about the late European recognition of latah are correct, his claims about the evidence of Malayan literature are more dubious. There is, in the first place, the question of the origin of the term itself, a matter which Murphy passes over without comment. It is true that earlier efforts at etymological speculation mainly illuminate European naiveté. In the case of Malay latah, O'Brien (1883: 144) noted in his early article that one etymologist had attempted to connect the term "in defiance of spelling, with *melata* [,] to creep." He went on to observe that this derivation was implausible and that he could not account for the antecedents of the current Malay usage. It now seems likely, however, that the origin of Malayan use is to be found in J. Gonda's (1973: 373) *Sanskrit in Indonesia*. Here a connection is suggested with the Sanskrit *lata-* ("defect; one who speaks like a fool, a fool").

Of course, such a derivation does not establish the antiquity or the origin of latah as it came to be later known, for an older term may be used to refer to a new pattern. The presence or absence of references to patterns similar or identical to present-day latah in older Malayan texts is thus of greater significance. Murphy (1972: 43; 1976: 11) evidently regards this evidence as important for his argument but asserts that while he is aware of two references to latah in such texts (often referred to as the *hikayat* literature but including other forms as well), these identify "a simple startle reaction or ticklishness and not the syndrome later called latah." While this statement is itself somewhat misleading (in that Malays themselves did not later identify latah as a syndrome, Europeans did), it is also based on a dubious reading of the sources. Murphy mentions two earlier references in Malay texts and cites Wilkinson's (1902) dictionary as one source. In fact, Wilkinson bases his (very interesting) entry on latah on not one but six different Malay traditional texts. His reference, following a brief, conventional, definition of latah is as follows:

... *Maka permainsuri pun latah-lah saperti orang gila tiyada khabarkan diri-nya*: the queen fell into a fit of *latah* and became as one mad, not knowing what she was doing; Ht. Koris. *Karena bonda Morah di-dalam latah-nya barang kata orang semuwa di-turut-nya*: Mother Morah is suffering from one of her fits of *latah*; all that people say she mimics; Ht. Koris. *Pura-pura latah*: pretending to be a *latah* subject; Sh. Bur. Nuri, 23.
Bukan-nya patah, ruwat;
Bukan-nya latah, di-buwut:
it is not broken but bent; it is not hysteria, it is only pretence; – a proverbial expression, the first line of which is often given to suggest the second.
L. mulut: a slight form of *latah* in which a shock causes the victim to fly into a paroxysm of coarse language but nothing more; Ht. Raj. Don., 4.

Latah is often used metaphorically of the madness of love. *L. wilangan*: id., Ht. Mas. [4] Ed. Ht. Perb. Jaya. *L. wilangan kesmaran*: id., Ht. Perb. Jaya. *Hanyah-lah tuwan hamba latahkan*: I am mad with love for you alone; Sh. Lail. Mejn. *Latah menyebut mas tempawan*: madly repeating "*mas tempawan*" (a term of endearment; Sh. Panj. Sg.) (Wilkinson 1902: 587–588)

In contrast to Murphy's inference, these references suggest that the range of behaviors (losing consciousness, mimicking, repeating, expressing coarse language, pretending) mentioned in the Malay texts are the same as those reported by later observers as latah. More effort might be devoted to establishing what was said about latah in these and other Malayan sources at various points in time. However, it would seem that real latah was well known to Malays before (perhaps long before) it came to the attention of Europeans.[2]

The later part of the latah story concerns the changes suggested in the European record of observation over time and in different places; that it moved from urban to rural areas and to new regions; and that it changed from being a syndrome likely to affect men as well as women, younger as well as older persons, and people of all social strata, to one affecting mainly women and poorer sectors of society. But is such a pattern really evident in the mosaic of existing accounts? Did observers make statements or provide evidence which lead to such conclusions, or if they did were they based on adequate knowledge? Or is the story of latah partly a consequence of the way that it has been told by different kinds of observers with varying perspectives over time? There is some reason to suppose that this is the case.

As we have seen, the instances of latah described by the earlier observers were of individuals they encountered in the course of their work and travels. In offering observations about the distribution of latah among the regions or peoples of the Malayan world they seem to have generalized, perhaps extravagantly, from their own experiences or from what others before them had written. The notion that latah first occurred equally among all Malays is based upon generalizations by several early observers (Fletcher and Fitzgerald are cited by Murphy [1972: 45] but Clifford [1898: 195] also observed that "people afflicted with latah are as often found among the well fed and gently nurtured, as among the poor and indigent"). Such assertions were not well supported by either full discussion or specific examples.

Perhaps the most interesting and important issue in the story of latah is the pattern of observation and interpretation concerning gender, and the question of whether this shows real change over time. The general assertions made by later observers about Malay latah and gender differ little from those of the late nineteenth century although most of the specific instances that are noted or described by the former are women. That latah in Malaya in the early period occurred almost as often among men as women is doubtful. It is true that, overall, the specific persons described in the early accounts are as frequently male as female. In fact, the latah persons in those reports written by non-medical observers in Malaya are nearly all males. However, there is good reason to suppose that the observers who produced the accounts were more likely to be familiar with Malay men than women. Further, all of these observers who commented on the frequency of latah among men and women claimed (or in the case of O'Brien implied) that it was more common among women than men (Clifford 1898: 195; Ellis 1897: 40; Gimlette 1897: 456; O'Brien 1883: 152; Rathbone 1898: 57; Swettenham 1900[1896]: 73).

There is also a significant difference between these accounts and those provided by medical observers. The medical reports, which became common around the turn of the century, noted only women who were latah. They were also based upon knowledge of particular latah persons, some of whom, however, were patients, including female patients. It is not clear whether such patients had sought help because of latah (unlikely), because of other problems, or even if they sought help at all. They may have been persons with psychological problems that were severe enough to lead them to seek therapy from a European doctor but which were incidental to latah. Nonetheless, the doctors probably had greater familiarity with Malay women in the late nineteenth and early twentieth centuries than did other European men.

There may have also been more subtle reasons why medical doctors more than other observers saw latah as a distinctly female problem. They were more inclined to define it in medical terms; that is, as a "syndrome," "illness," etc., which warranted diagnosis (and, occasionally, experimentation) leading, perhaps, to prevention and alleviation. A variety of medical and psychological ideas, including hysteria and hypnosis, were applied in such medical efforts; none except hysteria really endured. As Dr. E. W. Ballard put it in a curt note to the *British Medical Journal* in 1912, it was "unnecessary to attribute latah to opium, hashish, betel chewing, climate etc., as some people have done." It was simply hysteria and hysteria was "commoner among women, and after puberty" (Ballard 1912: 652). Matters progressed further once psychoanalytic notions came into circulation and the study of latah was taken up by colonial psychiatrists in the early 1920s. Freudian perspectives were in fact something of a revelation. The long-noted, but previously only circumspectly described, coprolalia and the newly revealed sexual dreams invited a diagnosis that latah involved a breakthrough of unconscious processes, and that it was caused by sexual repression. In any case, the Freudian revelation also explained latah as a female pattern, a possible consequence of which was that male latah was subsequently neglected. Finally, latah, which was certainly held to be very strange, would appear to fit with such racial notions of Otherness better than it did with the earlier conceptions of a universal human nature; it was held to be a racial characteristic, as we have seen – something which the Malayan race and perhaps some of the other Brown ones had but that Europeans (and here no cognizance was apparently taken by the European Malayanists of the French Canadian "Jumpers" in Maine) lacked.

Changes in opportunities for observation and in modes of interpretation thus probably account for at least part of the changes in the proportions of male and female latah persons to be seen in European reports over time. Such changes are further diminished if the British reports are distinguished from those concerning the Netherlands Indies. Like those concerning Malaya, the early reports about Java state that latah is mainly a female pattern. It is also the case, however, that many fewer latah men were reported in the early accounts about Java than in those about Malaya. This probably reflects in part a different pattern of interaction between Europeans and natives, and hence of opportunities for observation. In nineteenth-century Malaya the non-medical accounts were written by men (most influentially by Clifford, O'Brien, and Swettenham) who were involved in an early phase of colonial empire building. To judge from the instances they noted, the Malays among whom they saw latah were males – household servants, policemen, bearers, boatmen, and companions. In Java most of the early reports were written by medical men (van Leent, Neale, van Brero) who, like their counterparts in Malaya, in some cases knew about latah among female patients, and thus similarly provided women as examples.

But it is also likely that non-medical observers in Java were more familiar with latah among other women, at least servant women, than in Malaya. Here domestic colonial society was far more established than it was in late nineteenth-century Malaya, at least outside of the Straits Settlements. The European resident in Malaya at this time was likely to be a single man who was surrounded by Malay men. But the European resident in Java was more apt to have lived in a family household which had female servants. The link between servants and observations about latah is present in the early accounts of both places, as already noted, though it came to be especially stressed in interpretations about the pattern in Java. The ratio of female to male servants in European households may therefore partly account for the generalizations (and expectations) about the prevalence of latah among women during the colonial period.

Finally, it is also possible that, whatever the exact ratio was, latah was simply less common among males in Java and adjacent areas than it was in Malaya – or, also, that it was less common generally and thus less likely to be observed among men. In any case, the accounts of latah in the Indies do not indicate any real pattern of change over time regarding the proportions of men and women who were affected. Van Loon's (1924: 308–310) survey in the early 1920s found that a very high proportion were women (one hundred and fifty seven to four men). In an account referring specifically to Sumatra that was published several decades later, Adam (1946) discussed a Malay woman and noted that latah was mainly a female pattern, referring, however, to van Loon's survey. In subsequent accounts, both Pfeiffer (1968) and Geertz (1968) report finding only women in the course of their enquiries. However, both of these efforts included far fewer latah persons than van Loon's broader survey, and concerned only specific regions of Java. There would thus appear to be little basis for inferring a decline in latah among men from either the late nineteenth century to the 1920s or ·from then to the 1930s and 1960s on the basis of these several studies.

In summary, much of the evidence cited in support of the claim that latah has developed in a manner analogous to that of an infectious disease seems weak upon close examination. However, two points remain significant. One which has already been noted is that it is puzzling that there is little if any European reference to latah before the middle of the nineteenth century, and relatively little before the 1880s. This however needs to be set against the possibility that latah in some form is an old pattern in Southeast Asia, a matter to which I shall return. The second point concerns the spread of latah into new areas and groups among which it did not formerly occur. This possibility forms the topic of a later chapter on latah in Borneo.

3   "Latah" elsewhere

At about the same time that widespread attention was drawn to Malay latah by O'Brien (1883), two influential accounts of exotic startle patterns elsewhere in the world appeared. One of these concerned what was called "Jumping" and occurred among French Canadians of Maine in one corner of North America; the other involved the inhabitants of northeastern Siberia who were said to be prone to *miryachit*. Gilles de la Tourette's first published account of the "tic malady" which now bears his name, was based upon his reading both of O'Brien's account of latah and of reports of Siberian *miryachit* and French Canadian *jumping* (de la Tourette 1884). De la Tourette initially thought that the behavior involved in these exotic maladies was the same as that which he had observed among his own European patients at Saltpêtrière, although his teacher and colleague J. M. Charcot subsequently pointed out that the patterns were not the same (Shapiro and Shapiro 1982: 17).[1] Eventually yet other, apparently similar, startle patterns were noted for both these same general regions and new ones. Some of these concerned areas adjacent to the Malayan lands (Thailand, Burma, the Philippines) while others involved aboriginal Japan, Arabia, and Africa. In most (though not all) instances the pattern was well known to the local inhabitants and identified with a particular term.

Once attention had been drawn to the similarity of latah to startle patterns found elsewhere, most scholars who wrote about one or another of them also made reference to the others. In his account of Malay latah Ellis (1897: 32) noted that it was "allied if not identical with" *miryachit* of the Siberians and Lapps, the Jumping Disease of America and *Bah-Tschi* of the Siamese. Gimlette (1897: 456) drew similar comparisons, mentioning the "emotional diseases of most other countries, for example those of Grinqualand, Norway and Iceland" and *Ramaninjana* of Madagascar. Later writers cited yet other instances – Fletcher (1908: 254) and Galloway (1922: 140) both made reference to Abyssinia while in a later account Fletcher (1938: 642) claimed that a condition similar to latah "was not uncommon among Hottentot half-castes in Southwest Africa" but gave no source.[2] Generally based on secondary sources rather than a reading of the original accounts, such references to startle patterns in other places were perfunctory and were provided as background or contextual information rather than as a problem for consideration; and they were often erroneous. Where efforts were made at explaining the distribution of the various instances, these usually concerned either climate or race, and in the latter case either some specific race (Malayan or Mongoloid) or "primitive races" in general.

Eventually more serious attempts were made to examine the comparative evidence. In 1952 both David Aberle (an anthropologist) and P. M. Yap (a transcultural psychiatrist) sought to explain Malayan latah in relation to similar patterns elsewhere. A central purpose of Aberle's account was to report new information on the reaction among Mongols and other Central Asians. But since the literature on Malay and Javanese latah was particularly extensive, he devoted considerable attention to these instances and to the question of its similarity to other startle patterns. Here he wrote that

Comparison of accounts of Malay latah, the imitative form of "arctic hysteria," the North African condition, and the French Canadian (or mixed French-Canadian and American) Jumpers of Maine, with the Mongol *"belenci,"* etc., and "acting" *belenci, etc.* indicates that all of these syndromes are identical, symptom by symptom, except that coprolalia is not mentioned for the Jumpers or for North Africa. (Aberle 1952: 294)

Aberle does point out that latah was quite different from one form of Arctic Hysteria with which it had earlier been confused, and he also concluded that it was clearly not the same as Tourette's tic malady. But with these exceptions he concluded that "latah" was an appropriate term not merely for the Malayan pattern but also for the others as well. Aberle was certainly not the first to use the term in this general manner but he was among the first to try to justify it.

A further purpose of Aberle's study was to determine how the existence of "latah" in different places could be explained. If highly specific reactions occur among a limited number of different peoples, it followed that these peoples should have something in common that is absent elsewhere. His conclusions on this point were negative. He of course dispensed with the notion that "latah" was linked to tropical climates – an idea already abandoned in Malayan latah studies – or to either hot or cold extremes of climate, as had also been suggested. Nor did he find comparative support for a link between "latah" and the "Mongol" race, or between "latah" and amok – an enduring, if controversial, idea in the Malayan latah literature (Fletcher 1908: 254–255). Nor did it seem possible at that point to form a theory of the nature of the distribution of "latah" throughout the world with regard to cultural areas, types of social structures or child-rearing practices. The only factors which thus appeared to be widely characteristic of "latah" beyond its own symptoms were features of individual personality.

P. M. Yap, who carried out an entirely separate study of latah (focused on the Malays) that was published in the same year, was concerned with much the same comparative issues. He noted also that French, Italian, English, and Dutch observers had long been using the Malayan term for non-Malayan instances, though he seemed at first less certain than Aberle that such use was justified, noting that "discussion of its [latah] nature betrays inadequate understanding" (Yap 1952: 515). Yap went on, however, to speak of "the latah reaction under its various local names" and proceeded to inquire as to what the societies in which "latah" occurred, and the individuals who had it, had in common. Here he was particularly concerned to dispel the notion that "latah" could have anything to do with race. Beyond this Yap was rather more confident than Aberle about specifying what various "latah" peoples did have in common: the "latah" reaction, he thus noted, was found in culture complexes which were "by comparison to modern civilization, both East and West, little developed. The peoples showing it (not excluding the Jumpers) are peasants, grazers, hunters and fisher-folk and are naturally possessed of unsophisticated mentalities" (Yap 1952: 550).

"Latah" as a theoretical paradox

Whether or not it was because the studies of Aberle and Yap appeared to leave little more to be said without fresh evidence on the comparative occurrence of "latah," interest in the comparative problem lapsed until Hildred Geertz (a cultural anthropologist) took it up again in the late 1960s. She wrote from the perspective of latah among the Javanese, about which many accounts had been written in an earlier period but which had been the subject of no real theoretical analysis since the studies of van Loon and van Wullften Palthe in the 1920s and 1930s.

Accepting the cross-cultural existence of "latah" as reported in the accounts of Aberle and Yap, Geertz suggested that in regard to the Javanese this constituted a "theoretical paradox," which she posed as follows: latah "fits" with Javanese culture in that it is a complete inversion of right and proper forms of behavior. As such it is a potent, if relatively harmless, means of expressing psychological trauma. While latah would be eccentric in any society, such eccentricity is especially meaningful to the Javanese in several ways: it controverts highly valued polite behavior and it involves the use of obscene language, which is particularly disturbing to the sexually prudish Javanese; it is provoked by shock or startle, which are especially dreaded by the Javanese; and it parodies superior–subordinate relations, which are one of the pillars of Javanese social structure (Geertz 1968: 98–99). Yet while latah is particularly, perhaps even uniquely, meaningful to the Javanese as an expression of deviance, it was found in many other societies – that is, ones beyond the Malayan world – which presumably have little in common with specific Javanese cultural prejudices. She asked that if "latah" were a culture-linked malady, how could it be so similar in diverse cultures (Geertz 1968: 103–104)?

Geertz thus posed a challenging question that can be answered in several ways. One is to suggest that the information on which its premise is based is incorrect, that "latah" does not, after all, occur outside of the context of Javanese (or more broadly and correctly, Malayan and adjacent) cultures, and the evidence that it does is faulty. An alternative answer is to accept the cross-cultural reality of "latah" and to suggest that it reflects a basic human tendency to react to startle in a limited number of ways which may, for whatever reasons, become developed in some cultures. There are perhaps other answers (including the possibility that each of the foregoing ones may be partially correct) but these are the two that have been proposed and rigorously argued about in several articles and exchanges by Michael Kenny (1978, 1983, 1990), a cultural anthropologist, and Ronald Simons (1980; 1983a, 1985), a psychiatrist and a cultural anthropologist.

Kenny's solution to the "latah" paradox is the first answer. He begins with Geertz's assertion concerning the relationship of latah to Javanese social norms. But he goes beyond those concerning social organization and modalities of interpersonal relationships and seeks to link latah to the most basic spiritual beliefs and values of Malayan cultures, that is those concerning "the alus–kasar [refined–coarse] distinction, ... local theories about the constitution of the soul, ... beliefs about spirits and the nature of mediatory activities between the spirit and the human world, and, in fact, to beliefs about the nature of reality" (Kenny 1978: 213–214). The core of his argument is that latah is a form of symbolic action, and that it symbolizes social marginality.

Having affirmed the close and essential symbolic relationship of latah to core elements of Malayan culture, Kenny deals with the problem of "latah" in other places in the world (which have different cultures) by the simple expedient of denying it:

Latah has been assimilated to superficially similar conditions, also involving voluntary obscenity or mimicry, in Siberia and elsewhere ... but so little is known about the latter, and little enough about latah itself, that any assertion of a fundamental similarity between them is unjustifiable ... If latah is specific to Malayo-Indonesia, as I take it to be, the question which thus arises is that of the factors specific to this culture area which have led to it (1978: 209–210).

Simon's (1980: 205) solution to the "latah" paradox is the opposite one: "The latah paradox disappears when latah is understood to be the culture-specific exploitation of a neurophysical potential shared by humans and other mammals." Unlike Kenny, Simons carried out field research in a

Malay village in Malacca and also studied American volunteers with particularly strong startle reactions (who do not, however, go into trance-like states, follow orders or engage in echoing behavior when startled). On the basis of these instances and on that of the comparative evidence in general he argues against "purely cultural explanations which fail to explain so many small specific features of the latah reaction in persons living in societies unrelated historically and culturally and [also] its occasional appearance in persons in societies without a cultural tradition to account for latah behavior" (Simons 1980: 205).

In contrast to Kenny's interpretation of latah as a complex symbolic activity, Simons tries to show that it is basically a very simple process, subject to a certain amount of cultural elaboration but readily explicable in terms of behavioral psychology. The question of why Malayan societies have culturally elaborated latah to the extent that they have is not pursued very far. Simons concedes the significance of cultural analysis, though rather hypothetically. He notes for example that Malays commonly gave him a cultural explanation as to why women are more likely than men to be latah. This was that women are vulnerable because they have less *semangat*, or soul substance. But Malays also told him simply that women could be teased with greater impunity than men. Hence latah would be more readily observable and better developed through recurrent provocation in women than in men (Simons 1980: 203). Such a behavioral explanation, he argues, also accounts for the greater prevalence of latah among poorer or lower-status persons – they are simply more vulnerable to abuse than others.

The non-Malay and non-Javanese instances

Given the interest that students of Malayan latah have shown in the various non-Malayan instances since the late nineteenth century (and conversely that scholars concerned with the latter have generally taken in the former) it might be supposed that the comparative evidence has by now been thoroughly examined, as well as argued over. This has not really been the case.[3] Even a cursory review of all of the principal patterns that have been referred to as "latah" or compared to it, has yet to be undertaken.

To begin with, several recent discussions of latah have drawn attention to imitative behavior among non-Western peoples in "first contact" situations (Prince and Tcheng-Laroche 1987: 14–15; Yap 1974: 97–98). The original accounts of such responses, which make no mention of any form of "latah," go back at least to the early nineteenth century and include one by Charles Darwin. In his journal of the voyage of the *Beagle*, Darwin (1839[1845]: 202) noted mimicry as part of the behavior of Indians upon the arrival of the ship at Tierra Del Fuego in 1832:

They are excellent mimics: as often as we coughed or yawned, or made any odd motion, they immediately imitated us. Some of our party began to squint and look awry; but one of the young Fuegians (whose whole face was painted black, excepting a white band across his eyes) succeeded in making far more hideous grimaces. They could repeat with perfect correctness each word in any sentence we addressed them, and they remembered such words for some time. Yet we Europeans all know how difficult it is to distinguish apart the sounds in a foreign language. Which of us, for instance, could follow an American Indian through a sentence of more than three words?

Darwin went on to say that "all savages appear to be excellent mimics" and that he had been told of the same behavior among Caffres and Australians. The similarities between such mimicry and "latah" are interesting but limited. Darwin does not indicate that the imitative behavior was occasioned by startle or severe fright or even that it appeared to be involuntary.[4]

Beyond these "first contact" patterns, which involve imitation without startle, and the Western cases of hyperstartle without imitation, the main non-Malay and non-Javanese instances involve the following: those of other Malayan and Southeast Asian societies, the French-Canadian area of Maine (*jumping*), northern Russia and Scandinavia (Lapp Panic), Siberia (*miryachit*) and northern central Asia (various local terms), aboriginal Japan (*imu*), and Africa and the southern Arabian peninsula (generally no local terms identified). Let us look briefly at the literature on each of these that has been cited in various studies.[5]

"Latah" elsewhere in Southeast Asia

The reports of "latah" or latah-like patterns in Southeast Asia concern both Malayan and non-Malayan peoples. Overall these reports, in some instances very old, are sporadic and provide little or no systematic information about the occurrence of "latah" among the ethnic groups throughout the region. References to startle patterns among the non-Malayan peoples in Southeast Asia are scattered. There are published accounts of "latah" among both the Burmese and the Thai. Information on the Burmese instance appears to be limited to a single account published in 1940 by R. M. L. Still, a British colonial medical superintendent. Still notes the complex is known as *young-dah-hte*, the literal translation of which is "to be ticklish and nervous," and suggests it is relatively common in heavily populated areas where there are usually one or two affected persons in every village. He provides no information on age, gender or status except that concerning four specific individuals (two are men and two are women) who are unlikely to be indicative of a general pattern. All four of the persons were observed at the hospital where three were patients and one was a worker. Of the patients, one was a woman, two were men. None had been confined because of *young-dah-hte* in itself, but for killing or assaulting others. The woman had killed her husband and had been found to be psychotic while the two men had struck others, in one instance fatally, as a result of being startled. Such instances not withstanding, Still notes that *young-dah-hte* is not locally regarded as an illness or a matter of stigma. As in the Malay and other Asian instances of "latah," the Burmese version occurs in two forms (one involving an exaggerated startle and the expression of an obscenity, the other imitation) and seems otherwise to reflect the general characteristics of "latah."

The Thai form of "latah" is known as *bahtschi* (spelled variously). It was mentioned as early as 1863 by Adolph Bastian (1863) and has been more recently described in some detail by the Thai psychiatrist Sangan Suwanalert (1972, 1984). The meaning of the Thai term is, like the Burmese, "tickle-madness." Suwanalert himself identifies *bahtschi* with "latah" to the extent of saying that the two are identical. This inference is based upon research on Thai *bahtschi* persons in 1972 in Central Thailand and on Malay latah persons in Johore in the early 1980s. Although his specific study focused on the Bangkok area, Suwanalert suggests on the basis of wider inquiries that the pattern is common in both the central and southern areas of the country and rare in the north and northeast. He reports regarding gender that, as with latah, most *bahtschi* persons are women, and that they are frequently ones who have moved in from the country to work as laborers in factories.

Instances of startle patterns occurring among Malayan peoples other than Malays and Javanese have been reported for a number of ethnic populations from Malaya through Indonesia to the Philippines, though seldom in great detail. For Malaya R. K. Dentan (1968: 138, 147) reports a somewhat ambiguous instance involving the Semai, an Orang Asli (aboriginal) people. The Semai recognize a startle pattern involving imitation which Dentan notes occurs most commonly among postmenopausal women, especially those who are midwives. While this would rather clearly appear to be latah, the Semai do not label it as such but rather as *chachau*. Nor does Dentan think that *chachau* is simply latah by a local term in that the Semai regard expressions or displays of sexual obscenity as *papaq* or "sexual insanity" instead. While he does not say that the Semai are not also aware of the term latah, it would seem likely that they are since he reports that both *chachau* and *papaq* are Malay loan words (the former [*kacau*: to confuse or disturb] of which is used very commonly by Malays in regard to latah). Further inquiry would likely show additional instances of latah or similar patterns among other Malayan Orang Asli groups, although whether or not these will turn out to be instances of recent diffusion from Malays remains to be seen.[6]

Reports of latah in Indonesia outside of Java are fragmentary but widespread. As a result of his survey of physicians van Loon (1924) found that sixty percent of the instances that were reported involved Javanese, about twelve percent Malays, a like percent "Batavians" (a composite group), and six percent Sundanese; the remaining ten percent included natives from other islands, Buginese, Madurese, Ambonese, Minangkabaus, and Achehnese. Some mention is thus made of latah for nearly the entire sweep of the Malayan Archipelago, from Ambon in the east to the tip of Sumatra in the west. The Malay-Javanese term latah itself is likely to be used over the wide areas where the pattern is found, but another term (*gigiren* or local reflexives) has also been reported from Bali and parts of Borneo, the latter to be discussed at length later on. In the case of Bali, Gregory Bateson (Bateson and Mead 1942: 92) noted in passing that latah occurred but mentioned nothing about it while more recently Unni Wikan (1989: 45–48; 1990: 296–297) reports that in north Bali it is known as *gigian* and that she had observed a few instances. Neither of these references indicates that the Balinese attribute much importance to latah or *gigian* or that it is very common on the island. This may be because, according to Wikan, while the Balinese attach great importance to startle (*tekajut*), its primary consequence is not latah but other more serious problems, including illness.

Finally, early in the century W. E. Musgrave and A. G. Sison (1910) provided a brief medical account of what they again presumed to be a version of "latah" found in the Philippines and known as *mali mali*. They described only one specific instance but noted that the condition is prevalent among the "lower class," principally women. On the basis of more recent inquiries, Simons (1980) reports also that "latah" occurs in the Philippines both as *mali* and (in some areas) as *silok*, but provides no further details.

French Canadian Maine: *Jumping*

The first description of a culturally-identified hyperstartle pattern to gain wide Western scholarly attention concerned what was referred to as *"jumping"* among French Canadians in rural Maine. It was published by J. M. Beard in 1880. Beard was a medical practitioner who, after being told about this strange reaction and reporting on it at the annual meeting of the American Neurological Association, visited the Moosehead region of Maine and proceeded to find and to conduct experiments with several of those affected. He told that in one instance when a *jumper* sitting in a chair was ordered to throw a knife the man did so, at the same time repeating the order, and that in another two *jumpers* followed an order to strike one another. Beard said that these and other such responses were provoked by startle or by commands given in a quick, lowered voice, and that the persons affected would also imitate sounds, throw objects or strike out at others, with or without an order to do so.

Beard did not, it should be said, mention that *jumpers* either imitated movements or that they exclaimed obscenities. He reported that while such persons were retiring and deficient in the power of self-assertion they "were not nervous," that they were strong and capable of hard work; and that they appeared to be as intelligent as others of their class (Beard 1880: 489). He offered detailed information on gender and age but said that women were rarely affected and that the pattern might be seen in children as young as four or five years of age. On the basis of fifteen instances which occurred in four families, he concluded that *jumping* was hereditary. However, he also suggested that it was "epidemic," which would indicate that it was socially transmitted, and supposed that it was like the "servant-girl hysteria" of the Middle Ages – a "transcoidal condition," a "temporary trance" induced by irrational fear.

As one of the occurrences discussed by Tourette, Beard's account of *jumping* assumed considerable significance in the comparative study of echoing and startle disorders.[7] However, it did not inhibit the view that such patterns were "exotic," and therefore to be explained by reference to arctic or tropical climates, non-Caucasian racial constitutions, and out-landish customs and beliefs. Thus of all of the "culture-bound" startle patterns to be described, *jumping* has come to be associated with some of the more bizarre misconceptions to be found in a field of medical and ethnological inquiry rich in errors of fact and interpretation.[8]

One of the possible reasons why this occurred was that Beard's description (unlike the late nineteenth-century accounts of latah) was not quickly followed by other accounts of other instances or of similar patterns in the same or related regions. With the exception of fictional or folkloric treatments little or nothing further was written about *jumping* until the mid-1960s when new interest was aroused as a result of an accidental encounter in the course of the hospitalization of a French Canadian man, followed by observation of two other individuals with similar tendencies.[9] Harold Stevens, the author of the report of these new occurrences, concluded that all three are "suffering from a common syndrome characterized by spontaneous onset in childhood, persistent, and associated with no focal neurological signs nor abnormal laboratory findings" (Stevens 1965: 313). While he supposed that the patterns displayed by the three individuals were all instances of *jumping* as described by Beard eighty-five years earlier, he did not say whether or not any of them identified themselves as *jumpers* or had heard of the term.[10]

While inquiries into this and other instances (Chapel 1970) were carried out mainly from a clinical and neurological psychiatric perspective,[11] a subsequent investigation reported by Charles Kunkle (1967) involved a deliberate effort to locate and study *jumpers* in rural Maine where they had long been a part of regional folklore. Kunkle found, interviewed, and examined fifteen such persons (thirteen men and two women). Of these, seven would automatically obey commands and two would engage in verbal echoing. He also sought persons affected by *jumping* among hospital patients and found four, three of whom were men. In these instances *jumping* had developed as a "well-defined sequel to illness." However, none of these "secondary jumpers," as he calls them, engaged in either automatic obedience or echoing when startled. Finally, like Stevens, Kunkle does not say whether or not any of them thought of themselves as *jumpers* or recognized the term.

Northern Eurasia: Lapp panic, *miryachit*, and *imu*

Outside of the Malayan lands of Southeast Asia, startle patterns have been most extensively noted and described regarding northern Asia. Actually, such reports concern a wide geographical range of peoples extending from the Lapps of the European Arctic to the Yakut, Yukaghir, Samoyed, Tungus, Koryak, and Chuckchee and other groups of Siberia, the Manchus and Mongols of central Asia, as well as the Ainu of northern Japan and Sakhalin. Many of these peoples are tribal groups that share various other ethnological characteristics including bear cults and shamanism, although the latter is distributed far more widely than elaborate startle patterns. In this region in general, startle reactions were often regarded as a form of "Arctic Hysteria." The use of this latter term to refer to certain behavioral disorders among the Eskimo led to the mistaken inference that "latah" was also found in the New World Arctic.

If the Lapps of Russia and Scandinavia are among the far northern peoples which have "latah," they represent the Western extremity of the northern Old-World distribution. The "if" here, however, is rather substantial. References to Lapp panic as a form of "latah" (or anything else) illustrate rather well the armchair character of much of the comparative literature. Both Yap and Aberle merely mentioned that it had been asserted that Lapps have "latah."[12] More recently, however, Simons states that "latah" in the form of "Lapp Panic" is found among the Lapps and cites Collinder's *The Lapps* as his source. Collinder, however, did not write that he himself had seen Lapp Panic. Instead, he based his description partly on the eighteenth-century accounts of Högström and Tornaeus and noted that "nowadays it is chiefly known from Russian Lapland" (Collinder 1949: 151). The latter assertion, he explained, was based upon stories told by the Fisher Lapps of Inari (in Finland) about Skolt-Lapp (a Finnish-Russian group) women who were said to be "silly and easily scared." Lapp Panic among the Skolts is thus, he continued, "partly rooted in superstition." And here the folkloric character of assertions about Lapp panic are particularly evident: "If a Skolt Lapp woman is frightened by a sudden cry, she may think that a bear is going to attack her." This, Collinder suggests, may explain the practice noted by Tornaeus of Skolt Lapp women exposing their private parts during an episode of panic. "It is known from different parts of Lapland that this gesture makes the bear ashamed and that he will not easily attack a woman if he can help it" (Collinder 1949: 151).

As to the actual accounts of Tornaeus and Högström – the apparent ultimate sources of all recent assertions concerning the identity of Lapp Panic as a form of "latah" – it appears from the passages quoted by Collinder that these are ambiguous. Tornaeus's account makes no mention of the classic characteristics of latah, although Högström's description does:

I have seen some Lapps behave in this way when someone has suddenly screamed, or a piece of live coal crackles. When they are thus frightened, they will jump to their feet, and do not mind if they have a knife or an axe in their hands, but hit the person who is next to them. I have also seen some of them imitate any quaint gesture of other people ... and when it is over they will ask whether they have behaved indecently, because they say that they do not know what they have been doing. (Högström quoted in Collinder 1949: 152)

In contrast to the literature on Lapp Panic, accounts of Siberian *miryachit* (in Russian *meriachen'e, meriachit'* or *emiriachen'e*; transliterated also as *myriachit*, or *meryachit*, etc.) involve real ethnographic documentation as well as folklore. Widespread European attention was drawn to *miryachit* at about the same time it was to latah and *jumping*. In this instance it was William Hammond, a prominent American neurologist, who published an article in 1884 which brought *miryachit* to the attention of Tourette and others. However, unlike O'Brien's report of Malayan latah and Beard's of *jumping*, Hammond's account was not based on his own experience. He had read a report by three officers of the US Navy of their observations in far-eastern Siberia which took note of a strange pattern of behavior whereby an affected individual would, when provoked, imitate the actions of another against his own will. The behavior was well known to the Russians and was said to be common, especially in Yakutsk "where the winter cold is extreme." The only individual instance that the officers witnessed was the ship's steward whose ethnic identity was not given (Buckingham, Foulk, and McLean 1883: 51). Hammond found the report particularly interesting because it resembled the phenomenon of *jumping* as described by Beard. He rather ambitiously titled his own paper "Miryachit: A Newly Discovered Disease of the Nervous System" and noted that to his knowledge it had not been previously reported in the literature on Siberia. The latter assertion, however, was quickly challenged in a series of communications which again showed the international character of interest in the pattern at that time.[13]

Subsequent to this initial flurry of reports and exchanges in the 1880s, further accounts of *miryachit* were published, sometimes as a part of ethnological monographs on particular tribal groups. However, scholars who have subsequently made reference to these instances have often relied on studies which are themselves secondary. Of the latter, M. A. Czaplicka's *Aboriginal Siberia* (first published in 1914) has been the most widely used. In a section titled "Pathology" and consisting of a single chapter on Arctic Hysteria – sometimes equated with *miryachit*, sometimes assumed to be a larger order of far-northern psychological disturbances – this author summarized various observations and accounts of *miryachit* that had been previously published.

While the early notes reproduced in the secondary accounts such as Czaplicka's refer to a pattern of behavior that is otherwise analogous to latah, there is one significant difference. Neither earlier nor later reports of Malayan latah contain reference to incidents involving more than one or two individuals. However, the literature on *miryachit* includes several accounts of groups of persons becoming affected simultaneously, one of which, moreover, links the occurrence to the consumption of a drug, which also had not been reported regarding latah or other hyperstartle patterns. In this instance (recounted by a Dr. Yankowsky as quoted in Stevens 1965: 312) fourteen soldiers became liable to fits of echolalia following the consumption of hemp oil at the settlement of Novokievsky in 1865:

All of [the soldiers] were in different positions: some walking, some lying, others sitting, and they all continued to behave in the same manner in presence. When I asked "what is the matter with you?" – all of them jointly answered "what is the matter with you?" ... In answer to each question they jointly answered the same question. The commanding officer of the company said that these people had eaten potato with hemp oil bought from a Korean. Having heard the word "oil," everybody started repeating "oil," "oil," "oil." Neither requests nor orders could prevent these patients from repeating the words uttered by some one of us or some of them.

While it was initially suspected that the incident was simply a consequence of the consumption of hemp oil, it was subsequently learned that the Korean trader who had sold the oil to the soldiers had been a *mirasha* (one who suffers from *miryachit*), and that only those soldiers who had seen him had been affected. This was proof, it was supposed, that *miryachit* was contagious.

The other incident, which is not reported to have involved a drug, is the most famous in the literature on *miryachit* – the mass affection of the

TransBaikal Cossacks of the 3rd Battalion, which both Czaplicka (1969 [1914]: 313) and Shirokogoroff (1935: 251), among others, retell and discuss. In brief: "During a parade of this regiment the soldiers began to repeat the words of command. The Colonel grew angry and swore volubly at the men; but the more he swore, the livelier was the chorus of the soldiers repeating his curses after him" (Czaplicka 1969 [1914]: 313). As should be clear, this report bears a strong resemblance – minus the hemp oil – to the previous one recounted by Yankowsty. It originally appeared in V. L. Pritkowski's *Three Years in the Yatkutsk Territory*, a travelogue published in 1890. However, Czaplicka notes that Pritkowski did not himself witness it but rather had recounted what he had been told by a Dr. Kashim. Like the incident of the soldiers and the hemp oil (and the Skolt Lapp women and bears) it tends to have a folkloric character. For his part, however, Shirokogoroff goes on to analyze it on the apparent assumption that it really occurred.

But to move to firmer if less colorful ground, of the primary accounts of Siberian startle patterns which have been used by later comparative scholars (Yap, Aberle, Simons, Kenny, and others), the most important are those of Waldemar Jocalson, on the one hand, and S. M. Shirokogoroff, on the other. The former were written at the turn of the century and are essentially descriptive.[14] They provide information on the startle patterns of the Koryak and the Yukaghir – more developed in the case of the latter than the former. In the case of both groups Jocalson (1908: 416) asserted that there were a number of nervous diseases which he took to be manifestations of Arctic Hysteria, which he attributed to the difficulties of adjusting to the far-northern environment and from which both the tribal groups and the Russian settlers who moved into it tended to suffer. He thus claimed that relative newcomers such as the Tungus had Arctic Hysteria more frequently and severely than did the Chuckchee and the Koryak who were ancient inhabitants and who had become, he thought, more acclimatized (Jocalson 1910: 30).[15] Jocalson further asserted that the pattern became more acute during periods of famine (1910: 31).[16]

Such observations about the Arctic context of the nervous diseases not withstanding, Jocalson's descriptions of Koryak and Yukaghir startle reactions are strikingly similar to those written about Malayan latah during the same period. *Meryak*, as the pattern was known in Koryak, and *irkunji*, as it was known in Yukaghir, both occurred in a mild form (an obscenity exclaimed after a sudden fright) and as well in a more severe one. The latter involved a hypnotic-like state in which the person affected would mimic sounds and actions and follow orders. Both forms occurred mainly among women. In the case of the Yukaghir he estimated that fully one half of the women of thirty or forty and older suffered from *irkunji* (Jocalson 1910: 33).

The other account of the Siberian startle complex that has been widely utilized is that contained in S. M. Shirokogoroff's classic *The Psychomental Complex of the Tungus*. Published considerably later than the reports of Jocalson, this study indicated that the Tungus pattern (known as *olon*) was much the same as Koryak *meryak* and Yukaghir *irkunji*.[17] Although it provided considerable descriptive information, it is also of interest because of Shirokogoroff's effort to analyze and explain *olon* in terms of its motivation and social functions, and its place within the larger mental scheme of the Tungus. Indeed, of all of the older accounts of the various Siberian instances it offers the most provocative and anthropologically sophisticated interpretation of social and cultural factors. He concludes:

... in so far as pure and simple *olonism* is concerned, i.e. when no other "pathological" conditions are intermixed, it is not an abnormal phenomenon in the Tungus complex; as it is regarded by the Tungus, it has a certain social function – as a performance and instructive observation, – without which the Tungus life would be impoverished; it is liable to diffusion, fashions, and variations, both individual and ethnical, is rooted in the normal psychomental complex and, as such, it must be separated from the facts gathered under the name hysteria. (Shirokogoroff 1935: 252)

It is particularly significant that Shirokogoroff does not regard *olon* as a disease, malady, mental illness, or psychosis.

This has not been so of the various accounts that have been published concerning *imu*, the Ainu version of the far-northern pattern and its eastern extremity.

While the Ainu peoples of the north Asian islands of Hokkaido and Sakhalin share a number of ethnological characteristics with those of Siberia, *imu* has always been treated separately from *miryachit*. Further, while *imu* was first described at least as early as 1903 by Sakaki and then at considerable length in the 1930s (by Uchimura in 1935 and by Winiarz and Wielawski in 1936), little if any wider notice was taken of it regarding latah or *miryachit* until later.

As with *miryachit* as described by Jocalson and Shirokogoroff, the basic characteristics and social context of *imu* appear to be the same as those of latah.[18] However, *imu* also seems to have unique features involving spirit possession and the serpent cult. Ainu often become *imu* as a result of being initially frightened by a snake (as is also the case with latah in Kelantan), but much more is involved. In such cases the initial behavior of an *imu*-person-to-be is not *imu* but physical illness, the cure for which is the induction of the sufferer into the snake cult. If this works the person is cured of the illness but becomes permanently *imu* (Munro 1963: 161). A further connection between *imu* and shamanism has also been noted, though this appears to be more tenuous. According to several accounts (cited in

Ohnuki-Tierney 1985: 104), while not all Ainu shamans are *imu* (nor all *imu* persons shamans) there is considerable overlap, and the Ainu formerly saw a connection.

Africa and Arabia

Although it has not been one of the major regions in comparative studies of "latah," references to instances from Africa began at an early point. Some of these were nothing more than simple assertions offered as background information that "latah" occurred in different places, including Abyssinia and Madagascar. In addition to such references, Andrew Gilmour published in 1902 a brief description of an instance of what he interpreted as "latah" among South African natives. A civil surgeon in South Africa, Gilmour had read about Malay latah and was impressed by having seen such a mental affliction among local natives: "Sudden and unexpected noises caused them to imitate these sounds, while words, musical notes, etc. were accurately repeated by the men. A sudden touch appeared to make them lose control of themselves, while all movements made by the experimenter were copied without fear of consequences" (Gilmour 1902: 19).

While Gilmour's account has been cited recently as evidence of non-Malayan "latah" (Simons 1983a: 171), the information it provides is meager when compared to reports of latah and *miryachit* in the same period. As the above quote indicates, verbal and physical imitations are clearly present. But it is not possible to determine whether the automatic obedience of commands are part of the pattern. Gilmour (1902: 19–20) himself noted that "A paroxysmal form of momentary duration in which coprolalia is a prominent feature has been mentioned in papers on latah among the Malays, but no cases were met with." Also, he did not specify the particular ethnic populations or regions in which such behavior occurred, or indicate whether any of the "latah" persons or others in question recognized "latah" as a distinct pattern. In addition to reporting that it was "not uncommon," he simply identified the three cases which he discussed as being "Kaffirs." He did note that while there were many "Malays" (that is Malayans) in South Africa, it was not possible to trace a relationship between them and the natives who happened to be affected. And he reported further that he had not heard of any cases among women.

Although not referred to in recent debates about non-Malayan "latah," more substantial reports began to appear in the 1920s concerning regions far to the north. These were written mainly by Italian colonial doctors who, like Gilmour, were aware of Malayan latah from the literature and were pleased to be able to offer as a contribution to comparative medical knowledge their discovery of it in a new area. The Italian reports concern areas of present-day Libya, Ethiopia, Somalia in Africa and Yemen in the Arabian peninsula. There is also a report by a French psychiatrist concerning the southern Sahara. Though in one instance a local term (*nekzah*: "to be easily startled") was also mentioned (by Sarnelli 1934: 752) in reference to Yemen, the authors of all of these reports refer to what they found as "latah."

The initial discovery of "latah" in Italian colonial Africa was claimed by Guiseppe Infurna in 1928. While serving in Eritrea (in Ethiopia) he had been informed that "latah" occurred in the region; he subsequently encountered and described several persons who were in fact affected. A few years later Guiseppe Penso (1934) described a single instance involving a boy of ten years he had come across while he was stationed in Italian Somalia. These accounts were followed by reports by Tomasso Sarnelli (1934) and Angelo Natoli (1937) concerning Yemen and Cyrenaica respectively, of which the former is most substantial. Sarnelli explained that while posted in Tripolitania (in Libya) in 1923 he had been told of a number of instances of "latah" and had personally encountered one. And because this individual was an Arab from Yemen, and because the five individuals previously reported by Infurna (1928: 560–561) had also been Yemenese Arabs who were living in Eritrea, he undertook a search for "latah" in Yemen itself. Here he found that it was common and described six cases.

The trail of North African "latah" diligently pursued by Sarnelli did not, however, lead only to Yemen. The subsequent report of Natoli (1937) referred to further instances of "latah" in Libya which involved indigenous inhabitants rather than immigrants or sojourners from Yemen. Further, A. Repond (1940), a French colonial doctor who reported on "latah" in the south Sahara, noted that it was found among various of the ethnic groups in that region, and that he had been informed by other Europeans that it also occurred in the far-western Sahara. And finally, having traced "latah" to Yemen, Sarnelli himself also raised the possibility of a direct connection with Malayan latah, pointing out that many Arabs that he met in Yemen had sojourned in Java and Sumatra and that they were thus familiar with latah in these regions.[19] He did not, however, claim that any of the Yemeni who were "latah" had themselves been to Southeast Asia or had close relatives or acquaintances who had lived or travelled in the region.

Similarity and its implications

What then is to be made of these instances? How "similar" does latah have to be to other patterns to be "virtually identical" to them, as Simons (1983a: 168) asserts, rather than having only "surface similarities," as Kenny (1978: 209) claims? Considering only the basic characteristics of Malayan latah and other reported instances of latah, it is not difficult to see that some are more similar to it than are others.

To begin with the simple matter of gender, about which virtually all accounts comment, in the cases of *miryachit* and *imu* and (for whatever it is worth) Lapp panic, it is mainly women rather than men who are said to be affected; in those of *jumping* and "latah" in Africa it is mainly men. Of course where the Muslim regions of north Africa and Yemen are concerned, it is entirely possible that observations concerning gender were strongly biased. The investigators were male colonial doctors who may have had little opportunity to examine or question native women. Some distortion of this sort was probably present in observations of Malayan latah and is more likely to have been so in the Arabic and African Islamic societies which secluded women to a much greater extent. Whether or not such bias was strong enough to leave the impression that the occurrence of "latah" in these instances was more common among men than women when the opposite was the case, there is less reason to suppose that Gilmour's assertion regarding "latah" in South Africa or those of Beard and more recent observers regarding *jumping* were similarly wrong. Further, if gender were all that varied between Malayan latah and these other instances, this would be further reason to suppose that the reports of the latter were wrong. This however is not the case.

There is also the matter of local cultural recognition. In the cases of *imu*, *miryachit*, and *jumping*, as in that of latah, the pattern is recognized and labelled with a term or terms which both identify and explain it. From the Malay or Javanese perspective, "it is latah" is all that really needs to be said to make an otherwise peculiar reaction intelligible and even normal, and the same is apparently true of *imu* or *miryachit*. What then is to be made of cases in which an outside observer describes what he takes to be a significant pattern of behavior but reports no local term for it and instead either creates one (as apparently with "Lapp panic") or refers to it as "latah" (as with most of the African and the Arabic instances)? It is possible in such cases that there is no local term, even though the pattern may be common, either in a normal recurring manner or as a response in highly specific circumstances. Alternatively, it is possible that there is a local term which the observer(s) did not learn. Either way, such reports are difficult to evaluate without further information.

For all of the discussion about the similarities of latah to other startle patterns, little systematic attention has been focused on which latah characteristics are and which are not common to other instances. Of the classic features of latah – coprolalia, echoing, and automatic obedience – it is readily apparent that not all are present or important in some instances. Coprolalia is reported not to occur in the case of South African natives; nor

Table 3.1. *Latah and other instances of "latah"*

	Malayan latah	Ainu *imu*	Siberian *miryachit*	Afro-Arab "latah"	Lapp panic	French Canadian *jumping*
Gender	mainly women	mainly women	mainly women	mainly men	mainly women	mainly men
Coprolalia	yes	yes	yes	usually not noted	not noted	not noted
Echolalia	yes	yes	yes	?	not noted	yes
Echo-kinesis	yes	yes	yes	yes	yes	?
Automatic obedience	yes	yes	yes	not noted	not noted	yes
Local term	yes	yes	yes	in some cases	not noted	yes

has it been noted either in most descriptions of north African and Arabic "latah" (the report of Sarnelli [1934: 752] regarding Yemen is an exception) or in *jumping*. The characteristic which appears to have led observers of non-Malayan instances to infer that what they had seen was "latah" has always been a pattern of behavior involving startle or some other emotional event followed by imitation. Both coprolalia and automatic obedience seem to have been secondary considerations, the absence of which was regarded as significant. However, imitation in Malayan latah takes the form of both echolalia and echokinesis. In some of the non-Malayan instances both types of mimicry have also been noted to be equally common, but in the case of African and Arabic "latah," echokinesis has been held to be more common than echolalia. Table 3.1 summarizes these comparisons.

When latah and the other startle patterns are compared in this way the results are fairly consistent. In all respects both *imu* and *miryachit* are highly similar to latah, and *jumping*, African, and Arabic "latah" less so, while Lapp Panic is, at best, very dubious. Therefore it would appear to be incorrect to state either that "latah" occurs among all of these different groups or that, conversely, it is found nowhere outside of the Malayan area and that all other instances involve only superficial similarities. Certain specific patterns of behavior reminiscent of "latah" do occur cross-culturally in a way which suggests they may be generally human. These include responses to startle and imitative behavior in "first-contact" situations of confusion and stress. They also include – as I shall also go on to note later – capacities for alterations in states of consciousness. On the other hand, the number of instances in which the various behavioral elements taken to comprise "latah" actually occur together is much more limited. I shall return to these issues in the final chapter; in the meantime, let us turn to Malayan latah in its present context.

Part II

Latah, society, and culture

4 Latah in Kelantan: an overview

The common assumption among both earlier and some more recent (e.g. Murphy 1972, 1976; Gullick 1987: 262) observers that latah is a passing feature of Malay life finds little support in the evidence from present-day Kelantan (or, as we shall see, from Sarawak). While latah may have declined in some regions of Malaysia along the lines suggested, and while it may also eventually do so in Kelantan as well, this does not as yet seem to have occurred to any great extent. Here latah is common both among rural and urban Malays and among some of the non-Malay populations as well. As I shall suggest later, there is some reason to suppose that it has increased in some places.[1]

My own information on latah in Kelantan mainly concerns Pasir Mas, a town and district of well over 100,000 inhabitants located near the center of the coastal plain.[2] The town itself sits on the east bank of the broad Kelantan River and includes a central business district of shop-houses and markets, near which are government office complexes and schools. The district spreads eastward from the river and contains some of the largest expanses of wet rice land in the state, though rubber and tobacco are also very important crops in some areas (Map 2).

The neighborhood on the eastern edge of town where (as in several earlier periods of research) I lived and concentrated my efforts in 1984–85 is typical of the rural and semi-rural areas which surround the town core. The Malays in this neighborhood include farmers (*petani*), laborers (*buruh kasar, kuli*), carpenters and other artisans (*tukang*), clerks (*kerani*), smugglers, traders, and hawkers (*peraih*), government school teachers (*cikgu*), religious teachers (*ustaz, tuan guru*), government officials (*pegawai*), and various trishaw, taxi, and lorry drivers (*driber*). There are Muslim prayer houses (*surau*), a mosque (*mesjid*), several traditional religious boarding schools cum religious communities (*pondok*), and several concentrations of coffee, snack, and provision shops where women visit and make purchases and men spend much of their leisure time drinking coffee, talking or playing checkers. Just beyond this neighborhood, both away from the main road and a little further along it, lie more distinctly rural areas. These in

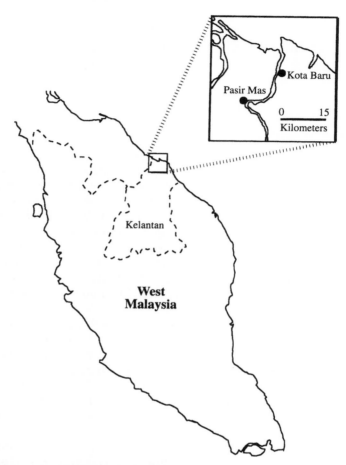

Map 2. Pasir Mas and Kota Baru Area

particular are currently experiencing much change: villages of rice-growers are turning into mixed suburban and farming communities.

The occurrence of latah

It should be noted initially that Malays and others in Kelantan tend to use the term "latah" in more than one way. Someone who is thought to be speaking foolishly or hastily may be said to be speaking or acting "latah," as is implied in the phrase "*jangan cakap latah*" ("do not speak latah"). As noted earlier, this may in fact have been the original meaning of the term and is close to its probable Sanskritic root, *lata* ("defect," "one who speaks like a fool," "fool" [Gonda 1973: 373]). It is also possible that such a phrase is a metaphorical reference to the pattern in much the same way that the phrase "don't be crazy" makes reference to the condition of insanity without really implying that the person addressed is insane. In any case, it should be kept in mind that Malays do not confuse such uses any more than Americans would the various meanings associated with "crazy." "Speaking latah" is therefore not the same thing as "being latah," as is implied in the phrase "*dia latah*" (he [or she] is latah).

Being latah therefore implies a particular pattern of behavior or a tendency to such a pattern. A person said to be latah (*dia latah*) may be latah at the moment or in the habit of becoming latah. In either case, however, it refers to actions that can vary much in intensity, duration, and other characteristics. It may refer to anything from a mild tendency to react easily to a slight startle (*mudah terkejut*) – that is to be "jumpy" – to reacting to a startle (or other stimuli) by losing or partially losing consciousness (becoming, as it is put in Kelantan, "*tak kabar*") and imitating movements, behavioral sequences, and sounds, or following orders. One of my Malay assistants, a young man in his early twenties, confessed to me at one point that he thought that he was a little latah, by which he meant that he was sometimes easily startled. Similarly Mak Soh, who I had known as a friend for many years, also told me that she was a little latah (*sedikit latah*). By this she meant that she was occasionally liable to be startled and exclaim something that would make others laugh and cause her embarrassment (*malu*). However, neither of these individuals or the many others like them were considered to be really latah by either themselves or anyone else.

When Malays in Kelantan refer to actions or persons as being latah, they generally make a clear distinction between two forms. The first of these concerns *kejut* or "startle." Persons who are said to be *latah kejut* are easily startled and prone to a strong reaction. This usually involves jumping, exclaiming an obscenity, striking out or kicking. The second involves an apparent loss of conscious and voluntary control over behavior and speech, and results in the imitation of sound and actions, or *mengikut* (literally "to follow"). Such a pattern is said to be "real" or "true" latah (*latah betul*). Individuals who are merely prone to exaggerated startle may claim that they are not latah because they do not *mengikut*. However, such a tendency to restrict the notion of latah to individuals who follow orders or imitate is a matter of ambiguity. In particular, there is a significant difference between men and women in this respect. Women who were merely prone to hyperstartle are less apt to be regarded as being latah than are men with such a tendency. They are more apt to assert that they are not latah but only liable to *kejut*. Men are less inclined to insist that they are not latah if they react strongly to startle but do not *mengikut*.

Such ambiguity not withstanding, there are many latah persons in the

Table 4.1. *Rural Malays (Kampung Belukar, Pasir Mas, Kelantan, pop. 770)*

Age	Men			Women		
	Latah kejut	Latah betul	Total	Latah kejut	Latah betul	Total
0–9			128			129
10–19			98	1		97
20–29			54	2	1	57
30–39	1		29	4	2	33
40–49			28	3	9	33
50–59			24	1	7	21
60–69	1	1	13	1	7	13
70–	1	1	5		4	8
Total	3	2	379	12	30	391

Pasir Mas area, and in Kelantan generally. This is certainly true of the eastern edge of Pasir Mas, and in the particular village of Belukar in which I did a complete household survey and interviewed all latah persons in detail. Here (see Table 4.1), in a total population of less than 800, there were more than forty persons who told of being particularly susceptible to startle, who were regarded by themselves and others as latah. Further out of town in this region the numbers of latah persons in specific Malay neighborhoods or villages appears to vary but there are probably none in which there are no latah persons at all.

Latah also occurs among urban Malays in Kelantan. While most of my research was done in and around Pasir Mas, with occasional forays made further away from town, I also made systematic inquiries in a Malay neighborhood in Kota Baru, the capital of the state, located some eleven miles down-river. My specific purpose here was to find out about the occurrence of latah among Malays in such an urban setting. While Pasir Mas is a "town" rather than a village it is hardly urban. Most of the Malay inhabitants live in neighborhoods which not long ago were villages, and which still have rural characteristics. And many of the Malays who work in the town center during the day live in surrounding rural villages.

Kota Baru, on the other hand, has been an urban center with a large town-based population for many decades. The court capital of the Kelantan Sultanate since 1839, it has Malay neighborhoods which have been present since the nineteenth century. And while some of the Malays who live in the older communities have moved in from villages, most are long-time residents. Such truly urban Malays have not been the focus of much sociological description. They are not farmers and villagers at heart but people who are descendants of several or more generations of urban dwellers. The men work as laborers, craftsmen, teachers, clerks, traders, and shopkeepers, as do also many of the women. The women have made the transition from chewing betel nut to smoking packaged cigarettes, which for the most part their rural counterparts have not yet done. Both men and women note the differences between themselves and *orang kampung*, or villagers.

In Kota Baru I worked in an area that I shall refer to as Jalan Atas Paloh, after the main street that runs through it. This is actually a residential area near the river rather than a cohesive neighborhood, and it is one of the old areas of Kota Baru. It is also socially diverse. Most of the houses on the side of the street near the river belong to squatters, some of whom have also been there for a long time. The inhabitants of these houses include some of the poorest Malay families I encountered anywhere in Kelantan. The dwellings on the other side of the street also contain poor families, but they also include middle-income and richer ones. Nearly all of the inhabitants of both sides of the street are Malay.[3] Finally, most of the inhabitants are commoners, though a few are members of the titled nobility of the state. While one of these families is rich, the others are scattered throughout the economic strata, from affluence through genteel poverty.

Latah is less common among the urban Malays of Kota Baru than in Pasir Mas but it is by no means rare here either. When I asked casually in Atas Paloh about latah in the area, or when I explained that I was interested in latah, it was sometimes suggested that I was wasting my time there and that I should go instead to the villages where I would find many latah persons. I think that these urban Malays responded in this way because they viewed latah as a part of rural Malay culture and therefore rooted in village society. The inhabitants of Jalan Atas Paloh saw themselves as more "modern" than villagers, and they associated latah with a more traditional way of life and mentality. However, they also appeared to know less about one another than their rural counterparts did about those around them. While the inhabitants of the neighborhood in Pasir Mas in which I lived generally knew about everyone in the area who was latah, the residents of Atas Paloh had little knowledge of who was beyond the next few houses. My own house-to-house survey (see Table 4.2) of the 112 families in Atas Paloh thus turned up more instances of latah than I had expected on the basis of more casual initial inquiries. Nor were the urban latah persons, who included similar numbers of women and men and of comparable age, transplanted villagers. However, there were fewer instances of "true latah" and more of simple startle than among rural Malays.

Finally, latah in Pasir Mas and in other areas of rural Kelantan also

Table 4.2. *Urban Malays (Jalan Atas Paloh, Kota Baru, pop. 742)*

	Men			Women		
Age	Latah kejut	Latah betul	Total	Latah kejut	Latah betul	Total
0–9			95			95
10–19			78	1		94
20–29	1		55	2		57
30–39	1		32	2		49
40–49			35			25
50–59	1		20		1	24
60–69			12	2	1	19
70–			6	1	1	8
Total	3		333	8	3	371

occurs among some of the non-Malays in the area. Most of the inhabitants of Pasir Mas town and district are Malays but there are also (in addition to a few families of Middle Eastern and Indian origin) important minority communities of Chinese and Thais. The Chinese in Pasir Mas, as in the state generally, form two broad ethnic types, known often in the region as *Cina Bandar* ("Town Chinese") and *Cina Kampung* ("Village Chinese").[4] The former have been in the region for several generations or more, but have retained many features of Chinese culture and are similar to the town-dwelling Chinese in other regions of Malaysia. They speak Malay as a second language and for the most part have not mastered the strong local Kelantanese dialect. The *Cina Kampung* are very different in several respects. They are all of Hokkien background and have generally been in the area for considerably longer than the town community, perhaps for several hundred years in some instances. What distinguishes them from those of the town and from some other rural-dwelling Chinese in Malaysia is that they have undergone extensive assimilation to the surrounding Malay and, especially in some areas, local Thai communities. They are all fluent in Kelantanese and tend to display the modes of interaction and patterns of behavior characteristic of rural Malay society in Kelantan. Although not entirely the same, they are thus a Kelantanese version of the *peranakan* or Baba Chinese communities found in some other areas of Malayan Southeast Asia. Many of them live in a series of villages strung out along both sides of the Kelantan River.

Like the Village Chinese, the Thai have been in the area for a long period of time and are fluent in Kelantanese Malay and, except in the realm of religion, are similar in life ways to rural Malays. In Pasir Mas the local Thai

Table 4.3. *Rural Chinese (North Pasir Mas, Kelantan, pop. 745)*

	Men			Women		
Age	Latah kejut	Latah betul	Total	Latah kejut	Latah betul	Total
0–9			101			102
10–19			90			76
20–29			54			42
30–39			40			31
40–49			30	1		32
50–59	1		20	3		33
60–69	1		34	5	2	29
70–			11			20
Total	2		380	9	2	365

communities are located further away from town than are those of the Village Chinese. Most of them are in the adjacent districts of Kota Baru and, especially, Tumpat. But some are situated in rural Pasir Mas, only a few miles out of town.

As for latah, of the two groups of Chinese, the *Cina Bandar* generally professed ignorance of latah – of either the term or the pattern – and I encountered no instances among them. The Village Chinese, on the other hand, were generally familiar with latah and able to identify specific latah persons in their own or surrounding villages. The results of the household survey that I did in a village complex lying along the river to the north of town (see Table 4.3) show thirteen latah individuals in a total population of seven hundred and thirty. However, latah among the Village Chinese mainly takes the *kejut* form.

The absence of latah among the *Cina Bandar* and its relatively common occurrence among the *Cina Kampung* strongly suggest the acculturative influence of Malays or Thais, with whom (in the case of the latter) these Chinese have intermarried in some instances. Latah in fact is more common among the local Thai than the Rural Chinese. The household survey (see Table 4.4) I did in a series of small hamlets to the east of town, which together had a total of 520 inhabitants, turned up a total of thirty-three latah persons, about the same proportion as among the Malays of Belukar and more than among the Village Chinese. Again, however, these Thai have considerably less imitative latah than do the rural Malays.

As in the case of the *Cina Kampung*, latah among the Thai may reflect an acculturative effect. It is true that since "latah" is known to occur among the Thai in Thailand as far away as Bangkok it might be expected to be

Table 4.4. *Thai (West Pasir Mas, pop. 523)*

	Men			Women		
Age	Latah kejut	Latah betul	Total	Latah kejut	Latah betul	Total
0–9			66			70
10–19			52			54
20–29			36	3		42
30–39			28	1		20
40–49			20	6		29
50–59			14	12		31
60–69	2		18	3		10
70–			13	3	3	20
Total	2		247	28	3	276

present among the Kelantanese Thai regardless of Malay influence. However, the linguistic evidence suggests at least a certain amount of acculturation. "Latah" in Thailand is generally known as *bahtschi* ("tickle madness") rather than as latah (Suwanalert 1972, 1984). And while the local Thai understand the literal meaning of the two lexemes which make up this phrase they do not apply it to latah, but instead use only the Malay term, as do the Village Chinese as well.

Social characteristics: age, gender, and socioeconomic status

Among the Malays (and the Village Chinese and Thai) latah is largely limited to adults. Although children may play at latah, and commonly provoke it, I encountered no instances among those of less than ten years and only a few ambiguous ones involving individuals of less than twenty. Latah is also less common in young adults than in those of middle age, and it is most common among older persons. However, observations about age can easily be misunderstood. Advancing age appears to increase the likelihood of *being* latah but it does not seem to increase the likelihood of *becoming* latah. Since persons who become latah tend to remain so, the number of such persons is much higher among the ranks of the old than among those of the young. But the ages at which different individuals first *become* latah are much more evenly distributed over the younger, middle, and mature periods of adulthood. Although many latah persons are very old, neither men nor women seem to become latah during the oldest decades of life. Further, in the case of women, the suggestion that the development of latah is linked to entry into post-childbearing years (e.g.

Kenny 1978: 221) is not necessarily correct. Some women do become latah at this time, but many others do so in earlier periods in their lives, especially in the period following the birth of a child. Nor, finally, should latah be confused with senility (*nyanyuk*) which Malays recognize as a separate condition. While in the case of a few older persons latah appeared to be mixed with the loss of memory, disorientation, and other characteristics of *nyanyuk*, the two patterns are clearly distinguished by everyone.

In addition to age, the occurrence of latah is a matter of class. As elsewhere, Malay society in and around Pasir Mas is stratified. Social distinctions are mainly a matter of traditional hereditary rank (*pankat*), wealth, and occupation, among which there tends to be some overlap, though less than in previous periods. Traditional rank, although significant, appears to be less important than in some regions. Relatively few families of higher noble rank live in the area and customary popular esteem tends to be focused also on Islamic religious leaders, who are commoners.

Wealth is undoubtedly important. It is traditionally based on land ownership but also clearly manifest in possessions, especially houses and furnishings. On this basis Malays tend to make distinctions which range from poor (*orang miskin* or *orang susah*) through those in the middle (*orang tengah*) to those who have it easy (*orang senang*) or who are said to be rich (*orang kaya*). To oversimplify somewhat, the poor possess little or no land and derive an income from sharecropping or laboring for others or from petty trade. Such families live in small, sometimes decrepit houses, often built with woven bamboo, sheet metal, and attap, and have few appliances and little or no furniture. Those in the middle range either own sufficient land to support a family or have income from wages, government pensions, or trade. Such families live in better quality houses which are generally built out of sawn lumber, painted inside and out, and have some furniture and a few appliances (always a television and perhaps a stereo and a sewing machine), and often own a motorcycle, but not usually an automobile unless it is used for trade or as a private taxi. The rich are those who either own larger amounts of land which generate substantial income from rent, own businesses or earn government salaries or, often, a combination of several of these. These families typically live in well-furnished houses, often built in a modern fashion of concrete or brick and finished with stucco, usually fenced with a gate, and generally furnished with upholstered chairs and sofas, dining tables, vinyl floor covering, and a full range of appliances as well as an automobile which is not used for commerce.

Occupational distinctions, which are also culturally emphasized, involve various lines of differentiation, but generally involve office work or teaching versus farming, manual labor, and petty trade. The former "new Malay middle-class" occupations tend to be associated with Western dress (for men), reading and writing, and the use of occupational titles (such as Mr. Teacher or Mr. Assistant District Officer So-and-so, etc.), as modes of address and identification. The latter occupations tend to be associated with Malay dress, oral communication, and the use of honorific family and kin terms (Older Brother, Father or Grandfather So-and-so) as modes of address and reference. Not all occupations (for example those associated with Islam) fit such distinctions in all respects and other skills and knowledge have social importance as well.

In terms of these distinctions, latah tends to be most characteristic of the poorer members of town and rural society in Kelantan, though not exclusively so. To confine the discussion here to Malay society, of the 236 households in Belukar, Pasir Mas, and Atas Paloh, sixteen are – in terms of the distinctions discussed above – distinctly rich, one hundred and twenty-seven are poor and another ninety-three are somewhere in between (see Table 4.5). Among these households, there are two instances of latah among the rich, and most among the larger number of poor. A substantial number of latah persons are also found among the slightly smaller number of middle-income households, although latah in these instances is less often of the imitative than of the simple-startle variety. Further, latah is far more common in the rural village of Belukar than it is in the urban neighborhood of Atas Paloh, even though poor families are no less common in the latter.

Finally, the status distinctions based on occupation are also relevant. Latah tends to be found in households (many of which, but not all, are poor) in which men work as farmers, laborers, trishaw or taxi drivers, and market traders, and in which women are farmers, laborers or traders, or village midwives. Latah is not common in households which form part of the new Malay middle class of school teachers, clerks, and government officials (who tend to be distributed among the middle and upper ranges of the economic strata). I generally found such Malays to be ambivalent about latah. Many have latah relatives and tend to see it as a part of traditional Malay life. Such Malays were often interested in what I thought about latah, in how I would explain it, and in its possible occurrence in other places, including the United States.

Latah, gender, and personality

While latah in Kelantan occurs among both men and women there are important differences. That latah is considerably more frequent among women than among men is among the most common of the observations that Malays tend to make when they offer information on the topic. This is sometimes suggested to be a matter of innate difference between men and women – that women have less *semangat* (soul) or less blood than men. The

Table 4.5. *Latah and the economic status of households among urban and rural Malays*

	Poor	Middle	Rich	Total
Latah kejut	9	12	2	23
Latah betul	25	9		34
Total	127	93	16	236

actual difference in numbers is substantial. In Belukar there are some thirty women who are identified as latah on the basis of their inclination to *mengikut* (imitate or obey) as well as a number of others who are prone to strong startle reactions but who do not follow orders or imitate others. On the other hand, there are but five men who are regarded by themselves and others as being to some extent latah, of whom only two are liable to *mengikut* and three others who are merely prone to react strongly to startle. The number of latah women in Atas Paloh is also much larger than the number of men.

Observations about the typical personality of latah women are a common feature in the literature which should be viewed with skepticism in light of my own information. P. M. Yap (1952: 553), for example, writes of latah women as "shy, retiring, nonaggressive, self-effacing, changeable and colorless ... with little individuality." When I first began to seek out and interview latah women in Pasir Mas I thought they did have certain personality characteristics in common, but that these were hardly the ones I had been led to expect from such generalizations; they were in fact closer to the opposite. These women did not seem shy and withdrawn at all, but rather talkative and gregarious. Nearly all of them were married and had families.

Because of this I wondered if those I came to know first were not a good sample. Many were traders (*tok peraih*) in the central market. Having arrived in town to study latah, I had wanted to make contact with as many different latah persons as quickly as possible. I had thus asked around about where I might readily find them. It was suggested that I go look in the market where there were many. This turned out to be good advice. There were a dozen or more latah individuals, mainly women, in and around the marketplace, who were quite willing to talk to me and point out others who were also latah. But because they spent their daily lives in continuous interaction with buyers and other traders I came to assume that they were not necessarily typical. I thus also began to seek out latah persons elsewhere, especially in and around the villages of my immediate neighborhood, particularly in Kampung Belukar where I eventually interviewed a large number and became familiar with a greater range of social types. I also came to the conclusion that in terms of readily-discernible personality characteristics they were, like the market women, not much different from other women of similar age and circumstance.

The more frequent occurrence of latah among women than men has various implications, some of which will be explored more fully in subsequent chapters. It may be noted initially that latah has fewer negative implications for women. Simple *kejut* latah is looked upon with amused indulgence, especially for women. *Latah betul* ("real latah") is also less stigmatizing for a woman, to the extent that it is at all. It has been argued that latah has a special meaning for Javanese and Malays because it contravenes basic cultural standards of human conduct. In so far as this is true – and, as I shall explain later, it may be overstated, at least regarding Malays – it is more true in the case of men than women. Men are expected to demonstrate less emotion than women and to maintain greater outward tranquility and composure. According to Malay Islamic ideas, men should be governed by *akal* (reason), rather than by passion or lust (*nafsu*), to a greater extent than are women. Sudden exclamations and sudden jerky movements are thus forms of behavior which are less excusable and more shameful for a man than for a woman. In the case of "true" or imitative latah, the behavioral patterns involved are ones which are particularly apt to be degrading for men. A latah man who is bent to the will of another, whose behavior he is imitating or whose orders he is following, is put in the role of a servant or child, and thereby demeaned. He has lost, at least temporarily, both his composure and his autonomy, and therefore his dignity. Men are thus more likely to resist becoming latah or being identified as such than are women.

This is all the more so since there is some tendency to associate latah in men with transvestism. Since true latah is noted to be both more appropriate for – as well as much more characteristic of – women than men, perhaps it is also assumed that it is likely to be found especially among men who dress as women or who otherwise behave in a feminine manner (*pondan*). This was made clear to me on one occasion when I was making inquiries among my neighbors about latah men. I asked Cik Zainah, who lived nearby, if she knew of any men around the area who were latah. She mentioned several that I already knew and who were only *latah kejut*. I thus asked if there were others around who were likely to be *latah betul*, perhaps in other villages. She thought for a moment and then said "Pak Su who lives in Kampung Belalang [a village several miles down the road], yes, he is latah." Pak Su of Kampung Belalang was known to be a *pondan*. When I sought him out I found that he did indeed have markedly feminine mannerisms, though he did not dress in women's clothes. He denied, however, that he was latah, or even that he was even a little vulnerable to startle. When I returned I reported to Zainah that it did not appear that Pak Su was latah after all. She supposed that I had wandered off and become lost and ended up in the wrong place or gotten the wrong Pak Su, the nickname (Father-the-Youngest) being extremely common. When I assured her that I had found the right Pak Su in the right village she turned to Mak Zaid, her mother-in-law, for confirmation. The latter also seemed certain that Pak Su was latah – because, she explained, he was a *pondan*!

On the basis of my surveys, interviews, and specific inquiries, I was never able to establish any actual relationship between male transvestism or tendencies to feminine behavior and latah, although this may exist. I was not able to determine how many of the men in the region who were explicitly *pondan* were also latah. There are few well-known *pondan* in the Pasir Mas area. One such man was Pak Ngah Kacang, a middle-aged individual who dressed as a woman and sold peanuts and other snacks outside of the town cinema, and who was, like Pak Su of Kampung Belalang, not latah. Against such possible links between male transvestism and latah should be set the various instances of male true-latah about which I did gain specific knowledge. Of the eight *latah betul* men I came to know, none was known to be a transvestite or in any way distinctly feminine. One was not married at the time but had been so on two previous occasions; all of the others were married, though most had been divorced several times. Nor were any of the much larger number of *latah kejut* men that I interviewed (all of whom were married) transvestites.

What has been said so far may suggest that latah men are likely to be socially marginal or to show other signs of instability. My own information indicates that this is so in some instances but not in others. To begin with, of the men who were *latah kejut* none seemed by their outward behavior or local reputation to be socially or psychologically maladjusted. They lived in circumstances and had personalities which in no way distinguished them from other Malay men of similar age and background. None seemed to me to be timid, nervous or unstable. While several were not especially forceful and could be provoked or teased with impunity, others were regarded as strong and potentially dangerous. In particular there is a well-known link in Kelantan between being *latah* and being skilled at *silat*, that is traditional Malay martial arts. One latah man in eastern Pasir Mas was a master *silat* teacher, while another was a shaman who had also studied *silat*; both were regarded as very formidable.

The true-latah men are a mixed case. Several of these were socially marginal and, in the view of other villagers, unbalanced. On the other hand, two of the true-latah men were respected members of their communities and were by all indications well adjusted. One of these was a *haji* (returned

Pilgrim) and a respected local religious leader with a successful marriage, a large family, and a nicely furnished house; another, though poorer, was also successfully married, had a stable family life, and was a community leader in traditional cultural and village activities. Between these two extremes the remaining several true-latah men appeared to be otherwise undistinguished from others of their age and circumstance.

The reproduction of latah

Latah is a highly stylized, more or less common pattern of behavior that has been replicated from one generation to the next for a long period of time – but how? Malays and others in Kelantan frequently say that latah may be inherited, and commonly identify *latah keturunan* ("descent latah") as a type. Heredity is also sometimes noted by latah persons themselves as a reason for being latah. Such observations may have led earlier European writers (Ellis 1897: 40; Gimlette 1897: 457; and Swettenham 1900[1896]: 66 among others) to the view that latah is a hereditary disorder.

It is true that those who are latah often have kin who are also latah. The number of latah persons about whom I gathered detailed information who have very close living or deceased latah kin is especially striking: nearly half have, or have had, a latah mother and nearly a third a latah grandmother. Latah sisters are also very common as are, to a slightly lesser extent, aunts. Conversely, only a few such persons have had no known latah consanguinal relatives. It is therefore reasonable to assume, as the Malays do, that latah individuals have often acquired the pattern from other family members or kin.

This of course does not mean that latah is necessarily genetically inherited. Parents transmit a genetic heritage to children but children also learn from their parents, their grandparents, older brothers and sisters, among others. A close genetic tie also generally involves a close social bond. My own information shows some slight reason to suppose that latah is socially reproduced rather than genetically transmitted within families. Women who are latah are much more likely to have mothers who were also latah than are men who are latah, even though latah men would seem to be equally apt to have inherited latah genetically from their mothers. (Since latah is less common among men than women, both have fewer latah fathers than latah mothers.) Further, with the exception of the fact that more latah men than women have latah maternal grandmothers, this pattern is consistent regarding senior female relatives. A substantially larger portion of latah women than men have both maternal and paternal aunts and older sisters who are latah. The very strong tendency for latah women more than men to have close senior female kin who are, or were, latah suggests that the latter have often served as models.

While in many instances latah is thought by latah persons themselves to be a matter of heredity, in other instances different causes were cited. Some thought only that they had become latah as a result of being provoked by other persons. Of the remainder, some explained being latah with reference to certain preceding circumstances or developments. Cik Mamat, a Malay man in his early sixties who had been slightly latah for about twenty years, recalled only that it had begun after he had studied *silat*. Similarly, Minah, a woman in her early thirties who had been latah for about three years, noted that it had begun after she had given birth to her second child and had just moved to a new residence, but that was all she could remember.

As with regard to these two explanations, there are again general differences between men and women. Like Cik Mamat, many Malay men who were liable to the *kejut* form of latah thought that they had become this way as a result of studying *silat* – this having made them more sensitive to attack. Women, by contrast, more often mentioned some personal or life crisis as bringing latah. A number of women mentioned that it had begun during one or another pregnancy while others said that it started after the birth of a child; both such periods are regarded as times of vulnerability (Laderman 1983: 201–204; Wazir Jahan Karim 1990: 50–54). Yet other women mentioned divorce or the injury or death of a child or grandchild as preceding latah. All such developments are regarded as weakening the *semangat* (soul) or affecting *angin* (mood, desire, motivation), and generally leaving one vulnerable to disruption and confusion.

Some latah persons were only able to recall such general emotional circumstances, but many others referred to specific incidents instead, or as well. Individuals for whom latah takes the stronger *mengikut* form were more apt to explain it on the basis of some specific incident or experience involving shock or trauma, though not all of them did so. Such incidents were often described in vivid terms which left little doubt about their emotional impact.[5] Wee Keng, a Village Chinese man from rural Pasir Mas, said that he had become latah as a result of an automobile accident which left him vulnerable to being startled. Other incidents involved deliberately violent actions of others, or situations which threatened physical harm. Limah, a Malay woman of Belukar, explained that she had become latah when she was about thirty-seven, after her husband had become crazy *(gila)*, struck her with a *parang* (cleaver), and had taken their daughter away. Similarly, Rosnah, a neighbor of the latter and a woman of forty-one years, said she was first latah about a year earlier. She had gotten up in the middle of the night to relieve herself and had encountered a burglar who had entered her house and then fled when she saw him, leaving her terrified.

Several men also associated the beginning of latah with encounters with other persons. Pak San, a retired Malay taxi driver and a neighbor of mine in Pasir Mas, told me one evening in the coffee shop where he spent much of his time how he had become slightly latah as a result of an experience that he had as a youth of seventeen years. He had gone to an orchard to pick a jackfruit and had suddenly come upon a couple in the act of fornication. He was both startled and badly frightened for he was acquainted with the persons and thus feared that he might be killed to prevent him from revealing what he had seen. In another instance Hussain, a Malay man in his early forties who had been latah since age twenty, said that it had begun with an incident in which one of his friends jumped out of a tree onto his back as he was walking along a lane at night. He thought that he had been attacked by a *hantu raya* (great ghost) which was known to lurk in the area. His friend had meant it as a harmless prank but he had been badly shaken.

Most often, however, the experiences held to be responsible for latah do not involve other persons. Several different women told me of becoming latah as a result of being severely startled by thunder and lightning and many others mentioned encounters with animals. Some such incidents involved harmless animals – such as a lizard or frog – in which case it was more a matter of being startled than threatened. More often however the animals were dangerous, or might have been. Two different latah men in the area thus told me of becoming latah as a result of being badly frightened by wild elephants that each had encountered while working in the forest in the interior.

The most common animal encounters described by both men and women involved snakes, especially large hamadryad cobras (*ular tedung selar*). One sixty-five year old man who had become latah about three years previously, told that it was because he had been wading in the padi field catching fish and a cobra suddenly appeared before him. Similarly, a woman aged forty-five, who had been latah for nine years, associated it with being frightened by a cobra while she was transplanting rice; a second woman of similar age said that she had become latah when she was bitten by a water snake while she was working in the field; and a third, a trader of sixty-three, recalled that what had caused her to become latah, more than forty years ago, was an encounter with a rat snake (*ular sawa tikus*) which, though harmless to humans, can be very large. She was winnowing rice and the snake had fallen from the rafters onto her winnowing tray. Other latah persons reported yet other such encounters. One man told of reaching into a fish trap (*bubu*) in muddy water to grasp a fish that turned out to be a snake;[6] another had a cobra rear up on a path in front of him; and another woman had one pass between her feet as she walked along a path.

In several of the instances of latah involving encounters with snakes individuals reported fainting or becoming paralyzed or acting in ways that were beyond their own control. In one, Bidah, a middle-aged woman in Belukar, said that on the occasion in which she had first become latah a cobra had appeared before her as she was transplanting rice. The snake had not attacked her but she was so badly startled that she could not move until other people came and led her away. Two other latah individuals from other villages told of similar incidents but with different reactions. One was an older Malay man who said that in the incident in which he had first become latah he had had a confrontation with a cobra, but that instead of fleeing he had managed to grab the snake and smash its head on the ground and kill it; he had, however, done so without realizing it until afterward. The other was a Thai woman who explained that when she saw a snake she would not run away but instead would lose awareness of what she was doing and go after it. This woman's mature daughter had been present and recounted that on one occasion she had returned home to find her mother sitting on the ground unconscious and holding on to the tail of a large cobra and trying to pull it out of the hole in which it was lodged.

In addition to such incidents, latah is linked in some instances to dreams (*mimpi*), though much less frequently than I had expected from the importance attributed to this connection in some of the earlier reports. I asked questions about dreams of all of the latah persons I interviewed in both Kelantan and Sarawak but with different results. While in Sarawak dreams were frequently mentioned, in Kelantan only a few persons told of having a dream at the time of becoming latah, or of having recurrent dreams that were associated with latah. In one instance Sabariyah, a Malay woman in Belukar, explained that she had first become latah after she had been *demam* (sick with a fever), during which she was dreaming or delirious. She did not recall what she had been dreaming about but her husband had struck the floor loudly in an effort to revive her.

It is possible that other persons also associated latah with dreams but did not wish to discuss it, particularly if the dream was of a sexual nature, as I found in some instances in Sarawak. "Yes I have dreams, but I don't associate them with latah" was the sort of reply I sometimes got when I raised the issue. It is not that dreams are devoid of significance. It is common knowledge that winning lottery numbers sometimes appear in dreams, that certain forms of love magic (*ilmu pengaseh*) operate through dreams, and that events which occur in dreams may subsequently occur in ordinary life. Sometimes dreams are the means by which a person receives supernatural protection or instruction. When I asked one woman whether she associated becoming latah with any sort of dream she said no but then went on to say that she had begun as a midwife as a result of a dream. When she was a young woman she had a vivid and beautiful dream in which she was visited by the Seven Heavenly Midwives (the *bidandari*) who told her that she should become a midwife and then went on to tell her everything that she needed to know about how to do it.[7]

The four latah persons who did associate being latah with particular dreams were Malay women, and all of their dreams concerned being attacked or chased by animals. One of these women, who was seventy-four, dreamed of being chased by a bull, while another about the same age associated her latah with frequent dreams of bulls and elephants, as the third, who was fifty-five, with being caught by a bull or a tiger. In so far as anything can be made of such a few instances, they are consistent with the accounts of actual remembered experiences that many persons did give as explanations of becoming latah.

The persistence of latah

However latah is conceived to begin, it is generally regarded as something which persists and about which relatively little can be done. Some individuals told me of first going through a period of *latah kejut* before becoming *latah betul*, while others claimed they were vulnerable to the latter from the beginning. Some said that their latah had remained the same over time while others said that it had become less or (more commonly) stronger with age.

However latah may begin or change over time, few latah persons pursue any of the usual courses of action often taken by those seeking relief from physical or mental illnesses or other maladies. Among all of those I asked, a few told of consulting *bomoh* (healers) about latah, without success. Most *bomoh* make no claim to be able to help with what is regarded more as a long-term habit (*tabiat*) or personality characteristic than an acute affliction. But while such notions tend to put latah beyond the scope of traditional medicine, they would not so readily preclude recourse to religion, another major source of relief from misfortune, for God is assumed to be all powerful and able to change anything. Haji Pak Su Amat, one of the true latah men mentioned above, told me that he had invited pious men (*tok lebai*) to recite prayers to rid himself of latah on several occasions. A few others, including Thai and Rural Chinese individuals as well as Malays, also told of seeking divine help through social rituals, but most latah persons of all ethnic groups had not done so. I encountered only one person who claimed to have ceased being latah. This was Citgu Omar, a Malay elementary-school teacher who lived in rural Pasir Mas. He told of having become *latah kejut* as a young man and then of overcoming it through his own efforts and God's will. He was, however, the only school teacher to have been latah that I met (or heard of) to begin with.

The fact that few persons actively seek relief from latah through medicine or ritual raises several issues that will be pursued further in subsequent chapters. The first is that while latah implies certain cultural notions of personhood, it is also viewed (at least by latah persons) as a social or interactive process rather than an individual one. When I asked latah individuals questions of a "how-often-are-you-latah?" sort, the answer was often some version of "it depends on how often other people startle me of course!" Similarly, when I posed questions about whether a person could get over latah a common answer was "I could only stop being latah if other people would stop bothering me." The second issue is the more fundamental one. The question of what latah persons do or do not do about getting over latah is sometimes the wrong question. Such questions imply that latah is necessarily an affliction which latah persons would rather not have and which does them no good. As we shall see, such an assumption, while not completely unfounded, involves an oversimplified view of a complex pattern which has a well-developed creative and expressionistic side as well.

5   Latah and Malay culture

The awareness that latah-like patterns were to be found elsewhere in the world not withstanding, it was axiomatic in many early accounts that latah had deep roots in Malay culture and character. However, since no one was very certain just what latah was in the first place, no one was very sure just how it related to other facets of Malay experience, culture, psychological makeup or environment. Once explanations became more theoretically oriented and the comparative evidence was examined more carefully, the problem of context and explanation emerged more clearly, but was not resolved. Recent interpretations, however, move in different directions. While Simons (1980, 1983a, 1983b) plays down the significance of the local context in favor of a behavioral explanation of broader human applicability, most other recent analysts of latah in both Malaysia and Java have sought to show how it relates variously to culture, mentality, and emotion in these particular settings (Geertz 1968; Kenny 1978, 1983, 1990; Laderman 1991: 42–43; Peacock 1978: 130–132; Murphy 1972, 1976; Siegel 1986: 28–33; Setyonegoro 1971).

In trying to understand the importance of the cultural basis of latah it seems significant not only to know whether or not something more or less exactly like it occurs elsewhere but also how common it happens to be. In many instances this information is not available. In Kelantan, as we have seen (and, as we shall see, in parts of Sarawak), latah is very common, and my own interpretation, which I develop in this and the following chapter, is based on this consideration. Latah is not, as we have also seen, limited to Malays in Kelantan. But there is some reason to suppose that the occurrence of latah among the Rural Chinese and Thai reflects the local immersion of these groups in Malay culture. It is not possible at this point to provide a cultural analysis of latah for all of the Malayan or Southeast Asian peoples in which it has been reported to occur, although it is likely that certain broad cultural continuities can be identified, as I shall go on to suggest.

74

Latah and startle

Given the central importance that Malays attribute to it in accounts and explanations of latah, startle (*kejut* [Javanese/Indonesian *kaget*]) is a good place to begin. From the perspective of scholarly interpretations, latah has been analyzed both as a startle reaction (especially by Simons [1980, 1983a, 1985]) and as a fear reaction (Yap 1952: 531–533). Startle and fear are, of course, closely related in the realm of experience for Westerners. An American, for example, who suddenly and unexpectedly meets another person at a corner or a door is probably as apt to say "oh, you frightened me" as "oh, you startled (or surprised) me." The latter would be the more correct response in that while some genuine fear may be involved it is likely to have been fleeting and to have derived from the startle rather than from the perception of any real threat. A Malay might or might not be as apt to confuse or merge *kejut* with *takut* as an American would startle or surprise with fear. However, there is clearly some association here as well. Some startling experiences, such as suddenly encountering a snake (often noted by latah persons as a reason for becoming latah) or suddenly seeing an automobile coming directly in one's way, are also genuinely frightening.

None the less, while startle is by no means the only thing which provokes latah, it is the one which Malays most frequently and emphatically note. A particularly common way of indicating that a person is latah is to say that he or she "cannot be startled," (*tidak boleh di-kejut*), by which is meant "cannot stand to be startled without reacting in a strong manner." A simple and less direct way of asking if a person is latah is to inquire if he or she is bothered if startled, or if people ever bother him or her in this way, and if so what occurs. While I learned this quickly in the course of my discussions and interviews with and about latah persons, it was independently confirmed by another investigator whom I met in the course of my fieldwork in 1985. This was a young psychiatrist from India on the medical faculty of the Universiti Sains. He had recently been assigned to the new University hospital in Kota Baru and wanted to learn about the mental and physical health of the Kelantanese villagers and had conducted a survey to this end. He had not heard of latah but told me that when his assistants inquired of individual villagers about their problems a frequent response by the person answering was that she or he could not stand to be startled.

Let us look then first at the startle pattern as it has been studied in behavioral terms. The classic behavioral studies of the startle reflex were done in the 1930s by Carney Landis and William A. Hunt (1939). The reflex as they describe it

... includes blinking of the eyes, head movement forward, a characteristic facial expression, raising and drawing forward of the shoulders, abduction of the upper arms, bending of the elbows, pronation of the lower arms, flexion of the fingers, forward movement of the trunk, contraction of the abdomen, and bending of the knees . . . The response is very rapid and follows sudden, intense stimulation. It is a basic reaction, not amenable to voluntary control, is universal, and is found among Negroes as well as whites, infants as well as adults, in the primates and in certain of the lower animal forms. (Landis and Hunt 1939: 21)

Landis and Hunt conducted carefully controlled laboratory experiments of startle which used film to record the reactions of human subjects to pistol shots and other sudden stimuli. They emphasize that it was only by capturing such reactions on rapidly moving film and then analyzing them frame by frame that they were able to determine what actually occurred in the startle reaction. (Anthropologists will note that the use of such a research technique is somewhat reminiscent of the efforts of Gregory Bateson and Margaret Mead [1942] to record and study sequences of Balinese cultural behavior during the same period.) Their demonstration of the nature of neurophysiological startle and their interpretation of its various manifestations and correlates within the carefully delineated framework of the methods and limitations of the laboratory seems indisputable. No cultural anthropologist, however convinced of the essentially learned and culturally varied basis of human behavior, is likely to doubt the innate nature of a basic startle pattern after reading their book. The *relevance* (in a positive sense) of what they show in regard to an explanation of latah is, however, more complicated.

To start with, the rapidity and the brief duration of the physiological reaction is clear. The basic, unlearned, response is measured in thousandths of a second. It begins within several tenths of a second and is completed within a half of a second of the occurrence of the stimulus. Everything that comes after this in the view of Landis and Hunt falls either into the category of a "quasi-learned secondary pattern" or into that of an acquired one. It would thus appear that all or nearly all of what is experienced and observed as latah comes after this initial half-second period and is therefore, in behavioral terms, a "post-startle pattern." The typical "immediate" latah responses of throwing, striking, shouting, etc. (not to mention the more lengthy ones involving verbal or physical echoing) might conceivably be initiated within the first half-second but they certainly could not be completed within this period.

The relationship between latah and the basic startle pattern as observed and defined by Landis and Hunt thus seems problematic.[1] In addition to being beyond the temporal sequence of the primary startle pattern itself, latah is in some important respects incongruent with it. Landis and Hunt find little association between variation in the intensity of the basic startle response and either gender or age. In contrast, latah varies greatly along these lines: it is much more common among women and older persons. Also certain commonly-noted latah behaviors – raising the arms, throwing or striking out or kicking – contrast with the contracting motions characteristic of the startle pattern itself. A further complication concerns the matter of habituation. The development of latah has often been assumed to be facilitated by repeated provocation. It has thus been argued that women and lower-status persons are more prone to be affected than others because they can be more readily provoked (Simons 1980). Landis and Hunt, however, found that habituation – repeating the stimulus over time, including longer as well as shorter periods – *reduced* the intensity of the reaction. If latah were merely an exaggeration of the basic neurophysiological startle pattern then it should thus be lessened by repetition, not enhanced.[2]

How then does latah relate to the basic startle response? It would be interesting to know how Landis and Hunt would interpret latah in light of their knowledge and perspective but they do not mention any such pattern. One possibility is that the motor and neural response described by Landis and Hunt as the startle pattern is more developed in some persons for one reason or another, or that it becomes so. And that having or developing a strong reaction leads directly to a deterioration or degradation of the conscious control mechanisms of personality, and with further conditioning (and deliberate direction by others) to "attention capture," echoing, and automatic obedience (Simons 1980). This would appear to be one explanation of latah. It would explain latah "directly" in terms of startle.

An alternative explanation, which is also suggested by Landis and Hunt's analysis, is that latah is more of a response to one or another of the emotional states produced by startle, rather than to startle itself. Landis and Hunt note that such emotional reactions which are secondary and, at least partly, learned, include annoyance (leading when sufficiently strong to anger and attack), fear (leading when sufficiently strong to flight, avoidance or defence), and curiosity (leading to the direction of attention to the source of the startle). Of these emotional states and behavioral tendencies, both fright (*takut*) and anger (*marah*) are ones which have been mentioned frequently in reports of latah, and they are certainly also mentioned in the accounts which my latah informants provided. Moreover, according to Landis and Hunt, unlike the basic startle response itself, these tendencies *do* vary, at least according to age. "The secondary reactions of children were more clearly defined than those of adults" (Landis and Hunt 1939: 141). Younger children showed a predominance of fear and flight. But with greater age, annoyance and curiosity increase. Finally, in addition to annoyance, curiosity, and fear, Landis and Hunt note a further category of secondary tendencies which they term "overflow effects." These include:

all those cases where the behavior does not seem to be rational and directed toward the stimulus but rather to be an overflow effect at some neural level, perhaps because the primary response is not sufficient to resolve all the motor tensions aroused by the discharge of the revolver. Changes in posture, nervous giggles, smiling, inconsequential remarks to the experimenter and the like are typical ... [Such verbal responses] take place on a symbolic level ... (Landis and Hunt 1939: 139)

A behavioral explanation of latah based on such secondary, culturally learned, emotional reactions to startle would be that the pattern was magnified out of "normal" proportions to the point that it overwhelmed the cognitive and moral guides and inhibitions governing behavior.

But why should this occur? If all human populations are equally prone to neurophysiological startle (and no one who has written about latah recently has argued to the contrary), why have Javanese, Malays, and some other peoples placed so much emphasis on it? It is true that it has often been said that startle has consequences for Malayan or Indonesian peoples which are particularly extensive and generally negative. Karl Heider observes in his recent study of emotions among Minangkabau and Javanese that while the notion of surprise has pleasant implications for Westerners, the unexpected is generally troubling for Indonesians, and that while this is particularly so for Javanese it is also true for other peoples in the region as well; in particular, startle is linked to confusion, disorientation, and disorder (Heider 1991: 64–67). In one way at least this certainly fits with latah. The term that my latah informants used most frequently to refer to being provoked by others was *kacau*, the more general meaning of which is to "confuse," become "mixed up," "to throw into disorder," as in the phrase "*dia suka mengacau saya*" (he [or she] likes to disturb and confuse me).

Startle, magic, and latah

Concerns about startle among Malays and other Malayan peoples are not limited to latah.[3] It is held to be dangerous during pregnancy and in the early life of a child.[4] In the case of infants, Malays in Kelantan told me that startle can lead to *sawan* (convulsions), an often fatal condition. Infants are thus handled in ways intended to protect them from sudden noises and movements. As children grow they become less vulnerable to the effects of *kejut* but they remain weak compared with adults. Beyond childhood women are thought to be more susceptible to the effects of shock than men. This is sometimes said to be so because they have less blood (*kurang darah*), or because their inner selves (*semangat*) are not as strong and thus more vulnerable to penetration and disruption. Many Malay women told me that they had first become latah following the birth of a child, a period in which the body has not yet regained its full equilibrium and can easily be knocked out of balance by a shock (see also Laderman 1983: 203).

It is thus true that Malay beliefs about startle carry over into the realm of magical and animistic notions as Kenny (1978; 1990: 132–133) has stressed. In several tales collected by Skeat (1966[1900]) and Gimlette (1971[1915]: 47) startle brings supernatural transformations, ones in which human beings are changed into animals or monsters. In the story of Princess Tehan a woman who is startled while bathing turns into a bear with white markings on its chest representing the soap not yet washed off her body (Skeat 1966[1900]: 187). Another such story recounts the metamorphosis of the small hornbill from a man. The man committed a murder and was then later startled so badly by seeing the feet of the man he had murdered protruding from a sheet that he changed into the bird (Skeat 1966[1900]: 129–130). Then there is the famous morality tale of the creation of the *penanggalan*, the female monster which sucks the blood of children. This demon was once a woman who was sitting immodestly in a wooden tub whereupon a man entered the room and startled her. The result was that in trying to escape she kicked her chin so hard that her head became detached and flew away with her entrails attached, the form in which the spirit is now seen (Skeat 1966[1900]: 327–328; Laderman [1983: 127] reports a different version).

But if startle is associated both with magical transformations in Malay folktales and beliefs and with latah, is latah also associated with magical power in a direct manner as Kenny (1978) has argued? An answer requires some discussion of Malay magic which, as reported and interpreted in the literature, is an enormous topic in itself (Endicott 1970). Malay supernatural notions, magical beliefs and practices, cosmological ideas, and religious traditions are both historically rich and complex, and subject to varying degrees of acceptance, interest, and skepticism by Malays (Firth 1974). Here is a brief overview of everyday notions of supernatural or magical power among Kelantanese Malays as I have encountered them in the course of fieldwork at different times. Such notions refer to objects and places as well as persons.

Certain objects which have properties we would refer to as magical are referred to by Kelantanese Malays as *bertuah*. Tok Su, the late *penghulu* of one of the village-districts of Pasir Mas who was very interested in such matters, owned a small *badik* (a kind of dagger) which he claimed was *bertuah*. He carried it with him, especially at night. It protected him from harm and, he thought, made him irresistible to women. Pak Lah, who lives in the same village, owned an old *keris* blade which also had such magical power. People occasionally asked to borrow it to see if it could be used to enable them to have dreams (*mimpi*) of a winning lottery number. Mat Zaid (a young neighbor and a cousin of Pak Lah) did not own a *badik* or a *keris* but had a piece of yellow cloth covered with Siamese writing which he carried with him everywhere as an amulet (*azimat*). It had been given to him by a Buddhist monk engaged by his mother to fight off the sorcery being directed against her by her husband's older first wife.

Places may also be magic. Many places in rural Kelantan celebrated in local history and legend are associated with supernatural powers, in which case they are referred to as *keramat*. Trees and graves are both commonly referred to in this way. In the case of a *keramat* tree this may mean only that the place in question is the home of a spirit who may cause harm to someone who relieves himself nearby or otherwise acts disrespectfully. *Keramat* graves, on the other hand, while also capable of causing harm, may be approached for positive purposes. There is a famous one in the town of Tumpat. Parents looking for help of a child about to sit for an important school exam will sometimes go there seeking assistance. *Kubor Datuk*, as it is known, is thought to be especially good for women suffering from infertility and for illnesses of children. The invocation of assistance from the grave, as from other such *keramat*, has been denounced by Muslim reformers and appears to have declined in recent years.

While *bertuah* and *keramat* are supernatural properties of objects or places rather than persons (at least in Kelantan living persons), magical powers of a similar sort are also attributed to living individuals. Here one such important term is *berkat*, which might be translated as "blessed" or even "saintly." In the Pasir Mas area there are (or were) several renowned religious teachers (*tuan guru*) who were widely reputed to be so endowed with spiritual energy. They regularly received visitors seeking help with various problems to whom they gave Koranic verses written on paper or water over which they recited verses. Rarer, and believed to be more powerful, are individuals referred to as *wali* (saint). Such individuals may, in the case of the famous "White Wali," be recluses who are said to be *mulit masin* (literally salty mouth) or oracles and to have the power to appear in two different places at once.

Finally, the most common form of personal magical power is associated with the notion of *ilmu*. Unlike *berkat*, which is given by God and cannot be obtained through individual initiative, *ilmu* can be acquired. The basic meaning of this term is simply "knowledge" or "science." But when it is said that a person "has *ilmu*" or that he has been seeking it, what is meant is that such a person has or has been seeking arcane knowledge used for ritual or magical purposes, of which there can be many. Obtaining *ilmu*, through study or, sometimes, through a dream (*mimpi*), is a traditional part of the process of becoming a curer, a midwife, or a warrior. Most young Malay men in Pasir Mas appear to take at least some interest in acquiring a little *ilmu* which can be used to influence women or to afford some protection against harm – dangerous as this can be for dabbling too much in *ilmu* is thought to be a cause of insanity (*gila*). In the case of men who seek to become powerful warriors (*pendekar*) through study and initiation into one or another of the *silat* (Malay martial arts) cults, the acquisition of *ilmu* focuses especially on *kebal*, that is invulnerability to being hurt by blows or cut or pierced by knives or bullets.

How then does latah fit with these various Malay ideas which in Western discourse are lumped together as "magic"? If one simply asks the question of whether magical or supernatural abilities of the sort outlined above are attributed to latah persons the answer seems to be no. Malays in Pasir Mas do not believe that a latah person *as such* can predict the future, provide a winning lottery number, cure an illness, help someone pass a school exam, win the affections of a man or woman, or do any of the other things which are sometimes thought to be accomplished or aided by supernatural assistance of one sort or another.

The matter of *kebal* (invulnerability) – a major area of traditional Malay magical interest – is more complicated. Latah persons are sometimes reported to successfully fight off or drive away tigers. In one of the early, famous articles on latah, Clifford (1898: 194) reported that Malays had many tales of latah persons frightening tigers into flight, while Fletcher (1908: 255) later reported a story in which a latah woman caused a tiger to become latah! Stories about latah and tigers continue to be told and occasionally reported in the newspapers. One which appeared in 1985 told of a latah midwife in rural Pahang who, after being startled by a tiger that had caught her goat, picked up a piece of bamboo and drove it away. Similarly, a latah man I interviewed recounted that his grandmother had survived an attack by a tiger because she became latah and confused it by imitating its movements. Since tigers figure prominently in Malay magical ideas as shamans' familiars and as wer-animals, the fact that latah persons are thought to get the best of them might well be an indication of supernatural power.

Stories are also told about latah persons and snakes. It is part of latah folklore in Kelantan that a latah person will not be bitten by a cobra. I was in particular impressed with accounts of encounters with snakes that were often given by individuals as explanations of how their latah had first begun. The thrust of several such accounts is that while the person is normally very afraid of a poisonous snake he or she will pursue and attempt to catch and kill it while latah. It is thus possible to infer from such stories that Malays believe that supernatural forces are at work. Both latah persons and others do suppose that latah behavior may involve remarkable feats. But at least in those many instances in which latah individuals described their experiences with snakes to me, no mention was made of magical powers or supernatural considerations. In some instances such persons did say that they were *tidak khabar*, that is semi-conscious or unconscious of what was occurring, a matter to which I shall return below. They did not, however, make any claims to being *kebal*.

However stories of the triumph of latah persons over tigers and snakes should be interpreted, there are other tales which have an opposite theme – that of vulnerability. Stories are thus also commonly told of things which happen to latah persons which injure or kill them. One latah woman of Pasir Mas told me of another latah woman who had been struck and killed on the south road out of town as a result of being latah. The latter was startled by the sudden approach of an automobile while walking in the road and, as a result, was unable to move. Another story is told of a latah *tok peraih* (petty trader) who sold lime for betel chewing in the marketplace in Pasir Mas. Someone came up and startled her and then pretended to reach into her lime jar, scoop up a handful of lime and eat it. The woman followed these gestures and filled her mouth with lime, swallowed it and died. I am not able to verify whether either of these stories has any basis in fact any more than I am the tales told about persons saved from harm by tigers or snakes by latah, but this is beside the point. To provide one further example, a first-hand account, Mek Sing, a rural Chinese latah woman, told me of an incident which happened to her. She is a market trader who makes daily trips across the border to Golok, Thailand. Once she was sitting in a cafe in Golok. One of the young men who worked there and who knew she was latah wanted to see if she would hurt herself. He came up quickly, startled her, set a nail upright on the table, and acted if he was going to strike the nail with his open hand, but then actually hit the table beside the nail. Mek Sing followed his gesture but actually struck the nail and drove it into her hand, producing a wound which left a scar she showed me. She was certainly not *kebal* (invulnerable). On the other hand, no one attributed incidents such as these to sorcery, witchcraft or the supernatural.

Latah men in the Pasir Mas area often said that they had become latah as a result of studying *silat* or traditional Malay martial arts. This was in fact the most common explanation of becoming latah that men gave. Further, *silat* defensive gestures – striking out with an arm or kicking – are the most common responses of Malay latah men to provocation. It should thus be kept in mind that the learning and practice of *silat* certainly does have ritualistic and spiritual as well as physical dimensions. Becoming adept is in part a matter of acquiring *ilmu* and not merely physical strength, speed, and skill. The supernatural context is made clear for example in Razha Rashid's (1990: 68–69) recent description of the sacred enclosure (*gelanggang*) in which *silat* takes place – one in which

... a guru can exercise his physical and mystical powers to the fullest without the intervention of mischievous or malevolent spirits, *jin* or *syaitan*. The entrance to the *gelanggang* consists of two poles (*penjuru*) upon which are wrapped layers of cloth (white, black, yellow, red) which have been 'blessed' (*jampi*) by the *guru silat* to prevent spirits from entering the arena. Each pole in the *gelanggang* is also blessed (*jampi/serapah*) by the guru in order to *pagar* (fence in or 'protect') the area, and neutralize all evil or potentially evil influences in it.

The fact that men frequently claim that they are latah because they have studied *silat*, and that *silat* has magical and animistic dimensions, again suggests that latah has supernatural connections. But while such links should not be dismissed out of hand, it is difficult to know how much significance to attribute to them. The Malay men who associate their latah with *silat* do not think that they are better at *silat* because of being latah, or that latah is a source of spiritual energy or magical power. They say that *silat* teaches them to be on guard (*jaga diri*) and to react instantly to movement or sound. It is true that this ability is itself thought of in spiritual terms; if you are adept you react *before* a move has been made by your opponent. Also, a *silat* contest between two men is very different from a cockfight, which has been taken as a metaphor of Malayan masculine aggression. The latter generally involves an immediate, frantic, and brief explosion of movement. In *silat* the participants begin by slowly dancing and circling one another gracefully, appearing to look away, moving arms and hands in a studied, leisurely effort to distract and to hide their intentions. Great emphasis is placed on control and equilibrium. A dance accompanied by drums and gongs, a *silat* performance is somewhat reminiscent of a *main peteri* shamanistic seance. In both cases there are rapid transitions in the action which are signalled or provoked by abrupt changes in drum and gong rhythms. And so while *silat* might seem to be the very opposite of latah (in that latah involves a loss of control while *silat* places great emphasis on its retention) both involve a sudden shift from one state to another. Both are also supposed to involve great speed – in *silat* when it comes time to stab, kick or strike, in latah in various actions which occur when a person has been startled.

There are other possible reasons why men may associate latah and *silat*. As noted already, being latah creates greater difficulties for a man than a woman. True latah involves a loss of control and the subordination of the self to the direction of another. A latah person who will imitate or follow orders can be made to perform amusing and demeaning acts against his or her will. The men who associate their latah with *silat* are not in this position. *Latah kejut* is, at most, only mildly degrading for a man and it lends itself to joking and amusement. By striking out with *silat* blows and kicks when provoked, a man greatly reduces the chances that he will be taken advantage of by anyone other than other men who are quick enough and strong enough to risk being struck. Dignity is thus protected from assault by women and children. Further, by associating latah with *silat* men link it with a traditional cult of male strength, skill, pride, and honor. It may thus also be that *silat* draws men who think they are easily startled. Several young Malay men I knew who were interested in *silat* told me that they thought that they were easily startled, although they did not regard themselves as latah. Further, of the dozen *latah-kejut* men I interviewed none seemed to be feminine, timid or lacking in self-confidence or otherwise poorly adjusted and uncomfortable with themselves. In this regard they contrasted with the much smaller number of "true latah" men, several of whom did appear to be nervous and to suffer badly in prestige, none of whom, however, associated their latah with *silat*.

Latah, shamans, and midwives

Since it has been suggested that latah is related to Malay magic, it has also been supposed that shamans and traditional midwives, as practitioners of magic, are likely to be latah. The issue here is reminiscent of the classic argument over whether shamans are apt to be mentally ill, unstable, or transvestite (Lewis 1989: 160–184). In the case of shamanism in Siberia and among the Ainu, a similar connection to *miryachit* and *imu* has also been sought. In all of these instances the existing evidence is at best ambiguous. The possibility of a link between latah and shamanism was raised by O'Brien (1883: 147) in the first important article on latah, but it was not pursued. O'Brien simply noted that one of the latah men that he knew happened to be a shaman. Richard Winstedt and Raymond Firth have offered different opinions on the matter. Winstedt (1969: 134), the leading colonial authority on Malay magic, raised the issue directly in his memoirs and suggested that latah was thought to be due to spirit possession, and that the latah person could serve as a medium through which spirits would speak. This was written late in his life and long after he had left Malaya, and appears to be the only place where he made the point. Firth (1967: 198), on the other hand, has argued that latah could not be controlled well enough for use in Malay shamanistic practices. Most studies of Malay shamanism (e.g. Gimlette 1971[1915]: 71–105; Cuisinier 1936; Laderman 1991) have been silent on the topic.

In present-day Pasir Mas, Mat Daud, one of the men in Kampung Belukar who is *latah kejut*, is a well-known *tok peteri* (a shaman, specifically a performer of *main peteri*, the most important of the Kelantanese seances). Among the Thai, the only male latah that I encountered in any of the communities where I conducted household surveys or about which I made other inquiries is also a famous shaman. And among the large number of Malay latah women I came to know or interviewed in various areas of Pasir Mas one was also a curer and shaman. These few instances need to be placed against the large number of latah men and women who have no particular involvement in shamanism or any other form of curing activity. Further, none of these individuals sees a connection. Mat Daud, for example, claims that being a *tok peteri* has nothing to do with latah, which he attributes in his case to *silat*.

Traditional midwives (known as *bidan kampung* or "village midwife" as opposed to *bidan kerajaan*, those trained and employed by the government) are identified in the literature as practitioners of magical and animistic ritual as well as "necessary" or "rational" activities relating to pregnancy and birth – though midwives themselves do not distinguish between such symbolic and functional realms of activity. Several accounts – including one by Gimlette (1897: 455) which concerns a Kelantanese woman – contain references to Malay midwives who were latah but, as in the case of shamans, do not make much of this connection or attempt to explain it. Another report (Gerrard 1904: 13) notes that a woman may have become latah as a result of witnessing a birth. But this was based upon the opinion of the woman's husband; the woman herself claimed she was latah as a result of being attacked by a crocodile. In any case, the woman was not a midwife.

In rural Pasir Mas latah is common among traditional or village midwives. There are presently two midwives in Belukar who are latah as well as another in an adjacent village; all in all four of the Malay latah women in Kelantan I found and interviewed were village midwives, none of whom was sought out for this reason.[5] Again, as in the case of shamans, the *bidan* themselves do not see any relationship between becoming latah and being a midwife. Tok Bidan Kalsun does not know why she became latah to begin with, and neither does Mak Soh. Macik Nah, a third midwife, said that she became latah after being frightened by a ram while Cik Essoh, the fourth, recalls vividly that she did so as a result of a snake falling from above her onto the winnowing tray she was holding. These women also emphasized that attending women at birth does not make them latah, and that latah does not interfere with their abilities to serve as *bidan* in other ways.

In the case of both shamans and midwives there may well be links between the symbolic realm in which both midwives and shamans operate and latah. However, there are other possible reasons, to be discussed below why – to the extent that the pattern is real – both types of ritual practitioners are apt to be latah.

Latah and trance

Another possible link between latah and the supernatural concerns altered states of consciousness. Persons who are latah behave in a manner similar to those who have achieved a state of trance through deliberate means or who have been made to do so through spirit possession or sorcery. H. B. M. Murphy has argued that Malayan peoples in general are strongly disposed to trance or dissociative states of hypersuggestibility as result of child-rearing practices.[6] Malayan infants and children are treated in ways which promote dissociation – the separation of body and behavior from will, thought from appearance and, in body movements, of part from the whole – as a normal and in some respects ideal mode of behavior:

Mothers throughout the region encourage the passive molding of the child's body to their own, and proceed from this to a manipulation of the child's body as if it were an extension of their own. In part this may be due to the cultural demand that the small child make certain religious and social gestures long before he is able to understand what he is doing. Whatever the reason, the result is that the child learns many body movements passively and in a dissociated fashion. Mead writes of the Balinese that virtually all motor learning, whether it be walking, eating, or something more complex, is "accomplished with the teacher behind the pupil, conveying directly by pressure ... the gesture to be performed. Under such a system of learning, one can only learn if one is completely relaxed and *if will and consciousness as we understand those terms are almost in abeyance*" (Bateson and Mead 1942: 15). Geertz writes similarly that "the kind of learning by being pushed and pulled through a simple pattern of motion" (Geertz 1961: 100) covers much of the Javanese child's first motor and linguistic development. As a result, one sees quite early in the Balinese photographs something that Mead and Macgregor call "dissociated body parts" (Mead and Macgregor 1951: pls. 51 and 56) which continues into adult life, both under normal conditions and in trance (Belo 1960). (Murphy 1976: 9–10; italics original)

But, Murphy continues, if latah seems to be consistent with certain basic features of Malayan personality as molded by infant and childhood learning patterns to produce a disposition to trance states, not all Malayan societies have latah. He thus reasons that latah is only *one* expression of such tendencies, and trance states involving possession are, in effect, a preferred alternative. Those Malayan societies which provide their members with ready access to other trance experiences are not likely to develop latah. The Malays and Javanese, on the other hand, who have less opportunity (which he attributes to the conversion to Islam) for culturally approved trance states involving spirit possession, have latah instead. The actual situation regarding both Malays and other Malayan groups is rather more complex than Murphy's brief summary of the evidence indicates and requires further explanation.[7]

To begin with, it may be noted that beliefs and experiences regarding altered states of consciousness are likely to be associated with distinctive views of the person. Strong cultural orientations to trance and spirit-mediumship or spirit possession as modes of affliction and healing are apt to involve a view of the human self as open to the influence of forces from without. "Personality" in such instances is likely to be seen as "interactive" rather than as isolated and autonomous (cf. Connor 1982 on such ideas among the Balinese and Heider 1991: 9–10 on Indonesians generally).[8] Amin Sweeney (1987: 196–197) argues on the basis of his studies of literature, folklore, and performance that a strongly interactive concept of the self (as well as a disposition to alternative states of consciousness) reflect patterns of culture and thought associated with oral tradition or partial literacy.[9]

Carol Laderman (1991: 42–43) relates such concepts of the person to shamanistic curing and notes incidentally, but significantly, that such notions are offered by rural Malays in Trengganu as an explanation of latah. In exploring the cultural assumptions of *main peteri*, she stresses the emphasis that is placed on internal processes of the self (the Inner Winds). But she also reports the prevalent belief that personality in some individuals may be permeable, that the gates which protect the inner self may not be fully closed. It is such individuals whose internal balance is easily upset, whose thoughts may become confused and overwhelmed by the words and actions of others, and who thus become latah. As we have already seen, a good deal of personal magical ritual tends to be concerned with "penetration" on the one hand, and with "guarding" (*jaga*), "gates" (*pintu*), "fences" (*pagar*), and "invulnerability" (*kebal*), on the other.

Malays in Kelantan recognize both deliberate and non-deliberate ways in which a person may go into trance. The process of deliberately entering into trance is known as *lupa* (a similar term [*luput*] is used by the Iban in Borneo) the more literal meaning of which is "to forget." In Kelantan this term has specific reference to achieving trance in the context of a shamanistic performance or seance, especially *main peteri* (Cuisinier 1936: 34). In the case of a shaman this involves the recitation of an incantation, swaying and dancing to music made by gongs and drums and other instruments, first slowly and then faster, and then by twirling the upper torso around and around. Other participants may also become entranced in a similar but more abbreviated manner. Although not the same thing, deliberately achieved trance states are associated with what is perhaps best termed "mediumship," that is the ability to transmit the words and actions of various spirits. In Kelantan, such trance states are an important part of the healing tradition and are thus regarded as beneficial and therapeutic (Gimlette 1971[1915]: 97; Laderman 1991). Non-deliberate trance states are a very different matter. In addition to startle, "involuntary" experiences which lead to alterations in consciousness include illness, sorcery, and attacks by spirits. Except (as occasionally occurs) in the case of individuals who are present at seances and drawn into unintended trance, possession is thought to be a matter of affliction; a cause of physical illnesses which do not respond to conventional treatments, or ones which seem to involve mental or emotional imbalance. Broadly speaking, involuntary trance is associated with "possession," which is to be under the influence or direction of something (a spirit) or someone else (as in sorcery). Very often it is supposed that the spirit causing the problem has been sent by a sorcerer on behalf of a client. While I was living on the edge of Pasir Mas in 1985 such an incident occurred in a nearby household in my neighborhood. Sabariah, a young, unmarried woman with several suitors about whom she could not agree with her parents, was fainting and having pain in one of her legs which could not be alleviated by the efforts of either practitioners of Western medicine at the local clinic or the traditional herbal medicines or massage therapy of Malay curers (*bomoh*). It was thus suspected that someone had used love medicine (*ubat guna*) or had obtained the help of someone who kept a *pelesit* (familiar spirit). At the time I left, consultation with various experts was still in progress.

As in this instance, trance activities in general, like latah, have an important relationship to gender. In the case of voluntary trance performances such as *main peteri*, the shamans and other players and performers who make up the groups are usually, though not always, men.[10] On the other hand, the individuals for whom such performances are held are, according to most accounts, as in my own experience, mainly women. In the case of other instances of involuntary trance and possession (as in that of latah) most of those involved are also women (Kessler 1977: 302). It is true with regard to Murphy's argument that most performances and activities involving voluntary trance have long been condemned from the perspective of official or orthodox Islam. Even in earlier periods when they were more widely tolerated by traditional Islamic leaders (and patronized in some instances by rulers), such activities were regarded as beyond the realm of *ugama* ("religion").[11] In the 1960s Muslim saints and holy men in rural Kelantan who had reputations for magical powers of the sort noted earlier, and who engaged in curing and other practical activities, did not, to my knowledge, make use of trance. Orthodox objection to performances and other activities involving trance has several bases. One of these is the supposed Indic-Hindu or at least non-Islamic character of the performance or ritual context; another the use of emotion rather than *akal* ("reason"); yet another the deliberate summoning of spirits. Ceremonial activities involving voluntary trance, however useful they may seem to everyone, and however relaxed local Islamic leaders may be about them, have thus for a long time formed a "peripheral cult" in relation to "official" or orthodox Islam in Kelantan, as is sometimes the case in other areas of the Muslim world (Lewis 1986: 94–107).

States of altered consciousness which occur as a result of accident are much less open to orthodox or other criticism. Unlike those who engage in activities involving deliberate trance, persons who are thought to have been put into a trance state without seeking it usually can not be faulted. Islamic critics may argue against spirits or sorcery as causes of what has occurred but even so the person affected has generally not made the claim. He or she is, after all, not conscious or aware. It is left to others to infer, divine or diagnose that an attack by a spirit or by sorcery has taken place. Further, whatever the cause it is apparent that there is a problem and that the person needs help.

Until recently access to trance experiences among Malays in some regions, including rural Kelantan, was not as limited as Murphy's (1976: 9–10) hypothesis supposes. If latah and possession are alternative trance patterns it is a matter of how common each may be, how much access the same sort of people may have to each, or the extent to which one may have declined as the other has increased. Such information about change over time is not readily available for either latah or spirit possession.

It does appear that throughout Malaya in general the places of voluntary and accidental forms of trance in Malay life appear to have changed over time in an opposite manner. On the one hand, organized seances and other ritual activities involving deliberate trance have almost certainly declined over a long period. Outside of Kelantan and Trengganu such activities appear to have disappeared decades ago as a result of secular Western and orthodox or modernist Islamic influence. On the other hand, the past several decades have seen the rise of previously unreported instances of involuntary trance and possession. Outbreaks of multi-person possession have occurred throughout Malaysia with some frequency. Now known commonly by the Western-derived term "*histeria*," such incidents have been the focus of much attention by the modern Malaysian mass media as well as scholars (Ackerman and Lee 1981; Lee and Ackerman 1978, 1980; Ong 1987; Tan 1963; Teoh and Tan 1976). Affected persons faint, scream, run about, and speak in strange voices. The incidents that have been described mainly have involved adolescent girls or young women and have occurred in one of two contemporary institutional settings. One of these has been modern Western-style schools, especially "Arabic" schools which offer instruction in religious as well as secular subjects and which attempt to enforce a more stringent Muslim code of dress and behavior on students than do other modern schools. The other has been the modern electronics factories located around the major cities of the west coast which employ large numbers of young, single women at relatively low wages and under monotonous working conditions.[12] Such incidents seem to be occasional rather than ongoing, though they may recur. In some instances they appear to have led to real benefits for those involved but in others they have not. While those who have written about these incidents have sometimes assumed that they are an example of a "traditional" pattern taking place in a modern setting, the earlier colonial accounts (Skeat 1966[1900], Gimlette 1971[1915]) of Malay magic do not mention them in any setting.

There may or may not be a relationship between the decline or disappearance in opportunities for traditional, voluntary forms of trance and spirit mediumship and the apparent rise of *histeria* incidents of trance and possession. The institutional settings of *histeria* are new, as is the presence of modern mass media to publicize them widely. Further, while the women involved in the latter incidents are young, those involved in deliberate trance performances are, or were, older. It does seem to be the case that states of altered consciousness associated with spirit mediumship or possession remain a familiar and culturally normal feature of broad sectors of contemporary Malay society.

As for Kelantan in particular, observers who wrote about Kelantanese shamanism in earlier decades of the century did not provide much information about the numbers of shamans who were active, about the frequency and numbers of seances held or the number of individuals who made use of them. The French anthropologist Jeanne Cuisinier who studied *main peteri* and the other magical dances of Kelantan in the 1930s reported that at that time they were very common at all levels of Malay society: "Les séances de *puteri* sont très populaires à Kelantan. Dans les villes, dans les villages, chez le plus pauvre paysan comme le Sultan, en toute occasion, sous tous les prétextes ... on organise des *permainan puteri*" (Cuisinier 1936: 93). In the 1960s and 1970s further accounts were published which suggested that was still so, at least in some rural areas.[13] While some types of seances described by earlier observers (Gimlette 1971[1915]; Cuisinier 1936) had become culturally extinct by the 1960s, *main peteri* at least remained very common (Firth 1967; Kessler 1977). In the Pasir Mas area where I attended numerous *main peteri* seances in the mid-1960s they were also common, though perhaps less so than in some areas. However, by the 1980s they had, as far as I could learn, ceased to be held at all. (See also Laderman [1991: 17] regarding Trengganu.) By this time Pak Derasah, the leading *tok peteri*, had died and his group had ceased to perform. Mat Daud, a second shaman who had been a part of the same group, was still living in Kampung Belukar but was no longer active. It was doubtless possible still to summon a shaman and group from another area for a *main peteri* seance but no one seemed to be doing so.

Has latah increased as other forms of trance experience have declined, as Murphy's hypothesis would suggest? As we have seen, latah in rural Kelantan is certainly now very common but there is little way of knowing if it was any less so in earlier periods. My guess would be that both latah and other trance experiences were both common in Kelantan over a relatively long period of time and that they were (and are), if anything, mutually reinforcing patterns rather than functional alternatives. And even if it could be shown that latah is now more common than formerly, there are other possible reasons – to be addressed below – that may also account for it.

6   Symbolic meanings and social uses

Part of the manner in which latah relates to the broader context of Malay and Malayan culture concerns its affinities with states of trance or dissociation which are familiar throughout the region. From the perspective of the comparative question, one would thus expect that analogies to the echoing and automatic-obedience form of latah that the Malays refer to as involving *mengikut* ("to follow") or as *latah betul* ("true latah") would likely occur in societies whose members are otherwise well acquainted with trance states and inclined to make use of them for various purposes. This is certainly so in the case of the Northern Asian instances. The various Siberian groups and the Ainu have both rich traditions of shamanism and spirit possession as well as versions of "latah" which are most like the Malayan one. Conversely, outside of societies with well-developed cultural traditions of trance and mediumship I suspect that echoing and automatic-obedience patterns will be found only among individuals who are otherwise clinically abnormal as well, that is as a part of distinct, biomedically established syndromes, and then only rarely. With the possible exception of the obscure case of the French Canadian Jumpers, this in fact appears to be so.[1]

But while the existing evidence indicates that cultural traditions of nurturing and creatively using states of dissociation appear to be necessary for imitative latah, it also suggests that these are hardly sufficient. Even if we include all of those instances which share only limited family resemblances with the Malayan pattern, the number of places in the world where "latah" has been reported is far smaller than the number where there are well-developed, normative patterns of trance. Thus there must be more to the context of latah than culturally recognized and approved inclinations to dissociation – but what? While such a question might well be asked regarding all of the instances in which some version of "latah" occurs, I shall limit my inquiry to the Malayan one.

Here a useful point of departure is another provocative conclusion about Malay latah reached by Simons. This is that not all latah is "genuine." Specifically, Simons (1980: 199–200) asserts that there are three types of latah: Immediate Response Latah, Attention Capture Latah, and Role Latah, by which he means in the latter case the deliberate enactment of either of the other forms in the absence of a genuinely startling or otherwise destabilizing experience. That not all latah is authentic in this sense is not exactly a novel observation. Earlier observers occasionally made such assertions. In his account of the Tungus, Shirokogoroff (1935: 250–251) argues at some length that much of *olon* is deliberate. Yap (1952: 527, 549–550) made somewhat similar observations regarding Malay latah, noting that cases varied along a continuum from those in which latah persons appear to be only "histrionic" to those which demonstrate the "full range and severity of symptoms." Putting it in less clinical terms, he also observed that some women were liable to affect startle and exclaim tabooed sexual terms, and that some did so in a very fetching manner. Simons however is much more emphatic and makes the distinction not merely as an observation but as a point of theory.

Malays also recognize that not all latah is "genuine." When I began to study latah in Kelantan I was struck by the apparent callousness of some of the things that I was told were done to latah persons which caused physical harm, not to mention humiliation. I thought that such incidents involved real cruelty and (assuming they occurred as described) still do. But it subsequently became apparent that some of the events involved skepticism that the latah person would actually do what he or she had been shown or told. Malays also often simply expressed doubt that some individuals were "really" latah, at least all of the time.

But why should anyone *act* latah? Simons suggests that this is done to attract attention. His explanation is that in Malay culture latah behavior is encouraged by the attention and actions of others who respond to it in a characteristic way. This encouragement nurtures both Real Latah and Role Latah. But Simons has had little or nothing to say about why Malays and other Malayans should be so attracted to latah, except that it is a part of Malay culture. He appears to regard it as a kind of accidental discovery. As is clear from his film on latah interaction (Simons 1983c), Malays find latah to be very amusing but he offers no further explanation.

Latah interaction

Assuming that latah cannot be adequately explained as either an organically or a non-organically based mental disorder and that some latah behavior is deliberate, then it must have some appeal. It is true to say that Malays and other Malayans may find latah entertaining, but why should they? An answer requires some consideration of the nature and uses of joking in Malayan societies. Here it may be useful to begin by looking at latah not only as a matter of individual psychology but also as a social activity. Thus as a part of the detailed discussions I had with all of the latah persons I interviewed at length (some thirty-eight Malay women and eighteen Malay men, as well as with another fifty non-Malay latah persons in Kelantan and Sarawak) I asked a series of questions about who, if anyone, deliberately teased them: "Who likes to make you latah? What kind of persons? Who in particular?" I also asked about which persons did not do so. Such questions made for some of the more animated parts of the discussions. A very few people replied by saying that no one tried to make them latah while a great many more said that *semua orang* ("everyone") did. Of those who answered "everyone" at first, as well as those who gave somewhat less inclusive answers, all went on to make finer discriminations among the persons they had some contact with in the normal course of their lives. Only in one or two instances did latah persons say that they were only provoked by persons who were "outsiders" (*orang luar*), persons with whom they had no significant relationships of one sort or another.

There are, however, differences between men and women. Malay men most frequently mentioned "friends" (*kawan* or *member*) as the persons who most commonly provoked them. While women also mentioned friends they did so less often than men. Similarly, women were more inclined to identify local children (*budak*) and neighbors (*jiran*) as types of persons who often teased them than were men; almost no men mentioned neighbors and only a few said local children were liable to startle them.

Whether or not latah persons said that they were provoked by everyone or "everyone who knows that I am latah," they either initially or subsequently noted certain specific individuals who did and did not do so. A few men and women said that their wives or husbands did so commonly or occasionally, but far more said that their spouses did not do so. Husbands and wives are supposed to respect (*berhormat*) one another, especially in public and in front of other members of the family. The relationship between siblings and between parents and children is also one of respect. Latah persons thus usually noted their own brothers and sisters did not provoke them. The differences between grandchildren and children are particularly significant. Grandchildren are very frequently noted to be culprits in latah incidents. Such grandchildren are generally described as *nakal* ("naughty"). Although grandmothers are supposed to be respected they are generally very indulgent of grandchildren. In a few instances grandchildren (*cucu*) were the only persons that forceful latah women said were able to startle them and get away with it – others, they claimed, were "*takut*" (afraid to try). On the other hand, mothers and fathers are much less commonly provoked by their own children and those who said they were often held that "everyone" teased them. Moreover, several of the women who said that their own children startled them explained that not all of the children did so. It was rather the younger ones who got away with being *nakal* much in the same way that grandchildren did.

In sum, it is clear that a large portion of the persons who commonly provoke latah individuals in Malay society in Kelantan are family members, kinsmen, friends, and relatives. The responses that occur when latah persons are startled or otherwise provoked include words and actions that are normally to a greater or lesser extent taboo, but which in relation to latah are permitted and encouraged and regarded as funny. Such behavior – both the provocation and the response – is reminiscent of a realm of activity of classic anthropological interest: joking.

In recent decades anthropological interpretations (e.g. Douglas 1975) have been mainly concerned with the cosmological and supernatural meaning of joking. For our purposes it is useful to note certain things which are taken for granted. Joking involves teasing and making fun of another person on the assumption that no real offence is intended or taken. The behavior involved which would in any other context arouse and express serious hostility is supposed to be taken as not serious, though it often has an edge and may lead to trouble (Basso 1979: 69). It involves a peculiar combination of friendliness and antagonism. Joking frequently, though not necessarily, concerns matters of sex and may involve ribald humor. ("When [Ojibway] cross-cousins meet they must try to embarrass one another. They 'joke' with one another, making the most vulgar allegations, by their standards as well as ours . . . Cross-cousins who do not joke in this way are considered boorish, as not playing the social game" [A. R. Radcliffe-Brown 1977 [1940]: 177, quoting Ruth Landis].) Joking behavior may involve only verbal exchanges or it may also involve horseplay.

Latah interaction often has such characteristics. There are, however, certain differences. Few latah persons I ever talked with were inclined to see being teased as a matter of harmless play (*main main saja*) about which they should not be angry, although many thought it very funny when it happened to someone else and admitted to provoking others on occasion. While even Role Latah cannot be simply reduced to a mode of joking, some of what has been written about the latter seems relevant.

In classic social-anthropological analysis, joking is paired with its opposite, which is "respect," and then linked with various axes of the structure of social relations. As is true of many things, the structure of joking and respect is clearest in societies which have unilineal descent and explicit, positive rules of marriage. Such arrangements produce situations in which cross-cousins joke with one another while parallel cousins do not, and the like. In Malay, Javanese, and other Malayan societies which lack unilineal descent and explicit marriage categories, the degree of respect in a relationship is a matter of gender, age, wealth, status, and familiarity, which may vary and configure differently in each case. Certain generalizations seem relevant, however. One is that members of the same generation (that is, brothers and sisters and cousins) are much more apt to joke than those of adjacent generations (that is parents and children or aunts and uncles and nephews and nieces). Joking is also common among members of alternate generations, that is between grandparents and grandchildren.

Modern studies of joking tend to assume that the relationship between the persons involved is equal and that the behavior is mutual. However, as Radcliffe-Brown originally noted, this is not necessarily the case: joking may or may not occur between equals and may or may not be reciprocal; the person teased may or may not respond at all or in equal measure. Latah interaction takes both forms but tends to be one-sided. The person who has been provoked can do little in the way of responding in kind if the person who provokes him is not also latah. There are, however, other ways of retaliating. Men who are simply vulnerable to *kejut* frequently respond to being startled by kicking or striking out with a judo chop. Latah women who have been provoked may also retaliate by hitting out or throwing things. This retaliation is often said to be reflexive, that is done without intent, but when I have (frequently) seen it, it often appears to be deliberate. The responses that some men make (either reflexively or deliberately) are often effective in that the person who has done the startling is made to jump or duck quickly in order to dodge the blow, which if he does not do will mean that he is at the losing end of the encounter. But the provoker may also lose his balance and stumble trying to get out of the way, thereby losing a bit of his own dignity in the process.

Latah interaction may also be three-cornered, that is involve another person beside the one who does the provoking. The third party is the person to whom the latah person's actions are directed. A situation that was sometimes mentioned to me as an example of what some latah men did involved a woman. The latah man would be startled and then told to embrace a woman who was in the vicinity. Needless to say such an attempt would cause outrage and embarrassment to the woman if it worked and was probably less common than the stories might suggest. Another, probably more common, involves a latah person striking another standing nearby after being startled by a third person. I can attest to first-hand knowledge of such instances, for I was the butt of such an encounter.

This occurred when I had gone to visit and interview Mek Sam, a Village Chinese latah woman who lived to the south of Pasir Mas. My assistant and I went first to her house, where we were told she was working in her son's provision shop down the road. We proceeded to the shop, met the son, explained why we had come and asked if Mek Sam was there and if we could talk to her. Mek Sam then emerged from the shop and approached me. Then I suddenly found myself thrown backward as a result, I realized, of being struck hard on the chest. Someone had startled her from behind just as she was about to shake my hand. Everyone was laughing, including Mek Sam. Expressions of concern, queries about whether I was all right and words of regret quickly followed. I was assured that no harm had been meant and that Mek Sam had not even been aware of what she was doing. Clearly, there had been a practical joke at my expense.

Why then has latah become elaborated into a kind of joking? I suspect that people anywhere are likely to find some latah incidents, such as the one just described, to be humorous and harmless fun. But I also imagine that many non-Malays are not only likely to have reservations about the implications of what sometimes occurs (as many Malays do, it should be noted) but to find it rather crude. Indeed it is hard in a sense not to suppose (but see below) that latah is quite out of character for Malays and Javanese who are otherwise very polite and restrained in their relations with one another. According to Hildred Geertz (1968) this is precisely the point of latah among the Javanese. It is so amusing because it is so contrary to the norms by which they otherwise live.

This suggests that part of the appeal of latah is that it provides opportunities for amusing foolishness, aggressive teasing, and sexual humor for people among whom other forms of joking are rather restricted. In his famous nineteenth-century essay on the races of the Malayan archipelago, Alfred Wallace drew a sharp contrast between the character of the Malay and the Papuan: "The Malay is bashful, cold, undemonstrative, and quiet; the Papuan is bold, impetuous, excitable, and noisy. The former is grave and seldom laughs; the latter is joyous and laughter-loving – the one conceals his emotions, the other displays them" (Wallace 1962[1869]: 450). Practical joking is thus "utterly repugnant to his [the Malay's] disposition; for he is particularly sensitive to breaches of etiquette, or any interference with the personal liberty of himself or another" (Wallace 1962[1869]: 448).

Various objections might be made to such assertions, especially regarding their applicability to the range of Malayan peoples to which they appear to have been intended. However, the general thrust is consistent with much that has subsequently been written about Malayan peoples (e.g. C. Geertz 1973[1960]: 232, 240–247 and H. Geertz 1959 on the Javanese; C. Geertz 1972 on the Balinese). In another famous description of Malayan character, Margaret Mead argued that it was not that the Balinese lacked strong emotion, it was rather that they could or would only express it in a theatrical context. "Only in the theater is the overt expression of emotion permitted. In real life the European is often at a loss to tell when two Balinese are quarreling, but on stage, emotions are so accurately delineated that no mistake is possible" (Bateson and Mead 1942: 31). Joking does occur among the Balinese, according to Mead, but it is limited to the teasing of small infants and children, to trance performances and to the theater. Elsewhere in the volume Gregory Bateson noted the similarity of what appears to be joking with men in trance and latah, which he mentions (though only in passing) also occurs in Bali; this joking involved "various grotesque and obscene orders" (Bateson and Mead 1942: 92).

Any analysis of the social uses of latah should take account of the gender and age-specific character of both the activities involved and the attitudes toward it. The implications of latah are different for women than they are for men. Latah of either sort is less demeaning for a woman than a man, for women are not judged by the same cultural standards as men by either women or men. Here in particular Geertz's thesis – that latah is so meaningful to the Javanese because it is so contrary to their standards of conduct – seems to need qualification. In another article she makes the point that there are significant differences in the public character of men and women: "Javanese women are less quiet and subdued than the men; they are much more expressive, and keep up a steady stream of conversation and joking most of the day. But this stream of chatter seems to perform the same function as reserve does for the men; it keeps people at a proper distance" (Geertz 1959: 226–227). Robert Jay makes a similar point but is more emphatic. He reports that while in an abstract way Javanese restrictions of politeness and refinement apply to women as well as men, women are in fact freer to express themselves directly and crudely than are men. "I have seen women of respectable standing in the community let loose barrages of verbal abuse at other women that left their spouses and male kinsmen on the scene speechless with embarrassment or studiedly indifferent" (Jay 1969: 44). "Women even in public frequently make use of vulgar language and manners in asserting themselves, and the men's reaction in public at least, is always studied indifference" (Jay 1969: 93).

Much the same point can be made regarding Malays in Kelantan. Here also men seem to be more preoccupied with dignity and poise than women. Malays themselves note this and say that both *ugama* (Islam) and *adat* (Malay custom) judge men and women differently. A similar point can be made regarding age. Although the patterns are not entirely opposite, Malay men seem to become more concerned with personal dignity and poise as they mature, while women appear to become less preoccupied with such matters. As is true in a great many societies, women in Malay (and I presume Javanese) society are most subject to restrictions when they are younger and least so when they are older. Younger women are considered more vulnerable to temptations and more likely to bring shame (*malu*) upon themselves and their families than are older women. Although rural Malays are aware of the Islamic proscription on physical contact between unmarried adult men and women it is not always observed. Older Malay women (as well as men) would thus sometimes take hold of my hand or arm and feel my skin. Older women thus take liberties in public that would be shocking for younger women. Heather Strange makes this point clearly regarding rural Malay society in Trengganu:

Only old women, those labelled by themselves and other as *orang tua*, are free from the restraints of modesty they have lived with during most of their lives. Their double entendre banter with young men is acceptable, even amusing and clever; similar behavior by a younger woman would elicit comments about brazenness. An old woman can relax on her porch, in full view of anyone and everyone, in a sarong clinched under her armpits, leaving shoulders, calves, and even knees exposed, without criticism. A younger woman can bathe at a well or engage in work near her house in such attire; but she cannot relax clad only in a sarong except in the privacy of her home. (Strange 1987: 23–24)

The situation in Kelantan is similar. Strange implies a sharp contrast between the behavior permitted old women and that deemed proper for all others. In my own experience the relaxing of restrictions (or the assertion of privilege) is more gradual over the course of adulthood. In any case, the basic point is that the occurrence of latah in regard to gender and age within Malay society thus seems to be more a matter of elaborating upon certain tendencies which are otherwise present than of contradicting them: the joking and double-entendre banter permitted *orang tua* women becomes in latah explicit sexual obscenity engaged in by both old and not-so-old women.

Latah as symbolic protest

The rather distinct position of older women not withstanding, part of the appeal of open joking for Malays and Javanese is doubtless its inversion of dominant cultural standards of polite and proper behavior. In this regard latah is also a species of privileged behavior. Ronald Provencher and Jaafar Omar (1988, also Provencher 1990) thus describe the similar attraction of modern Malay humor magazines such as *Gila-Gila* in the political and social environment of contemporary Malaysia, and cite the specific example of the editorial writer who wrote humorous and satirical but serious-minded columns under the pen name of *Manasasau* [son of] *Minah Latah* (1988: 91). This is also part of the attraction which Malayan audiences have to the clowns in the theater, whose abrupt, crude (*kasar*) movements and direct, unrefined discourse places them in opposition to the formal heroes and heroines who display all of the ideal virtues and say all of the right things. It is in fact highly likely that the joking and buffoonery of clowns in both theatrical and (in Kelantan anyway) shamanistic performances are models for latah behavior and for audience responses to it.

Aside from being generally contrary to "proper" conduct, clowning and joking reflect several patterns of behavior commonly associated with latah. One of these, already alluded to, is deviant or explicit sexuality. The anthropologist James Peacock (1968: 156–157) thus notes that the clowns in Javanese proletarian drama may engage in what would off-stage be grossly improper behavior, as in the following instance: "Finally, the clown pokes his hands up under his shirt (which hangs down to his crotch) and begins doing the dance motions under his shirt, in front of his genitals, smiling dreamily. The master of ceremonies angrily slaps his hand." Does anyone doubt the answer to the question that Peacock then asks: "Might the hand motions about the genitals allude to masturbation – which evokes a slap on the hand from authority?" Carol Laderman (1991: 93) similarly refers to the appeal of bawdy humor in Malay *main peteri* performances in rural Trengganu: "Miss click-clack (Mek Ketuk-ketak), a spirit who appears in Mat Din's seance . . . is hot after a man – almost any man will do. The Mute Spirit (Hantu Bisu) is a favorite with audiences in Merchang. All he wants is to get laid, and he conveys this message by the universal symbolism of a finger moving in and out of a circle made by the joined thumb and forefinger of his other hand."

Another pattern common to both theatrical and shamanistic joking is mimicry. Here again Peacock (1968: 159–160, 242) notes both the importance of imitation in Javanese theater ("The clown's favorite game is to imitate the gestures and words of somebody other than himself – a creditor when he is actually a debtor, a master when he is actually a servant, a girl when he is actually a man, a policeman when he is actually a thief" [1968: 73]) and its reflection in latah, which he terms the Javanese "national neurosis." But here matters become much more complicated. While the theatrical mimicry of which Peacock speaks is deliberate, the intentionality of latah is ambiguous. In his attempt to explain Javanese latah – which he also presumes to be a form of mental illness – the anthropologist James Siegel attempts to make a distinction between "compulsive imitation" and "mockery," the former being innocent of deliberate malice, the latter mordant sarcasm:

Small children, hearing foreign languages spoken, are inclined to repeat what they take to be the sounds of that language. This has an element of mockery to it. When I heard myself imitated not by children, but by some young women, I felt I was being mocked. I am now inclined to think that this was not the case. The women were neighbors of mine and were among the people with whom I felt on the closest terms. On no other occasion did they show any behavior that I interpreted as hostile. Moreover, they did not mimic my English, but my Javanese . . . That [this] was not a case of mockery but of a certain compulsion on their part to imitate is, I believe, shown by the fact that, not only in this incident but in each case where they mimicked me, my pronunciation when I said the phrase *"ora apa apa"* was distorted. I had thus reproduced the situation that occurs in *latah*, where indistinct pronunciation leads to associations that ought to be suppressed. (Siegel 1986: 31–32)

In this passage Siegel makes reference to a hypothesis that has frequently been proposed (most fully by Murphy 1976): that Malays and Javanese are taught from birth to learn through imitation, and that latah is a compulsive, pathological expression of the resulting tendency. While compulsive tendencies to imitation may be a part of "genuine" latah, it is also true in my experience that Malays have quite deliberate recourse to mockery. Kelantanese Malays, for example, have a rich vocabulary of expressions which imitate the sounds of speech of Europeans, Chinese, Indians, and other Malays (not to mention the sounds of animals, machines, and other things) which they routinely employ in conversations about such persons. This use can take the form of both harmless joking and deadly ridicule. And again, deliberate mockery and ridicule are frequently used in shamanistic performances in which demonic spirits may be shown to be drunken, too dumb to count or lecherous.

Involving as they do both bawdy sexual references and imitation, such theatrical and shamanistic forms and clowning blend readily into satire and sarcasm and provide opportunities for the expression of social criticism and animosity. Such tendencies have been stressed by I. M. Lewis as an explanation of the commonness of spirit possession or ecstatic religion throughout history and among various cultures. Lacking other means of effectively securing their interests or getting even with those who have oppressed them, both women in general and lower-status men are inclined to use trance and possession to gain attention and other benefits, exert influence, register thinly-disguised protest, and in some instances mobilize the support of others in similar positions. This theory of trance and possession has been criticized on various grounds (e.g. by Kapferer 1983: 93–99)[2] but it has also been argued that it fits well with both traditional Malay shamanistic seances in Kelantan (Kessler 1977: 301–302) and possession *histeria* among young Malay factory women (Ong 1987: 207).[3] To what extent does it illuminate latah?

The circumstantial evidence of the occurrence of latah in Kelantan fits with such an explanation. We have already seen that it is most common among women, poorer persons, and individuals in older age categories, though we have also noted that there can be various plausible reasons that such persons are likely to be affected, and that the behavior of such persons may be privileged in other respects as well. In any case it is notable that where Pasir Mas and Kota Baru are concerned, latah appears to flourish especially neither in the most traditional and deeply rural areas nor in the most modern urban ones but in the villages and neighborhoods on the edge of town. Over the past several decades communities such as Belukar and surrounding communities in Pasir Mas have been buffeted by currents of change that have been pervasive in Kelantan but which have been especially strong in the expanding interface of town and country.

While in the past nearly all of the inhabitants of Belukar were farmers (*petani*) this is no longer so much the case. Some still plant padi, especially in the great expanse of open fields to the north. But as noted earlier, many of the households are now supported by other means. Many of the men work as laborers, taxi drivers, trishaw peddlers, policemen, teachers, and traders in Pasir Mas and elsewhere. Part of the rice land has been converted into house sites. Thus like many of the villages in the region, Belukar has begun to take on the characteristics of a suburban bedroom community. It is connected by a small dirt lane to one of the main roads leading out of Pasir Mas. The inhabitants thus have fairly easy access to the center of town which is three kilometers away. A few of the men own automobiles which they drive to work elsewhere, including Kota Baru, the state capital, about twenty kilometers away. Some of the men also travel much further and do not return home at the end of the day. They work as far away as Kuala Lumpur and Singapore and return home every several months for the major holidays and when their terms of employment expire.

Belukar, like most of the other Malay villages on the fringes of Pasir Mas, is also a community which is now less homogeneous than it once was. There were always differences in wealth and status and religious expertise. Even when nearly all of the men were farmers there was considerable variation in land ownership. A few families owned many acres while many owned only a few and some none at all and worked as laborers or share-croppers. But now differences in wealth are more pronounced and have less to do with land ownership than with occupation. Those who form the wealthier strata of the village are families in which the men earn salaries as teachers or government officials, or are successful businessmen. Moreover, such differences are readily apparent in the houses of the village.

The houses of the poorest villagers are small, sometimes constructed in part of palm thatch and split bamboo, unpainted and bare or sparsely furnished. The houses of the richest villagers are large brick, concrete, and stucco (*rumah batu*) two-storied structures, brightly painted and furnished with Western-style stuffed chairs and couches, floor coverings and appliances which proclaim their owners not only well-off but modern. In addition to the small number of the largest and fanciest houses and the larger number of small or decrepit dwellings are many more that are somewhere in between. However, the houses of the rich and the poor are not set in different areas but are close by, in some instances in full view of one another. Everyone is well aware of such material distinctions and what they imply about wealth, but they are also socially confusing for the newly-rich villagers are generally not the sort of hereditary aristocrats that others were taught by tradition to respect.

The religious changes which have also moved through Malay society over the course of the past several decades have also been strongly felt in Belukar and the other villages and neighborhoods on this side of town. This area has been marked by a particularly strong traditional commitment to Islam. In the past there were a number of active religious boarding schools (actually communities of students and pious followers) presided over by a senior teacher and leader. The Islam associated with these religious communities and espoused by the religious elders and pious men (*alim* and *lebai*) of the region is devout but also tolerant of local customs and practices and did little to interfere with the relative freedom of movement of women. As Islam in the region became heavily politicized in the 1960s, religious ideology was directed more toward Malay nationalism than into criticism of Malay culture.

The phase of religious reform known generally as the *dakwah* is a different story. Originating among sophisticated, often university-educated West-Coast Malays, this movement has been directed at the religious practices and life-ways of Malays. Locally the movement was resented and in some respects religious life continued as it had. However, Malays in the area have also come to accept newer, more stringent modes of religious behavior as a basis of a proper life. As locally interpreted, this has meant a focus on externally visible patterns of behavior and dress, especially involving women.[4] Further, the previous acceptance of traditional shamanistic and theatrical performances has ceased.

It is also apparent that such economic, technological, social, and religious changes have been most strongly felt by those types of persons already most likely to be latah: those in middle and later years of adulthood, women, and the poor. Older Malays are thus confused and disoriented by the rapid changes in the region in ways that have some likely connection to latah. Being startled by traffic was sometimes mentioned by latah individuals and, as noted earlier, a latah women was said to have been struck and killed by an automobile. Somewhat similarly, several persons told me that television (especially American wrestling) was among the things that made them latah. The new patterns of work which take many men away from the village, in some instances for prolonged periods, have also left older persons and women of all ages in situations of isolation that were uncharacteristic of traditional life. In addition, in the case of women with husbands working and living in distant places there is concern about the possibility of relationships with other women, for even if a man is devoted and loyal there is the chance that he may be trapped through sorcery. And finally the effects of change may have something to do with the commonness of latah among the midwives of Belukar and surrounding villages.[5]

In sum, the sorts of persons who are latah are often of the same type that have been held to be typical candidates for spirit possession. The social and cultural processes that give rise to states of possession thus provide a better explanation of latah than does the notion that it is a form of neurosis or psychosis or evidence of an organic neurological disorder. At the same time, the social and cultural dynamics of latah and possession are not entirely the same. Here it is useful to consider an example from my experience.

During the course of my last stay in Pasir Mas I went on one occasion to visit and to eat supper at the house of Pak Ngah and his wife Zainab in a village in rural Pasir Mas. They are a couple I had known well since my first period of fieldwork twenty years before. He is an occasional carpenter and farmer with relatively little land with the result that the family is relatively poor even by local standards, but hardly marginal in village society. While waiting for the meal to be prepared I brought up the topic of latah. Although I already knew most of the other families in the area and was not planning to do a household survey, I casually asked if anyone in the neighborhood was latah. Pak Ngah remained silent but Zainab said yes, there was. I asked who and Zainab replied that she herself was "*sadikit*" ("a little"). Pak Ngah remained silent but did not seem pleased by this disclosure. I was quite surprised for I had never heard it before. She was only a little latah, Zainab explained, and then only occasionally. Then she went on to recount an incident that had recently occurred. She said she had been riding in a local private taxi in the village with several other locals including Haji Wan Leh. The latter is a religious official at the local mosque, a wealthy landowner and a member of the opposite political party from that of Pak Ngah and Zainab, and someone they did not like, though none of this information was part of the story – I already knew it. The taxi hit a bump and she was startled (*kejut*) and blurted out "*palak Tok Haji*" ("the Haji's prick"). Everyone else in the taxi laughed she said, but the Haji had just sat quietly. She laughed a little when she told the story, perhaps because she was embarrassed, perhaps because she was amused or perhaps because, as I think, she was a little of both. Pak Ngah continued to look as though he wished she had never brought it up.

While the social dynamics of latah, as in the incident recounted to me by Zainab, have certain similarities with those of spirit possession, it is not the same. As we have seen, even the *kejut* form of latah is rare among younger women who are typically possessed. Further, although older women have greater freedom to make joking allusions to sexual matters and to utter sexual obscenities, they are still engaging in risque, tabooed behavior if they do so openly. These, however, are relatively minor points. The more basic question is whether latah serves as a means of protest similar to spirit possession along the line noted by Lewis (1989) and, if so, whether this may help account for its prevalence in contemporary Malay society in Kelantan. Lewis argues that spirit possession cults are *not* merely a means by which women (and lower-status men) "symbolically" (or "unconsciously") protest their position *vis-à-vis* their husbands, family, and kinsmen, or society in general; but rather that they are also a means of *improving* it through the acquisition of property (new clothes and jewelry), prestige, and influence, and through the development of new social relationships. If nothing else, the appearance that spirit possession has occurred requires the acknowledgment that something needs to be done to alleviate the problem.

In contrast, the incident described to me accomplished little or nothing for Zainab except perhaps some satisfaction and amusement in recounting it to others – which she did voluntarily in my case. Haji Leh is unlikely to have supposed it had anything to do with the fact that he was rich and she was poor and resented it. He may or may not have supposed that she was "really" latah. All that I can say for certain is that she told the incident freely and without any evident encouragement of her husband, perhaps mainly to entertain me. It does, however, seem to have been another instance in which the butt of the latah incident was not the latah person herself but a man in the vicinity, that is Haji Leh. It is also an incident that, if not a joke at the time it happened, became one in the telling. And here the person at whose expense the story was recounted to me was another man, Pak Ngah, to whom, however, she had been successfully married for thirty years. Unlike most Malay couples I have known, Pak Ngah and Zainab did joke with, or about, one another. This often focused on meals and cooking and was at her expense. My impression was that she was, in a small way, getting even.

The extent to which latah evokes sympathetic assistance from relatives, family members or friends varies. Westernized or university-educated Malays may be likely to regard latah from a psychiatric perspective and suppose that the person may be in need of help. For example, in Kuala Lumpur one urbane Malay man who was involved in administering the grant program which sponsored my research expressed an interest in latah which went beyond conventional politeness. He told me that his aunt had recently begun to develop latah, and that he had taken this to mean that she needed more looking after by the family, and perhaps psychological counseling. Doubtless such an attitude is common among some sectors of

Malaysian society but I found little evidence of it in rural Kelantan. Here the prevailing attitude is that latah is amusing, that latah persons are not really harmed, and that teasing is all right as long as no physical injury is involved. Not everyone shares this attitude and the actual situations vary. In some instances the teasing that occurs is of a friendly and gentle character, and in others family members make an effort to protect the latah person from harassment by outsiders. But there is little inclination to see that latah means that a person needs active care. In some instances latah persons seem quite able to look out for themselves; indeed, some of them are very forceful. Further, unlike spirit possession, latah is not an acute problem about which something can be done, but a continuing state for which there are no generally recognized means of alleviation. Thus while the social and psychological bases of latah may have some affinity with those that have been held to encourage attacks of spirit possession the differences are also significant.

Part III

Borneo comparisons and perspectives

7 Latah in Borneo

In the past two chapters I have tried to show how latah is and is not importantly related to other elements of Malay (and where it seemed appropriate to generalize, Malayan) culture and social practice. In the next two chapters I extend my analysis to Sarawak, and to the Iban in particular. Sarawak is one of the two modern Malaysian states in northern Borneo, and is both geographically far larger and ethnically more varied than Kelantan (Map 3).[1]

It is useful to preface what follows with a brief discussion of what drew me to Borneo in the first place. Broadly put, my interests were comparative. I wanted first-hand information on latah in a different ethnic and cultural setting. While most descriptive accounts and efforts at explanation have concerned the Malays and Javanese it has long been known that latah is not limited to these groups. F. G. H. van Loon, the Dutch colonial psychiatrist who worked on latah in the 1920s, noted on the basis of his survey of physicians serving throughout the Netherlands Indies that instances had been noted among various Indonesian peoples in addition to Malays and Javanese (van Loon 1924: 308).

Such awareness not withstanding, much of the analysis of latah, especially Javanese latah, has focused upon hierarchy and its various social, cultural, linguistic, and psychological correlates. The Dutch colonial observers were fond of pointing out that latah in Java was especially common among servants, particularly servants in European households, and more recently it had been suggested that it had its origin in the evolving pattern of European dominance and native subordination in the mid-nineteenth-century Malayan world. The anthropologist Hildred Geertz (see also more recently James Siegel [1986: 30–32, 132, 284–285]) had offered an explanation of latah based on the inference that the distinctly Javanese values involved were rooted in class differentiation and language levels, social indirectness and sexual prudery. While there are certainly also continuities among the Malayan peoples of the region, there are also differences. Although some Bornean groups are hierarchically ordered, others lack a pattern of class differentiation, are socially direct and not

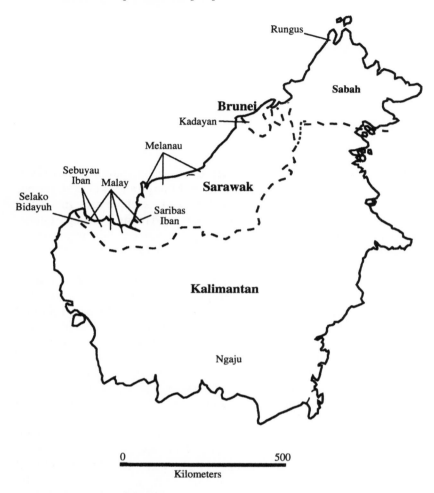

Map 3. Latah in Borneo

prudish about sexual matters. Further, the colonial history of the region has been very different from that of Malaya and Java. What then of latah in such a setting?

I was drawn to Sarawak in particular by a report of an earlier survey (Chiu, Tong, and Schmidt 1972) showing that latah was common among Iban as well as Malay populations. Moreover, this report was as interesting for what it did not say as for what it did. It mentioned nothing about latah among other Dayak groups and it did not make clear whether latah was characteristic of all or just some Iban. Here was an issue of classical ethnological interest, among other ways in regard to Murphy's assertions that latah has undergone a pattern of expansion, change, and decline over time. While my original interest in Sarawak was thus a matter of gaining limited comparative information on the occurrence of latah among the Iban, what I found initially led me to a broader and lengthier survey involving other groups as well. Before turning directly to the Iban, I shall discuss the larger pattern and its development.

Latah in Sarawak

In addition to many Chinese, the population of Sarawak includes Malays as well as the indigenous Dayaks. Like those of most regions of Insular Southeast Asia, Sarawak Malays derive from Muslim immigrants from other regions, including Java and Sumatra and the Malay Peninsula as well as long-time Malay inhabitants of Brunei descent (see, for example, Harrison 1970: 147–159; Leach 1950: 33–37; and Sanib Said 1985: 1–10). Some also descend from Dayak groups that were driven seaward by wars and the expansion of more powerful interior tribes and that, obtaining sanctuary with coastal and riverain Malay chiefs linked to Brunei or the Brooke regime, eventually converted to Islam and assumed a Malay identity. The Sarawak Malay population is concentrated mainly in the coastal areas of the westernmost part of the state where they support themselves with fishing and farming. There is also a substantial urban or semi-urban Malay population in Kuching and other towns along the coast and the lower reaches of the major rivers, especially the great Rajang.

Little needs to be said at this point about latah among Sarawak Malays. My own inquiries were made around the towns of Lundu and Kuching, in villages and hamlets on the Saribas River, and in the river towns along the middle and upper Rajang River – Kanowit, Song, Kapit, and Belaga. These showed knowledge of latah to be general and latah persons to be present in most communities. In one Malay village complex in Betong, Saribas, in which I did a complete household survey (see Table 7.1), there were eight latah persons in a population of 727. In other areas with large Malay populations the number of latah persons appears to be similar.

The Dayak sector is diverse (Lebar 1972: 147–197). Today the term "Dayak" is used to refer to the indigenous non-Malay population of the state, which includes many different local ethnic populations, all speaking Malayan languages, some (such as Iban and Selako) very close to Malay, others much more distant.[2] From the perspective of stratification there are two traditional patterns. The coastal Melanau and the various *Orang Ulu* (up-river peoples) – the Kenyah, Kayan, Sekapan among others – are ordered hierarchically; they have hereditary chiefs and systems of rank and

Table 7.1. *Sarawak Malays (Kampung Rendah, Betong, Saribas, Second Division, pop. 716)*

	Latah		Total population	
Age	Women	Men	Women	Men
0–9	0	0	130	128
10–19	1	0	66	72
20–29	0	0	61	62
30–39	0	0	33	28
40–49	2	0	32	19
50–59	4	0	26	28
60–69	0	0	10	11
70–	0	0	2	8
Total	7	0	360	356

recognize broad distinctions among nobles, commoners, and (formerly) slaves (Rousseau 1990). On the other hand, the Iban and Bidayuh (or Land Dayak) have an egalitarian social order, one that lacks such systems of class, rank, and leadership. Of these two patterns, the hierarchical is closest to that of the Malays and Javanese, although far less well developed.

In the past most Dayaks dwelt in longhouses situated on hillsides or along streams and rivers, engaged in slash and burn cultivation involving dry rice, and practiced warfare focusing on headhunting. Rich traditions of belief and ritual focused upon these and other concerns and involved shamanism, spirit possession, collective feasting, animal sacrifice, elaborate augury, and extensive taboos. With the exception of headhunting, major portions of this way of life remain in effect throughout large areas of the interior. However, conversion to Christianity or much less often Islam, increasing reliance on wage-labor (especially in logging) and cash-cropping, urbanization, and the spread of Western education has also been extensive in many regions. This is especially true in the western area of Sarawak (First Division) where most of the Dayak groups have shifted from hilltop and mountainside villages to lowland settlements and single family houses, to pursue mixed farming and become Christian.

Table 7.2 provides a broader summary of the results of my inquiries about latah in central and western Sarawak, including the specific groups and sub-groups involved, the areas where my efforts were concentrated, and my estimates of the commonness of the pattern. It shows that latah is present in some regions or sub-groups and absent in others; specifically that it occurs among Bidayuh, Melanau, and Iban in some areas but not in all others. Such a pattern suggests, to begin with, that in this region latah has

Table 7.2. *Latah among Dayak peoples in Central and Western Sarawak*

Ethnic group	Sub-group	Occurrence	Research areas
Bidayuh	Selako	Common	Lundu (1st Div.)
Bidayuh	Bukar-Sadong	Unknown	Monkos (1st Div.)
Iban	Sebuyau	Very common	Lundu, Kuching (1st Div.)
Iban	Saribas	Common	Betong (2nd Div.)
Iban	"Up-river"	Unknown	Ulu Oya (3rd Div.), Middle Rajang, Lower Baleh, Lower Mujong (7th Div.)
Melanau	Christian and Pagan	Unknown	Dalat, Oya River, Kut River, Middle Igan River (3rd Div.)
Melanau	Muslim	Common on coast but uncommon up-river	Dalat, Mukah towns, Oya and Kut rivers (3rd Div.)

little or nothing to do with a hierarchical rather than an egalitarian social order.[3] It is also apparent that latah is not associated exclusively with a set of ethnic groups defined in terms of language. Nor for similar reasons can religion be a decisive factor.[4]

If the occurrence of latah in Sarawak has little to do with ethnic or language divisions, hereditary social hierarchy or religious affiliation, it none the less shows a clear pattern. It is at the present time a coastal (broadly conceived) rather than an interior pattern. It thus seems certain that its occurrence must reflect conditions or developments relating to this zone. I once discussed the ethnic pattern of latah in Sarawak with a Melanau government official who, perhaps jokingly, suggested that there might be something in the environment – such as the effect of the tides or the coastal climate – which caused latah. This seems unlikely, unless it can be shown that latah is related to some sort of yet-unnoted dietary deficiency common to coastal populations. It is more likely that the occurrence of latah here reflects processes of social and cultural change which have taken place within this region. Almost certainly a major part of this process has been the influence of Malays or of other Malayan Muslims (Javanese, Boyanese, Minangkabau, communities of which are all present in the area) from other regions.

There is first of all the term itself. All of the groups in central and western Sarawak who have latah, that is, who recognize a hyperstartle pattern among themselves and so label individuals, refer to it as *latah*, that is by the widely used term of Malay (or Javanese) origin, rather than by a local word.[5] Further, latah is found in areas where there are large numbers of Malays, as there are throughout much of the First Division, or where Malay influence has otherwise been historically very strong, as among the Muslim Melanau.[6] Conversely, latah is apparently lacking in the deeper interior areas where there are few or no Malays. Even among the Melanau there are differences from one region to another which are linked to the religious divisions noted above. Most of the specific Melanau latah individuals whom I located and interviewed lived in or near the old river-mouth trading towns of Oya and Mukah. These are the areas where the population is most heavily Muslim and where Malay influence from Brunei has historically been strongest.

It is thus apparent that latah in central and western Sarawak has spread readily from Malay or other Malayan Muslim groups to Dayak populations in polyethnic coastal and estuarine areas. But the conclusion that latah has simply diffused in this way needs to be qualified in several ways. To begin with, elsewhere in Borneo the occurrence of latah may or may not have such direct origins. The apparently widespread occurrence of "*gigiren*" (e.g. among the Kadayan of Brunei [Maxwell 1990]) and its reflexives (e.g. *giren* among the Ngaju [Schiller 1987, pers. commun.]) also suggests a common external source. However, the use of local terms such as "*obingsalah*" by the Rungus Dusun of Sabah (Doolittle 1991) and "*bibiran*" by the Timogun Murut, also of Sabah (Brewis 1992: 11–14), do not. Nor in Sarawak has Malay influence necessarily always been direct. In some cases it seems possible that latah was learned from other Dayak groups rather than directly from Malays. Finally, as I shall go on to suggest below, indigenous Bornean beliefs, practices, and traditions also appear to have influenced the spread of latah and the development of some of its features.

Latah and Dayak culture

Most of the characteristics of latah in Sarawak are the same as in Kelantan, although there are also certain differences. As in Kelantan, people who have latah associate it above all, though not exclusively, with startle. Among the Iban, for example, the term for startle is *tekenyit* (Richards 1988: 156), which appears to have much the same range of meaning and implication that *terkejut* has for Malays. Persons who are latah are said to be vulnerable to *tekenyit*. Those Iban who are familiar with latah also distinguish between a simpler and briefer hyperstartle pattern involving a sudden exclamation and various physical responses, and a more extended one involving imitation or "following" (*ngikut*), merging into altered consciousness (*luput*). However, the tendency to insist on the distinction between "simple startle" latah and "following latah" and, in some instances, to claim that only the latter pattern is "true" latah, is not as important among the Iban or in Sarawak generally as in Kelantan. In both places there is occasional ambiguity regarding whether or not a person is really latah or not but generally in Sarawak individuals who are regarded by others as latah also readily acknowledge being so. As in Kelantan, where latah occurs in Sarawak it is not regarded as something about which much can be done. Latah persons among Malays and among other Muslims in Sarawak only rarely told of inviting prayers, visiting shrines, or making vows as efforts to stop being latah, and few non-Muslim Dayaks mentioned consulting *dukun* (healers). Nor is there evidence that latah itself is thought of as a form of insanity or illness among any of the Bornean groups in which it occurs, though this is not to say that it is never associated with instability or personal difficulty.[7]

A more striking difference concerns gender. In Kelantan, as we have seen, both men and women are latah, although women more frequently so than men. In Sarawak, on the other hand, all of the latah individuals I found were women. My inquiries about latah men generally elicited the reaction that "men are not latah." My statements that latah occurred among men in Kelantan often produced amusement and sometimes references to transvestites – an association sometimes made in Kelantan as well, although everyone there knew of latah men who were not. While one Bidayuh Dayak man told me that he had heard of a Malay man in a coastal village who was latah, I was never able to find any specific instances.

A further difference, which requires more lengthy discussion, concerns the role of dreams. These are matters of great importance among the Iban (Freeman 1967; Jensen 1974: 117–120), and among other Dayak peoples (see for example Metcalf [1982: 58–59] on the Berawan). While, as we have seen, dreams were not commonly accorded much importance regarding latah in Kelantan, some earlier writers reported that Malays and Javanese emphasized them. In Sarawak dreams were more frequently cited as bringing latah or as being associated with its perpetuation. Of the thirty-six latah persons I interviewed in detail (eight Iban, eight Melanau, eight Selako Bidayuh and twelve Malays), about half said that they had dreams in relation to latah. Further, such dreams are quite different from those few reported in Kelantan. The latter, as we have seen, all concerned being chased or attacked by or struggling with animals – rams, bulls, elephants, tigers. Of the Bornean dreams only one concerned animals, specifically snakes and monkeys. The others all concerned ghosts, demons or persons. Further, whether or not dreams of animals of the sort told by a few Malay women in Kelantan are to be regarded as implicitly sexual, many of the dreams recounted by latah Dayak women in Sarawak were explicitly so.[8]

Throughout Borneo dreams are accorded importance as a means of communication between the human and the supernatural worlds. In dreams the soul may wander and in dreams the person may be penetrated and possessed by a spirit. Dreams may reveal future events and they may be a means by which a person is given knowledge and instruction. Becoming a shaman or medium often begins with dream experiences with spirits.[9] Further, since they are regarded as a communication with spirits rather than as a reflection of the private emotional state of the dreamer, dreams are often a matter of public discussion, and may require action by others. Finally, the spirits which appear in dreams are often motivated by carnal desires.[10]

Dreams about spirits which sexually desire or possess humans are thus common in Borneo and are often a matter of public concern rather than private guilt or shame. Moreover, they are often a part of the experience which leads to the assumption of a role of shaman or medium. In some instances this is a matter of seduction or unwanted sexual harassment while in others, as in that of Bidayuh priestesses (*borih*), it involves a legitimate marriage between a spirit lover and a woman. Given the prevalence of such beliefs among Bornean peoples it is not surprising that latah should become associated with dreams, in some instances with sexual dreams involving spirits. As we have already seen, some reports of latah have emphasized the occurrence of dreams in relation to the beginning of the pattern or to its recurrence.

The dreams recounted to me by latah persons among different ethnic groups in Sarawak also vary somewhat though there are commonalities. Those that Malay women described in relation to becoming latah included being attacked, being murdered; in one case a Malay woman, Putit, told of waking up with a snake on her face. She also told me of recurrent dreams of snakes and monkeys and of men trying to catch her. Ibu Bibi, sixty-six at the time, said that her dream was of men hanging in shadows; they were, she thought, *hantu latah*, latah ghosts. This was the only reference that any of the Malay women I interviewed in Sarawak made to dreaming of spirits or to being bothered by spirits. However, among latah women of the Dayak communities such dreams are common. Sometimes they involved visits by dead family members. Giah, a seventy-six year old Sebuyau Iban woman, said that the dream she had when she became latah included the ghosts of her mother and father, while Siti Hawa, a Melanau woman of fifty-five, dreamed of her dead son who has continued to visit her regularly in her sleep. Drama, a forty-two year old Selako Bidayuh woman, told how she was reunited with her dead children and grandparents in her latah dream. In other instances the spirits in latah dreams are strangers. Ipot, a seventy-four year old Melanau woman, said she was visited by a groups of ghosts who took her away and kept teasing her until she became latah. And Rosni, another Melanau woman, attributed her latah to a dream in which a Haji (she is a Muslim) chased and caught her and carried her around.

As the latter suggests, latah dreams may involve carnal intercourse with spirits. While some Dayak women only hinted at this others were quite frank about it – again reflecting the public character of the pattern. Giah, whose latah dream included visits by her mother and father, also said that a devil (*iblis*) had come and slept with her. Several different latah women mentioned such encounters, while two others told me that they had consulted *dukun* or *manang* (shaman) and were informed that spirits lusted after them. Two such experiences were recounted by pagan Selako women in rural Lundu. In one, Gingo, about sixty, said that a spirit had come to her at night and as a result she had become pregnant and given birth to a child who had lived for several months and then died. In her grief she ran into the forest where she lost consciousness and then had a dream in which she saw a spirit, a *hantu ara* which attacks women at childbirth. The spirit told her that the body of her child should not have been put in a tree, as it had been, for it was already too old, and that she would go mad. She did not become mad but she has been latah ever since.

Another such latah dream experience has particularly strong shamanistic overtones. It was recounted by Jejak, a Selako midwife of sixty-five years. About six years previously, she was returning from delivering a baby. As she passed through the graveyard she saw a burial mat flying through the air, even though there was no wind. Then she saw a large white head and a body. The head had a handsome face but for arms and legs there were only bones. The spirit tried to catch her and chased her home where she fell down on the steps unconscious. Her sister called a *dukun* to wake her. She revived but became very ill. At dusk she died and remained dead until early the next morning. Being dead was like a dream. She had a *parang* (chopping knife), a basket, and an axe and went to collect firewood. But when she arrived in the forest she found she did not have the *parang* so she returned home. Then, however, she went back but discovered her axe was missing and went home again. The same thing occurred with the basket. At this point she awoke and realized she had been dead. The house was full of people, as when someone dies. They told her that she had stopped breathing and that her body had turned white. This was still before she had become latah. Shortly after Chinese New Year, she had several dreams of a spirit that had a human body but the head and legs of a wild pig. The spirit chased her home and she slammed the door. The spirit's human body could not pass through the door but its feet and legs did. Then the spirit changed into the form of a man she knew in the village. The man could not speak and simply made a noise – "mnn, mnn" – but tried to get her to sleep with him. After this she became latah.

The importance of dreams in relation to latah suggests that it has blended readily with important existing Dayak beliefs and practices. I have already pointed out with regard to Malays (and more generally Malayans) that familiarity with states of dissociation and trance are an important part of the cultural context of latah. Such states are also familiar to Dayak peoples in Borneo. Indeed they are accepted with much less ambivalence as a fundamental part of religious experience and healing practice than among present-day Malays in Kelantan. As in Kelantan, I found no indication that latah itself is associated with magical powers. However, there are important parallels between latah and the assumption of roles of spirit medium or shaman in Bornean societies. Individuals often become shamans or mediums at about the same age that persons become latah – the middle years of adulthood. This is especially so when becoming a medium or shaman is the result of a sudden decision or necessity rather than a long period of study. Further, as with the beginning of latah, the assumption of the role of spirit medium or shaman is often preceded by a trauma. Both, moreover, are perceived to involve a permanent transformation of the self, not a "role" that can be entered and exited at will. Bornean mediums and shamans are widely believed to be what they are because of overwhelming spiritual forces. And finally, shamans and mediums (or less frequently "priests") are often women. In some cases (as among the Bidayuh and the Rungus) certain such ritual specialists are exclusively women. In other instances, while both men and women may become shamans or mediums, women often predominate. In those societies, such as the Iban, in which shamans are generally men, there is a symbolic link between shamanism and transvestism, even though actual transvestite shamans are presently rare (Winzeler 1993b). The tendency to suppose that latah men would be transvestites has already been noted.

8   Latah and the Iban

Having traced the general outlines of latah in Sarawak, let us turn to a specific instance. I have noted earlier that I was first drawn to Borneo because of a previous account of latah among Iban in Sarawak, and that while I found latah to be present among various Dayak populations in the coastal and lower river areas, my inquiries showed it to be especially frequent among some of the Iban. In this chapter I thus look more closely at the Iban and suggest some reasons why it may be particularly common in this instance.

The Iban are the largest and most widely distributed of the indigenous non-Malay Bornean populations of Sarawak, and they are no longer a homogeneous ethnic population. Significant differences have by now come to exist and to define Iban populations in some areas as a result of varying histories of migration and contact with Malays and other non-Iban peoples, especially over the past century and a half. At the one extreme are the Iban of the middle Rajang and various other rivers of the interior. These are the more "traditional" or, perhaps more accurately, "pioneering" shifting cultivators of Derek Freeman's (1970[1955]) well-known account of the Baleh River dwellers. At the other are the Sebuyau Iban of the Lundu (see, for example, Low 1848: 165–168; Pringle 1970: 46) and the Kuching areas. The Sebuyau Iban migrated from the Sebuyau River, near the lower Batang Lupar, around the beginning of the nineteenth century either before (according to Sandin 1968: 6–7) or after (according to Low 1848: 166–168) wars with the Sekrang River Iban. As a result of his survey of the ethnic groups of Sarawak Edmund Leach (1950) went so far as to classify the Sebuyau as "para-Malays." This term is hardly justified in that the Sebuyau had already by that time become Christian rather than Muslim and had retained their own language and identity, as they continue to do today. But it does suggest that the Sebuyau Iban were at that time even more fully Malayized than the Iban of some other areas that were also in longstanding acculturative relationships with Malays. Today they recognize themselves as a distinct community within the larger population of Iban. The men are no longer tattooed, and all are at least nominally Christian. Many Sebuyau,

Table 8.1. *Sebuyau Iban (Kampung Sungai Dayak, Lundu, First Division, pop. 498)*

| | Latah | | Total population | |
Age	Women	Men	Women	Men
0–9	0	0	50	49
10–19	0	0	64	65
20–29	3	0	40	25
30–39	2	0	23	26
40–49	5	0	26	19
50–59	4	0	24	26
60–69	5	0	18	16
70–	2	0	12	15
Total	21	0	257	241

especially those in the Kuching area, are educated urban dwellers. Some are government clerks and laborers, saw-mill hands and the like, while others are still swidden farmers.

As is true of some of the other Dayak peoples of Sarawak, latah is found among the Iban of some areas and not of others. It is very common among the Sebuyau Iban who dwell in the vicinity of Kuching and Lundu (see Table 8.1). Latah is also fairly common among the Iban in some areas of Saribas River and it occurs at least sporadically in the Sibu area on the lower Rajang River. Conversely I found little or no evidence of latah among the Iban in the interior or upriver regions of the country. For example, while I made extensive inquiries at longhouses along the middle Rajang from Song to Nanga Baleh, in the lower Baleh up to the Mujong, as well as in the lower Mujong, I turned up neither any instances nor any real knowledge of latah.[1]

As in the case of Dayak groups generally, the spread of latah from Malays to Iban can thus be seen simply as a part of a larger pattern of diffusion and transformation in the coastal regions of Sarawak. The context in which this has taken place is readily apparent in some of the polyethnic towns. One of these is Lundu, where I have frequently stayed throughout the past five years in which I have been doing research in Sarawak. Lundu is a small riverside market and district-administrative center which appears to have changed little in form or function since it was established as a colonial outpost of the Brooke regime in the mid-nineteenth century. Surrounding the town core – a characteristic little Sarawak colonial bazaar consisting mainly of three rows of Chinese shops set in a square around a park open to the river – are a series of very discretely delineated ethnic village-neighborhoods: Malay, Sebuyau Iban, and, further out of town, Selako Bidayuh. The village of Sileng on the edge of town, for example, is composed of both Malays and Sebuyau Iban, each occupying a separate section, differentiated from one another by a small open field, the Malay part known as Sileng Melayu, the Sebuyau part as Sileng Dayak. Members of all of the various communities mingle in the Lundu bazaar and the government offices and share the same buses that transport people and goods over the dirt roads in and out of town. Members of each group speak their own language but frequently know those of the other communities, especially Malay. The impact of Malay culture on the Sebuyau Iban as well as the Selako Bidayuh is obvious. The people of both groups in the Lundu area have abandoned longhouses entirely and live in Malay-style dwellings. The absence of a mosque or prayer house, or in some instances the presence of a Christian chapel, is the only indication that such a village is not a Malay community.

The relationship between latah and a broader pattern of Malay influence among the Iban is also evident in Betong, another small colonial bazaar town and administrative center, in this instance on the Layar, the main branch of the Saribas River. Here Malay influence on the Iban has occurred over a period of several centuries.[2] However the Saribas Iban, no matter how strongly affected by Malays, have not (as of 1987) abandoned longhouses in favor of separate Malay-style dwellings set in Malay-style villages adjacent to Malay communities, as they have long since done in the Lundu and Kuching areas. Nor are Malay and Iban communities situated as closely to one another as they are in Lundu. It is perhaps in part because of these differences that latah appears to be less common among the Saribas Iban of the immediate Betong area than among the Sebuyau Iban of Lundu. While one large (over forty doors) longhouse in Betong had four latah women, and another of comparable size had three, several others had none.

The strong acculturative influence of the Malays in such places as Lundu and Betong is thus partly responsible for the particular commonness of latah among the downriver Iban. In addition, as noted earlier, the Iban share the general complex of beliefs and experiences involving dreams and trance experiences which are closely associated with Malayan latah generally. Our concern here, however, is with a third set of factors which may also help to explain the frequent occurrence of latah among some of the Iban. These involve social tensions, on the one hand, and social uses, on the other. In the case of the Iban these relate to gender in particular.

In order to understand this, it is useful to review briefly the study of gender relations among the Iban. Such a review will show that the now-substantial literature suggests that while the status of women and the relationship between men and women in Iban society are similar to what is characteristic of other Dayak societies, there are also notable differences that are pertinent to the matter of latah.

Warrior traditions and their perhaps inevitable emphasis on aggressive masculine virtues notwithstanding, gender among Bornean peoples has often been described in sexually egalitarian terms (see especially the collection in Sutlive 1991a). Generally speaking, domestic life shows relatively little sexual domination. Moreover, in some groups, such as the Rungus and the Bidayuh, important parts of much of the traditional ritual life of the community were in the hands of women.

The older accounts of missionaries and administrators (Howell 1963a[1908], 1963b[1910]; Low 1848: 196–199; St. John 1862 [vol. I]: 47–57) give little indication that gender relations among the Iban varied much from the general pattern. It was noted that Iban women inherited equal shares of property, chose their own husbands, and that men and women shared the tasks of food production, though with men doing the heavy work of clearing and women doing much of the routine work of cultivation. Men sought prestige through headhunting though women approved and, in fact, were to some extent responsible through their inculcation of values of bravery and revenge into male infants, and through their taunting of young men who had not yet taken heads and through their adulation of men who had (Gomes 1917: 5; Richards 1963 [1909]: 118–120).

Such views were not, however, based on substantial ethnographic fieldwork, which did not begin among the Iban or many other Bornean peoples until after the Second World War (Leach 1950). The literature published since that time thus presents a more complex picture. Following two years of fieldwork among the interior Iban of the Baleh River, Derek Freeman (1970[1955]) produced an initial report of Iban agriculture and social organization which, in so far as it dealt with female–male relationships and the position of women, added validity and depth to the previous picture. Notably Freeman demonstrated absolute male–female symmetry in certain basic areas of Iban social organization such as post-marital residence and inheritance. However, in subsequent publications dealing specifically with headhunting, shamanism, and symbolism he presented a somewhat different picture (Freeman 1967, 1968). In these he focused on sexual attitudes and emotions which he interpreted from a Freudian perspective. He suggested that male and female (including parent and child) relationships were marked by tension and conflict. Michael Heppell (1975), Freeman's student, provided further documentation of Iban domestic tension and conflict and noted the role of sexual transgressions as sources of fights, killings, and feuds.

In particular these later studies show the existence of a strong double standard in post-marital sexual morality and custom. This provided that a man away from his own longhouse was considered a bachelor, and thus free to seek sexual favors as he chose, whereas women had no such opportunity. Though free to take lovers before marriage, Iban women were prohibited from engaging in adultery. An Iban man who caught another man in the act of sexual intercourse with his wife had the right to spear him to death (Freeman 1967: 340). More generally Freeman argued that traditional Iban society was dominated by male values. These concerned especially head-hunting, including both the practice – which after having been suppressed for a decade or so had recurred against the Japanese during the war – and the cult by which men enhanced their prestige in a series of extensive celebrations. They also concerned the practice of men spending long periods away from home in trading ventures or work. Headhunting and journeys are in turn associated with the practice of tattooing which among the Iban was limited to males. Only men who had taken a head had the right to have the backs of the hands tattooed. Other tatoos were added after the completion of a journey, so that a body covered with tatoos indicted many trips away from home.

It has been further argued that these practices and the ritual celebration of male virtues had a strong effect upon women that was manifest in several ways. Both Freeman (1967) and Clifford Sather (1978) emphasize sexual dreams of a pathological sort and Freeman also argues that Iban women were prone to forms of envy and antagonism toward men that were expressed in various ways:

It is not uncommon to see an Iban mother fondling, in an admiring way, the penis of her infant son. This is erotically stimulating to the child but it is also, I would suggest, threatening, for to look on an object not one's own with intense longing is also, in most cases, to envy its possessor. This is seen when a mother and young son quarrel, as they often do. Then, the boy, enraged, will shout at his mother (as in a case I observed): "Your vulva! Your vulva." And the mother, also angry but partly in mockery, will retort: "Your stiff penis! Your testicles!" ...

Again, during head-hunting rituals which are occasions for the celebration of the preoccupations and narcissism of men, bands of women as comically dressed transvestites complete with grotesquely ornamented phalli, for hours on end will chant songs in which they mock male pretensions and denigrate the male genital. (Freeman 1968: 387–388)

It is thus also clear that whatever they show about envy and other emotions, the expressive activities of Iban women take an overt rather than a "symbolic" or repressed form. If traditional Iban women were inclined to feel envious toward – or angry at – Iban men they also had some ritual means of directly expressing such feelings. Freeman himself interprets the experiences and behavior of Iban women in psychoanalytic terms, asserting for example that incubus dreams "together with my direct observation of the oedipal behavior of Iban girls, suggests the hypothesis that the incubus, at one level, is a disguised father image, and that the unconscious springs of the incubus dream lie in psychic formations resulting from the Oedipal situation" (1967: 338). The interaction between Iban mothers and sons and the customary mocking behavior of Iban women during headhunting celebrations are similarly interpreted as classic penis envy.[3]

The matter is further complicated by the social and cultural changes that have taken place. The emotions and behavior of the Iban that Freeman describes concern the still highly traditional population of the Baleh River area in 1950. While *gawai* (festivals) relating to the head cult continue to be held occasionally in the interior, the extent that either they or the particular activities of women continue to occur in the form in which he describes them is a matter of uncertainty. The various possible emotional correlates of the extensive social and cultural changes which the Iban have (very differentially in various areas of Sarawak) undergone have now also begun to be described. However, material of the sort provided by Freeman and Heppell concerning the more traditional interior Iban has not yet been published in comparable detail by those scholars who have studied the more changed Iban of downriver, coastal, and urban areas. It is likely that some of the facets of traditional Iban life which gave rise to female animosity at male privilege and pride diminished as the Iban were brought under European and post-European domination, especially as active headhunting and warfare were suppressed.

However, while recent accounts (Mashman 1991, Kedit 1991, Davison and Sutlive 1991) vary in this regard, they suggest that not all bases of tension between Iban men and women have been eliminated as a result of modern developments. There is, for example, the practice of male journeys known as *bejalai* as described by the Iban anthropologist Peter Kedit (1987, 1991) and others (Freeman 1970[1955]: 222–226; Jensen 1974: 49–53). *Bejalai* includes lengthy journeys or expeditions to distant places to collect jungle produce, engage in trade or wage-labor, or to serve in the military but which, in any case, have as a primary purpose the achievement or validation of status. In the modern period *bejalai* are undertaken above all for wage-labor in logging camps, oil fields, and on cargo ships. Hence the practice merges with the circular labor migration activities of men of most Dayak populations of Sarawak and of much of the Third World in general. However, among the Iban, the practice is institutionalized and ritually elaborated to a greater extent than among other groups, and it continues to be common among downriver as well as interior Iban. Indeed it has generally been argued that as headhunting was suppressed it became more important. Men returned with goods and tales of adventure and distant places as they had formerly returned with trophy heads and stories of raiding.

Like headhunting, *bejalai* is thus a male pursuit. Women have no culturally sanctioned means of going on journeys and thus escaping the routines of longhouse life and the work of cultivation. Since they are not expected to do so, women may have much less desire to travel than men. However some women do leave the longhouse and migrate to towns but those who do are presumed to be engaged in prostitution rather than in worthwhile, status-enhancing activities (Sutlive 1978: 163–165; 1991b; Kedit 1991: 297). While *bejalai* for wage-labor has economic and other benefits it also has drawbacks for women. These include being left behind, being required to perform the agricultural labor normally performed by men as well as that done by themselves, being uncertain when men will return or whether they will return at all. For married women with absent husbands the drawbacks include loneliness and the temptation to engage in adultery (Kedit 1991: 313).

But if the sources of tension between men and women in Iban society have not necessarily diminished as a result of modern developments, it would appear that opportunities for women to express these seem to have lessened. As the Iban have been drawn closer to the more modern sectors of Malaysian society the opportunities for sexual clowning and ridiculing men that were a part of traditional ceremonies have diminished. This is so at least among the Sebuyau Iban. A possible part of the reason that latah has become as popular and widespread among the women of this group as it has is that it has certain parallels with the traditional sexual joking behavior of Iban women.[4] Consider first the pattern which Freeman describes as pervasive among the Baleh Iban circa 1950:

One of the forms which this mockery [of men] takes is for two women to share a nickname (*emperian*) which they regularly use in addressing one another in a bantering tone of voice. It is always a nickname directed at males, and usually at the male genital. (Freeman 1968: 388)

By way of comparison here is an instance from my own experience involving latah with the Sebuyau Iban in Lundu in 1986. During the course of my house-to-house surveys and interviews with latah persons, in Sarawak as in Kelantan, I occasionally became the object of what I have interpreted to be latah joking. Such incidents occurred several times among the Sebuyau. In one instance, during the course of an interview with Miti, a Sebuyau woman of thirty-seven years, I dropped my pen. Miti was startled and quickly said "Oh, you dropped your penis," then laughed and said she was *malu*. On another occasion we were working on the survey in the same area of the village. We went to the house of Lumut, Miti's older sister. Before long Miti herself appeared, sat down and listened to the conversation. I completed the interview without incident, but when I arose awkwardly from sitting cross-legged on the floor I forgot that a pressure-lamp was hanging just over my head, and I hit my head on it. Lumut became latah and said "you bumped your penis." Everyone – me, my assistant, Lumut, and Miti – burst into laughter, and Miti quickly said "have intercourse with me." This in turn provoked riotous laughter.

Here it is also important to take note of who teases and jokes with whom. Sebuyau Iban women, like other latah persons, reported that they are often provoked by other women, including their own friends, and they also readily acknowledged that they tease others. Miti told me that Lumut was among those who teased her and that, even though she does not like to be startled, she likes to provoke others because of what they say and do. Lumut and Miti are in fact among a number of women in that end of the village who are well known for latah. I had in fact been warned by other villagers to watch out for them. That such a pattern of joking and teasing among Iban women reflects elements of protest and animosity seems likely for several reasons. Miti and Lumut have both had somewhat difficult lives. When she was young Miti had a child out of wedlock. She subsequently married and was then divorced from a Chinese man. She has been married to her current husband, a Malay, for the past eleven years. Three of the six children to whom she had given birth have died. Her husband is poor, having previously been a sailor and now a farmer. They live with her parents who are now both old. Since she converted to Islam, they are the only Muslims living in the Dayak part of the village. Lumut is also poor and somewhat socially marginal, although to a lesser degree than Miti. While her husband, like most of the other villagers, is a Christian, she has remained a pagan.

Among the Sebuyau Iban, as among other groups which have latah, such behavior is regarded as naughty or deviant but only slightly so. To openly express the sexual obscenities which are blurted out in the course of latah, or to follow orders or to engage in behaviors which are foolish or obscene is to violate standards of proper, dignified behavior. But the violations are not usually that serious and in any case they are excused by the accepted view that latah persons are not responsible for what they say and do. Men here also may harbor suspicions that women are not necessarily really or always unaware of and unable to control their actions, but this does not seem to make a great deal of difference. As is generally the case, the Sebuyau women who are latah are mainly from the poorer economic strata. Such women are perhaps especially in need of a little attention and somewhat less concerned about the possibilities of a loss of prestige in the community. However, women may be latah and also pillars of respectability.

Part IV

Conclusions

9 Explaining latah: paradigm and paradox, syndrome and ritual, nature and culture

Since it was first noted in the nineteenth century, observers and theorists have suggested many possible cultural, historical, psychological and social variables to account for Malayan latah in one place or generally. Those proposed in the recent period include reference to child-rearing practices (an emphasis on rote-learning and imitation which promotes dissociation and distinctive views of the body and the self as composed of detachable body parts [Murphy 1976]); a hierarchical social order, especially a colonial one in which there are also strong elements of confusion in the modeling of appropriate behavior (Geertz 1968; Murphy 1976) and in the use of appropriate language codes (Siegel 1986); sexual prudery (Geertz 1968: 99–100) or sexual repression and penis envy (Murphy 1976: 16); concepts of the soul and supernatural empowerment (Kenny 1978). Some such explanations refer to a series or combination of factors.

To be broadly relevant it would seem to be necessary for any such explanation to fit the range of Malayan societies in which latah occurs. This would cast doubt on those arguments formulated with specific regard to Java which emphasize elaborate class-hierarchy, colonialism, and linguistic stratification, which do not fit well with Borneo. In my own view several factors are broadly applicable and otherwise important. One of these is the prevailing familiarity with trance states, as indicated in the common occurrence of possession as a mode of affliction and of shamanism and spirit-mediumship as modes of healing. True or imitative latah is frequently a form of trance and needs to be understood in this light. I have already mentioned that Malays and other Malayans often described latah to me in the same terms they use to discuss other forms of dissociative behavior, as involving changed awareness and a greater or lesser loss of memory and control. To say this does not mean that all or most instances of latah involve radically altered states of consciousness. Most occurrences are fleeting disruptions of the normal stream of conscious experience and some may be a matter of performance. But latah for some individuals on some occasions involves deep trance.

Another such factor is a general preoccupation with startle, which brings disorientation and confusion and renders the individual vulnerable to entry or manipulation (cf. Laderman 1991: 42–43). Familiarity with trance states and particular concerns about startle thus imply certain views about the person as permeable and liable to influence from without and of the self as interactive rather than autonomous. Latah itself is taken to be a primary reflection of susceptibility to startle but various illnesses are also explained in such terms. Malayans are hardly unique in their beliefs about startle but they appear to place particular emphasis on it.

Finally, there is the Malayan preference for limiting the overt expression of strong emotion – including anger and humor – to ritual contexts including theatrical and shamanistic or spirit-mediumistic performances, or, in Borneo, to festivals, dances, and celebrations. Long stressed by European observers of Malayan peoples, this preference has perhaps been overstated, and it is more common among some peoples (the Javanese and Balinese) than others (the Iban and other Dayak groups). But it appears to be a general feature of the Malayan cultural personality. The importance of latah in this regard is that it constitutes an acceptably ritualized form of behavior and interaction and thus lends itself readily to teasing and joking. While latah cannot be simply reduced to this, it frequently displays some of the features of classic humorous, often bawdy, ritual insult and response. Such features include inversion and parody. But while it has been claimed that the particular meaning of latah is that it contradicts normal standards of conduct this is only partially true. Latah behavior is partly a matter of contradiction but it is also partly a matter of exaggeration. As noted above, latah is uncommon among younger women, for whom expressions of a sexual nature would be most contradictory and embarrassing, and common among mature and older women who are already permitted greater freedom in such matters.

The latah paradox diminished

Discussions of latah in recent decades have been animated especially by reference to a seeming paradox. The difficulty here is not only in specifying a set of cultural features which explain its occurrence among a variety of Malayan peoples but in reconciling these with its occurrence elsewhere as well. How can latah be explained in specific regional cultural terms if it occurs in distant geographical and cultural settings as well? My own solution to the latah paradox is to nibble away at it from several directions until little of it remains.

To begin with, assuming that the neurobiological potential for hyperstartle reactions and trance states is common to humanity, cultural differences are also fundamental. Among other things, some societies expect, nurture, and encourage trance experiences while others do the opposite (Ornstein 1977). Such differences must be part of the explanation of latah. Various observers have reported simple hyperstartle reactions among modern Western individuals and, in some instances, have interpreted these to be instances of "latah." But such reactions (with the exception of rural French Canadian *jumping*) do not involve or lead to sustained command-obedience or imitative patterns, that is to trance states. Writing recently about a person affected by a severe startle reaction in Holland which he takes to be "latah," the psychiatrist J. A. Jenner (1990: 196) suggests that the reason that such individuals do not develop echoing reactions may be because *imitative* behavior is not acceptable in Western culture, which emphasizes individuality. This may be true as far as it goes, but it is also the case that Westerners tend to distrust and stigmatize trance states in general as religiously marginal, fraudulent, or mentally pathological.

Progress can also perhaps be made on another part of the latah problem – its apparent occurrence in many different places. Discussions of "latah" often assume that it is cross-culturally more common than it is. Such assumptions rest in part upon an overly broad definition of "latah." In the article on the case of hyperstartle in the Netherlands, Jenner (1990: 194) refers to "The occurrence of latahs all over the world . . ." This and similar generalizations can be misleading. Instances of simple hyperstartle may occur among individuals all over the world but true imitative or command-obedience "latah" does not. While not necessarily exhaustive, my earlier review of the comparative evidence indicates that true "latah" occurs extensively only in two regions: (1) in Southeast Asia among Malayans and to some extent among adjacent and immigrant peoples; and (2) in an arc across far northern Asia from the Ainu of Japan through Siberia to (possibly) the Lapps. In both of these regions the "full" latah pattern (startle combined with the expression of sexual obscenity in some individual instances; the loss of consciousness, imitation, and automatic obedience in others; and cultural recognition and labeling) are present. The occurrence of such a pattern indicates diffusion, at least within each region (for which I have presented direct evidence regarding Borneo) rather than broad cross-cultural occurrence and psychic universality. Both such regions, moreover, have in common well-developed traditions of trance and shamanism.

Other instances of "latah" have been reported in north Africa and Arabia, but these (like French Canadian *jumping*) are either so rare or so obscurely documented that they are difficult to evaluate. They may be a matter of individual or highly localized aberration rather than of cultural patterning. Beyond these instances, the occurrences that have been cited appear to be either cases of "startle neurosis" *without* imitation, command-obedience or other indications of dissociation (as with the Western hyperstartlers described by Jenner [1990]; Simons [1980]; Thorne [1944]; and others) *or* of imitation *without* startle or other "latah" features (as in the various "first-contact" displays of mimicry reported by Darwin [1845(1839): 202]; Gilmour [1902]; Gajdusek [1970: 61]; and others). If all of these instances, which show only one or another characteristic of Malayan latah (or Siberian *miryachit*) are lumped together as "latah," then the pattern is more common.

Either way, however, the paradox of latah is substantially diminished. If "latah" is taken to include any of a variety of behavioral forms, its wider cross-cultural distribution can be demonstrated but its significance as a highly particular pattern is lessened; conversely, if it is more closely defined as an integral complex of behavioral features, then its comparative occurrence turns out to be much more narrowly circumscribed than has often been claimed. For some the paradox may remain. True imitative or complex "latah" definitely does (*pace* Kenny 1978, but see also Kenny 1983) occur outside of a single area and this is a matter of real ethnological interest. But it does not seem to be a great paradox, given the highly imperfect state of ethnographic and ethnological knowledge. Geertz herself originally hinted that the paradox might turn out to be more apparent than real.

Syndrome and ritual

While discussions of latah have been animated especially by reference to a seeming paradox, the *study* of latah and of the culture-bound syndromes in general has its own paradoxical character. Although the very notion of "culture-bound syndrome" as formulated by Yap has been held by some scholars to be seriously if not fatally flawed it has, nonetheless, grown in importance and been applied to an ever wider range of instances. Developed originally out of earlier notions of "exotic psychosis" and the like to deal with certain cases of apparent mental pathology in non-Western societies which did not appear to fit standard Western psychiatric categories, the concept has been increasingly applied to a variety of Western or post-industrial maladies. An approach which some anthropologists have found to be untenable in comparative ethnographic terms has been found by other anthropologists (and some psychiatrists) to be highly relevant for explaining obesity, anorexia, agoraphobia, para suicide, flashing, non-economic shoplifting, and even adolescence and menopause in America or England (Littlewood and Lipsedge 1987).

But if the older classic non-Western culture-bound syndromes are a good model for analyzing various post-industrial afflictions, the reverse may be less the case, at least where latah is concerned. The "new" culture-bound syndromes have been discussed in particular in terms of "medicalization," the creative or transforming process by which socially recognized behavioral patterns or conditions come to be defined as *illnesses* and brought within the scope of official medical authority. As Littlewood and Lipsedge (1987: 298) stress, medicalization provides "mystical sanction" for the maladies and gives them meaning as biomedical afflictions rather than as individual eccentricities, accidents of nature, or patterns of deviance, and offers the possibility of relief through therapy.

In the case of latah, medicalization has occurred mainly at a distance, as it were. It is certainly true that when Western observers first became aware of latah they tended, with an occasional objection, to define it as an exotic mental disorder ("a disease of the brain and not the body"). But while Western views may be spreading, the medicalization of latah has yet to be widely adopted in Kelantan or Sarawak, or apparently elsewhere in Malayan society.[1] The large number of Malay and other Malayan latah persons that I came to know certainly did, for the most part, regard latah as a problem, but seldom as one that could be helped. Most thought that latah was due to the actions of others and that if a person was not startled or teased he or she would not be latah. A small number of individuals reported consulting curers, with no success, and a few told me that they had sought the help of religious elders, again with little success. One Pasir Mas man informed me that he had gotten over being latah by his own efforts and the Will of God. Most latah persons regard latah as an enduring aspect of the self that is, however, affected to a large extent by those around them.

If latah is not a culturally medicalized *illness* the question remains as to whether it may none the less be a syndrome in another sense, that is a biomedically recognizable *disease*, as Western observers have often held it to be. But the culture-bound syndromes in general turn out to be very problematic in this regard. In their survey of the literature, Littlewood and Lipsedge (1985: 118) make the notable observation that "Whether a particular pattern is described as a 'ritual' or a 'syndrome' often seems to depend on which type of Western professional first described it." The distinction between ritual and syndrome that they are getting at is a matter of "utility" and "pathology." Biomedically oriented psychiatric studies that treat apparently pathological patterns as syndromes do not necessarily assume that they are entirely without utility. Reference is sometimes made to the benefits (attention, support, sympathy) that an individual derives from suffering from a syndrome as "secondary (or hysterical) gain," and to the useful consequences it may have for others as "social function." It is assumed, however, that syndromes as such are basically maladaptive. In contrast, the individual and social values of "ritual" are taken to be primary rather than residual. The fact that latah was first brought to widespread Western attention by a non-medical colonial observer notwithstanding, it got put in the syndrome category early on and here it has, until recently, remained firmly established as a "disorder" with which persons (frequently referred to as "patients") "suffer." Yap (1952: 550) and others have noted that latah may have its benefits and uses but assume that it is basically a form of psychopathology, a view opposed especially by Kenny (1978, 1990).

Part of the problem of latah in this regard is the nature of the existing record. Over time those who have written about latah have tended to be drawn to the more dramatic instances. In the course of interviewing large numbers of latah persons I also encountered some fairly striking examples. However, these – a small portion of the total – are comparable to those which a reader of the literature is likely to regard as typical. Many observers of latah have attempted to do more than provide colorful anecdotes about vivid behavior, but the more ordinary instances they mention tend to recede into the gray background of the record, especially as information is replicated in second- and third-hand accounts. Further, latah is subject to local folkloric embellishment. All of this has the effect of making the pattern appear less a part of normal social interaction and more pathological than it commonly is.

It is true that the biomedical status of latah is also complicated by the fact that several of its most striking behavioral features are associated with various forms of mental pathology noted in Western persons, some of which, moreover, appear to have an organic or neurobiological basis. Excessive startle responses have been well documented in a number of different diseases, particularly chronic encephalopathies (Kunkle 1967: 356–357).[2] Echolalia, echopraxia or echokinesis, and coprolalia are also latah characteristics which, for a long period of time, have been noted in clinical descriptions of severe abnormal behavior. Such patterns include schizophrenia, alcohol psychosis, and epilepsy (Carluccio, Sours, and Kolb 1964).[3] It is assumed that in some instances (that is, those involving either alcohol psychosis or epileptic seizures) the mental pathology has an organic basis (Brain 1965: 57).[4] As noted earlier, some discussions of "latah" have also drawn attention to the occurrence of imitative behavior among non-Western peoples in "first-contact" situations as indicating confusion and stress (Prince and Tcheng-Laroche 1987: 14–15; Yap 1974: 97–98).

Such observations suggest a possible link of some form between latah and biomedically recognized mental pathology. Yet specifying the nature of such a link is inherently problematic. To take a related example, while spirit possession has also been labelled a culture-bound syndrome (e.g. by Yap 1960) and interpreted as a manifestation of mental disorder, scholars who have studied such patterns closely have cautioned that appearances cannot be taken at face value. In an analysis of possession states associated with Melanesian cargo cults, Theodore Schwartz (1976) makes a distinction that is pertinent to latah between "pathogenic" and what he calls "pathomimetic" patterns. The former refers to behavior, such as seizures, shaking or trembling which has its basis in neuropathology, while the latter refers to apparently identical patterns which do not. "Some of the extreme behaviors observed in cults are *modelled* [emphasis original] on pathogenic behaviors that occur under other circumstances. However, the coma and convulsive seizures appearing in the cults do not require that the enacting participant be either epileptic or under extreme stress" (Schwartz 1976: 184). In situations which encourage cargo-cult activity, pathomimetic behavior is expected, even encouraged, and culturally patterned.

Possession behavior also has certain sociological consequences that are relevant to latah. As Lewis (1986, 1989) in particular has stressed, possession can absolve the affected person of responsibility for behavior that might not be otherwise tolerated. Both possession and latah attract social interest. However, while possession incidents generally provoke a local crisis and demand immediate action, latah is regarded as an enduring pattern and may evoke amusement, teasing, and abuse to which, however, the latah person may respond in kind. There is also a certain amount of overlap between the kinds of persons who are liable to spirit possession and those who become latah, though again there are also differences. In both cases considerably more women than men are affected. But in contemporary Malaysian society at least, younger women, who are seldom latah, are more likely to be affected by possession *histeria* in contrast to older women who appear to be less prone to attacks by spirits but liable to latah. In both Kelantan and Sarawak I found latah to be especially common in regions in which change appears to have been hard on older persons and on women, and in which other, more traditional, rituals of solidarity and support have declined. Noting such sociological parallels in crude summary manner makes them both sound more consciously contrived and less complex than they really are, but they are significant.

The distinction between psychogenic and pathomimetic possession is reminiscent of Simons's (1980) distinction between his two forms of "real" latah and "role" latah. However, while referring similarly to "role" possession, Schwartz points out that individuals manifesting the same behavior can vary widely in the extent to which alterations in conscious ego control are involved. He suggests that the range begins with conscious sham involving collusion of the whole group and goes through conscious or unconscious acting out of culturally defined cult behavior to real trance or autohypnosis. The problem for anthropologists is that "present methods of field observation cannot help us resolve the actual state of the person observed" (Schwartz 1976: 185). Although Simons (1980) argues that by using ethological techniques of observation it is possible to readily distinguish real latah from role latah, the more complex, less readily segmented continuum Schwartz proposes for possession states may be more appropriate.

Recent work on spirit mediums and possession in Borneo is also significant in this regard (see Winzeler 1993b). Among Bornean Dayak peoples generally two paths to religious authority are common: the "priestly" and the "shamanic." The first path involves study, is closely associated with broader authority, is often monopolized by men, and is oriented to extensive prayer and the performance of sacrifice. In contrast, the shamanic path, while also requiring some study and initiation, often involves initial affliction or at least powerful dreams which indicate the attention of spirits. Bornean shamans commonly lack wider authority, are sometimes mistrusted or regarded as eccentric or unstable, but they also often attract considerable interest and admiration and are deemed essential for certain types of curing and other ritual activities. They make use of trance and spirit mediumship and sometimes perform dramatic feats of exorcism. Shamanism in Borneo is culturally patterned and socially mediated. It is much more a matter of "ritual" rather than of "syndrome."

As with cargo-cult possession, Bornean shamanism, spirit-mediumship and the like, latah may in some individual cases involve neurobiological pathology. Along with innate normal tendencies to echo reactions in certain extreme situations, this possibility may help to explain the origins of latah as a cultural pattern but have, if anything, only a limited role in its perpetuation over time. Once it was established, cultural learning, expectation, and individual need and social use appear to be an adequate explanation for the existence of latah and, as I found in Borneo, for its spread into new areas.

Glossary

This glossary includes some of the vernacular Malay (or Malayan) words and phrases which appear in the book, specifically those which refer most directly to latah, to the forms of behavior and emotion associated with it, and to closely related matters. It also includes other vernacular terms for the various patterns which have often been taken as instances of latah and with which I have dealt in the book with under the general rubric of "'latah' elsewhere." Unless otherwise indicated, the terms given are standard (Malaysian) Malay, although they also occur in other Malayan languages as well.

bahtschi (*Bah-Tschi*) Thai term for "latah" in Thailand.
bibiran term for "latah" among the Timogun Murut of Sabah.
bidan kampung traditional (literally "village") midwife.
bidan kerajaan government midwife.
bomoh (*bomor*) curer or shaman.
buruh kasar laborer.
cakap to say, to speak.
cerita story, tale.
Cina Bandar (Kelantan) Town Chinese, but also meaning the less locally acculturated Chinese.
Cina Kampung (Kelantan) Village Chinese, but also meaning the locally acculturated Chinese; comparable to the *Peranakan* or Baba Chinese of other areas.
demam fever, feverish.
dia she, he.
dukun (Sarawak) common Bornean (and Indonesian) term for curer.
gawai (Sarawak) Dayak festival.
gigian Balinese term for "latah," probably reflexive of *gigiran, giren*.
gigiren, giren, gagiran terms for "latah" reported for various areas of Borneo.
gila crazy, insane.
hantu spirit, demon.

hantu latah (Sarawak) latah ghosts, encountered in dreams.

hikayat epic.

histeria uncontrolled, unconscious behavior often attributed to non-deliberate possession by a spirit or to sorcery.

ilmu literally "knowledge," but also traditionally meaning magical knowledge and implying spiritual power.

imu (also *imu:*) Ainu term for "latah."

irkunji Yukaghir term for *miryachit* or Siberian "latah."

jaga to guard, to be on guard.

jampi magical formula, incantation, spell.

jumping, jumper terms for the behavior pattern interpreted to be a French Canadian version of "latah" in rural Maine and related regions.

kacau most literally "to disturb and confuse" but used very commonly by latah persons in regard to efforts of other persons to provoke latah.

kaget Javanese/Indonesian term for startle.

kampung village.

kebal invulnerability.

kejut term for startle; *terkejut*: to be startled.

keturunan descent, heredity, as in *latah keturunan*.

kuli laborer.

latah the basic Malay, Javanese, Iban (and often other Malayan) term for exaggerated startle, to be distinguished from "latah" as used in Western discourse for all instances of hyperstartle (*latah, mali mali, bahtschi, imu, miryachit, jumping*, Lapp Panic, and others) which have often been taken to be the same behavioral pattern. The quotation marks used here and throughout the book are intended both to distinguish the generic term from the vernacular Malayan one and to indicate the ambiguity of the former.

– *betul* (Kelantan) literally "true latah." Used to mean "very latah" but most specifically the imitation and auto-obedience version.

– *kejut* (Kelantan) most literally "simple-startle latah." Often used to refer to vulnerability to startle involving the expression of obscenities but not the loss of conscious control, imitation or automatic obedience.

– *mulut* literally "mouth latah." Used sometimes to refer to verbal imitation or the expression of obscenities.

– person the term "latah" or *latah* has sometimes been used alone in Western discourse to refer to a person ("he is a *latah*") as well as to a pattern of behavior ("he is *latah*"). The former use is misleading in that *latah* is not used in Malay (or, to my knowledge, in other Malayan languages) in this way. The correct Malay is *orang latah* ("latah person"). The term *pelatah*, which also means latah person, is grammatically proper but seldom used in my experience in Kelantan and Sarawak. This is also true of the verb form *melatah*.

lupa (Iban *luput*) literally "forget" but used in relation to shaman performances and seances to mean deliberate trancing.

main literally "to play"; *main main* means to fool around or to joke, sometimes used in reference to pretending to be *latah*.

main peteri literally the "play of the Princess," the name of the Kelantanese seance or possession performance involving trance, theater, clowning, joking, music, the most common purpose of which is curing through exorcism and spiritual rejuvenation.

mali mali term for "latah" in the Philippines.

malu shame, shyness, modesty, embarrassment – one of the most important of all Malay and other Malayan emotion-concepts; often mentioned by latah persons as a consequence of being latah.

manang (Iban) shaman.

marah anger, to be angry.

mati to die, death, to be dead.

mengikut literally "to follow"; used in reference to latah to mean automatic imitation or obedience.

meryak Koryak term for *miryachit* or Siberian "latah."

mimpi dream.

miryachit (*myriachit, meryachit*) general term for Siberian forms of "latah" (also Arctic Hysteria).

muda young.

mudah easy, easily, as in *mudah terkejut* ("easily startled").

nakal naughty, mischievous, annoying. Often used in regard to latah to refer to "privileged" young children who startle older relatives in a form of inter-generational joking.

nekzah term reported to mean "to be easily startled" in relation to "latah" in Yemen.

ngikut Iban term meaning "to follow" (see *mengikut*).

nyanyuk feebleness of mind and forgetfulness in the elderly; clearly differentiated from latah.

obingsalah the Rungus Dusun term for "latah," the literal meaning of which is "to misspeak."

olon Tungus term for *miryachit* or Siberian "latah."

orang person, human being.

orang tua an old person.

orang ulu (*Orang Ulu*) literally "up-river person or people"; in Sarawak the "Central Bornean" ethnic groups of the deep-interior.

pangkat rank.

parang chopping knife, bush knife; sometimes mentioned in accounts of injury inadvertently inflicted by latah persons.

peraih (*tok peraih*) in Kelantan a petty trader, often a woman, very commonly represented in the ranks of latah persons.

petani farmer, cultivator.

pondan transvestite.

sakit sick, sickness; infrequently referred to in relation to latah.

sedikit (Kelantan: *sikit*) a little, as in *sedikit latah*.

semangat spirit of life, soul.

silat Malay martial arts, the fighting dance.

silok term for "latah" in the Philippines.

takut fear, frightened.

tekajut Balinese term for startle.

tekinyit Iban term for startle.

tidak khabar (also *tak khabar*, *tidak sedar* etc.) to be unconscious, in a state of trance.

ular snake; frequently (especially the cobra) mentioned as an object of fright and original psychological trauma in accounts by latah persons.

young-dah-hte Burmese term for "latah" noted in at least one firsthand account.

Notes

INTRODUCTION: THE PROBLEM OF LATAH

1. These include, for Malaya, Clifford (1898); Ellis (1897); Fitzgerald (1923); Galloway (1922); Gerrard (1904); Gimlette (1897); O'Brien (1883); Rathbone (1898); Ridley (1913[1897]); Swettenham (1900[1896]); and for Java (van Brero (1895, 1896); van der Burg (1895, 1897); Forbes (1885: 69–70); van Leent (1867); Metzger (1887); Neale (1884).
2. Allbutt and Rolleston (1910); Castellani and Chalmers (1919); Manson (1910, 1950); Scheube (1903); Osler (1944); Meth (1974); Price (1941); Strong (1944).
3. Barnouw (1985: 370–374); Bourguinon (1979: 280, 284); Honigman (1967: 403–405); Kluckhohn, Murray, and Schneider (1953: 696); Levine (1973: 29); Linton (1956: 115–116); Opler (1967: 133–134); Wallace (1970: 218).
4. Foster and Anderson (1978: 83, 96); Helman (1990: 235); Landy (1977: 340–341); Moore *et al.* (1980: 212); McElroy and Townsend (1989: 279).
5. Nor were the culture-bound syndromes, either as a general category or in specific instances, recognized by official Western psychiatry and included in the third edition of the *Diagnostic and Statistical Manual* of the American Psychiatric Association (DMS-111). This prompted various responses including assaults on the cultural biases of this official organ, discussions of where and how the culture-bound syndromes could fit, and expressions of hope that they would be included in future editions. See especially the 1987 (11) issue of *Culture, Medicine and Psychiatry* devoted to this and related matters concerning the culture-bound syndromes.
6. Notable exceptions include Foulks (1972) on Arctic Hysteria, Hufford (1982) on Old Hag, and Rubel, O'Nell, and Collado-Ardón (1985) on *susto*.

1: THE STUDY OF LATAH

1. It seems more likely that what Logan witnessed was an instance of what subsequently became known as Tourette's Syndrome rather than latah. De la Tourette initially thought that the behavior involved in latah, *miryachit*, and *Jumping* was the same as that which he had observed among his own European patients at Saltpêtrière.
2. O'Brien thus wrote in a footnote that he had "been collecting for some time past cases as regards *latah* subjects who have also committed amok, but the facts that I have collected are as yet too spare for me to venture upon matured generalization" (O'Brien 1883: 153). Such facts never appear to have been published.

3. I have already noted that I did not find this to be the case in my own study.
4. For my own part, I found little evidence of a link between latah and dreams in Kelantan but a strong one in Sarawak.
5. For his part Kenny (1990: 125) notes in a short sentence that the latah person "may or may not be fully conscious" as if this is a mere detail of no importance in comparison to the matter of what latah symbolizes. In Simons's case, as with dreams, the matter of changes in consciousness in latah is avoided altogether. Here as elsewhere the firm behaviorist, he labels imitation and automatic obedience forms of "attention capture" and explains them as a result of arousal.

2: LATAH, HISTORY, AND GENDER

1. E.g. Marsden (1783, 1984[1812]). Thomson (1984[1864]: 170), whom Murphy does not mention, clearly identified and then described latah in his account of his early life in Malaya. However, while this may have been as early as 1839 or 1840 when Thomson first lived there, his account was not published until much later and does not clearly indicate when the incidents he described took place. And in any case, it is not so much earlier that it would undermine Murphy's argument. A fuller examination of Dutch sources regarding the Netherlands Indies might do so.
2. P. J. Zoetmulder's (1982) dictionary of Old Javanese, which cites latah as appearing in five texts, suggests that this may also have been the case with the Javanese, although here the meaning is given simply as "bewildered, perplexed, dumbfounded."

3: "LATAH" ELSEWHERE

1. None of the three exotic echoing maladies involves the grimaces and jerks or "tics" which were principal symptoms of Tourette's Syndrome. However, the possibility of a link has continued to persist, or reappear, in medical handbooks and encyclopedias, and has been raised anew in a recent discussion of latah and the culture-bound syndromes (Prince and Tcheng-Laroche 1987: 14).
2. Some accounts also include the Lapps (Sammi) of the Eurasian Arctic.
3. The two scholars who seem to have considered the comparative material most fully are Yap and Aberle. Of these Yap cited or included in his bibliography much of what was then available but noted that he had not read all of the sources. Those which he did not list included all of the Italian accounts concerning north Africa and the Arabian peninsula. Aberle, on the other hand, relied on one source regarding the latter region (Repond), cited one other source (Natoli) but noted that he had not read it and, curiously, neglected entirely the case of *imu* among the Ainu, which would have strengthened his argument. Of the more recent studies of particular concern here, Simons cites a variety of non-Malayan instances, though fewer than Yap and about the same number as Aberle; then there is Kenny who after initially dismissing the entire body of non-Malayan literature as old and unreliable without apparently reading it, subsequently examined the main accounts of Siberian *miryachit* (which he declared to be surprisingly but accidentally like Malayan latah) while again declaring that the other instances need not be considered.

4. Later accounts of similar behavior provide further information but still do not fully clarify such issues. D. Carlton Gajdusek (1970) reports mimicry in first-contact encounters in both South America and Melanesia with four totally different groups:

> In our contact with primitive peoples, this mimicking behavior appears to be carefully balanced between fright and anxiety, flight or fight reactions, and playful smiling and laughter. It is not unreasonable to propose that to mimic and attempt to respond in such a way as to behave like a strange newcomer, who is a source of fear and anxiety, may be an unconscious anxiety-alleviating mechanism aimed also at evoking a reciprocal controlled and controllable, and thus friendly, response in the strange visitor. Imitation and mimicry have had high survival value in natural selection. (Gajdusek 1970: 61; quoted in Yap 1974: 97–98).

Such inferences again raise the possibility that echoing behavior reflects an inherent, primordial human tendency in confusing and highly emotional circumstances. But also again there is no mention of startle *per se*, or of the expression of obscenities, both classic features of latah. Further, Gajdusek does not say how any of the groups in question regard imitation, or if they use it in ritual or in other social contexts. And while he notes that what he saw is not unlike the behavior described in the neurological literature concerning certain pathological states, he makes no mention of any form of "latah."

5. I should stress here that I make no claim to having done an extensive search for all primary, let alone secondary, accounts of non-Malayan startle patterns beyond those cited in the comparative treatments of "latah" dealt with here.

6. Dentan (pers. commun., 1993) has more recently informed me that

> Latah among the Semai is interesting. I don't think that in the 1960s, when I wrote the article in *Bijdragen*, people recognized a connection between echolalia and coprolalia. I asked about it systematically in 1992–1993. My impression, like yours, is that it's commoner in communities of Semai in fairly close contact with Malays. I suspect that it may have something to do with the same Malay gender biases that have led to an upsurge in transvestism (*pondan*). Most Semai don't know the Malay word, so I had to describe the symptoms to get a response – which means I didn't elicit the ethnopsychological grouping they would have made. A lot of people never encountered it; most of those who did called it a Malay phenomenon.

7. It is also interesting that Beard reported that while *jumping* appeared to be restricted to the northern part of New Hampshire, Maine, and Canada, cases had been reported for "the Malays upon the other side of the globe." This observation preceded the publication of O'Brien's 1883 paper through which Malay latah had generally come to be widely known. Beard did not cite the source of his information on Malays.

8. A Russian synopsis of Beard's article published in 1884 thus reported that *jumping* was an affliction of gymnasts. (This observation presumably derived from a misunderstanding of Beard's statement that in one instance a startled *jumper* had thrown a tumbler to the floor. The translator presumably, in addition to associating *jumping* with gymnastics, had assumed that "tumbler" referred to an acrobat rather than a glass.) More serious perhaps, in a later article on *imu* (the Ainu version of the startle pattern), first a Japanese (Uchimura 1935) and then two Polish scholars (Winiarz and Wielawski 1936:

185) reported that *jumping* occurred among the "Red Indians of North America." Further, in his survey, Yap devoted much of his analysis of the *jumpers* to their presumed association with Anglo-American religions. Beard himself had mentioned the "trance practices" of some American revivalist religious groups including the Shakers, who rolled on the floor and jerked with frenzy, but he did not, however, claim any generic connection between *jumping* and "holy rollers"; no *jumpers* were noted to also be "holy rollers," the children of "holy rollers," members of pentecostal churches or even of communities in which there were such churches. Yap, however, sought to derive *jumping* from the activities of the Shakers, which, he noted, were religious folk originating from the Methodist Congregation of Wales whose devotions involved *jumping*, shaking, and the utterance of incoherent gutturals or "barking." Such behaviors, Yap went on to suggest, were a consequence of the Shakers' prohibition of marriage and the requirement of celibacy for all members which was sexually frustrating for both men and women. Such an effort to derive French Canadian *jumping* from an Anglo-American religious movement seems strangely out of place in an otherwise judicious and critical account. The religious affiliation(s), or heritage, of the *jumpers* has not been reported.

9. The first was discovered to have a markedly strong reaction to startle which took the form of *jumping* but did not involve coprolalia, echoing or automatic obedience. Neurological laboratory tests revealed no abnormalities, as was also the case with two other patients who subsequently appeared. One of the latter was a fifty-two-year old woman who was found to have similar symptoms but who would also occasionally echo the words that had been spoken to her; another was the niece of this woman, who was twenty at the time and less severely affected, but who had been so since she had been eight years old.

10. Stevens's paper and the discussion which followed its initial oral presentation at the annual meeting of the American Neurological Association focused on psychiatric and neurological rather than ethnographic matters of cultural awareness or context. A colleague suggested that the pattern "looked like a myoclonic seizure with which one often sees nothing on the EEG except under unusual circumstances" (Stevens 1964: 67).

11. However, Reuben Rabinovitch (1965), another psychiatrist and neurologist, published a note linking *jumping* to games played by children in rural Quebec, which in turn he had traced back to the horseplay of lumberjacks in all-male winter camps. In an observation reminiscent of Clifford's objection to the medicalization of latah, he suggested that "If one had to make a disease of this" it should be mass hysteria or conditioned reflex (Rabinovitch 1965: 130).

12. Yap (1952: 517) noted that Scheube listed Lapps as one of the peoples among which "latah" occurred in his *Diseases of the Warm Countries* [!], and that Scheube had listed as his source "Högström," after whose name Yap placed a question mark, indicating that he was unable to identify him. This was presumably Pere Högström, the Swedish clergyman who published *Description of the Lappmarks of the Crown of Sweden* in 1746. Aberle (1952: 294), on the other hand, cited the Netherlands Indies colonial physician P. C. van Brero regarding his assertion that it had been said that the Lapps had "latah."

13. An Italian denunciation of Hammond's discovery was soon followed by claims of Russian authors to have first described the disease. These included a response

to a reference in a Russian journal to a review article in a Spanish publication.

14. Jocalson was a Russian who was exiled to Siberia and who subsequently participated in the Jessup North Pacific Expeditions and produced ethnological studies of both the Koryak and the Yukaghir as a part of the monograph series resulting from this enterprise.

15. In the case of the Koryak the antiquity of one of the symptoms of Arctic Hysteria was reflected in its presence in a folktale in which Big Raven's niece, when startled by Grebe-man, exclaims, "The penis hangs, the vulva hangs."

16. Seemingly inconsistent with this line of argument, however, is Jocalson's assertion that the nervous diseases were more common among the inhabitants of permanent settlements than among those who led a nomadic life. Those Yukaghir who lived in skin tents and wandered about the tundra with their reindeer herds seldom suffered from hysteria. This would seem to suggest that social and cultural factors as well as (or rather than) climate were involved, for nomadic tent dwellers would seem to be more vulnerable to environmental stress than house-dwellers. Jocalson did not, however, discuss such a possibility.

17. Shirokogoroff thus noted that *olon* was very common among the Tungus, that the term meant "to be suddenly frightened," that the spirits were not held to be responsible for it, and that while both men and women were affected, it was especially common among younger women.

18. However, in a recent analysis of *imu* based partly on the older literature and partly on her own limited information, the anthropologist Emiko Ohnuki-Tierney (1985) notes much apparent variation from one region to another. Such variation probably indicates more than anything else inadequate or incomplete information. Ohnuki-Tierney (1985: 100) also reports that in the mild version of *imu* persons mumble nonsense words rather than exclaim obscenities, and that the latter are expressed in the trance-like version. It is also reported for some Ainu groups that the usual pattern of automatic obedience is reversed, so that the *imu* person does the opposite of what has been ordered (Munro 1963: 108; Ohnuki-Tierney 1985: 100).

19. The evidence here is mixed. If Arabic "latah" had derived from the Malay countries the term itself would likely also come to be used, which apparently was not the case. Further, since nearly all of the specific "latah" persons noted in the African and Arabic instances are men or boys, if the reports are accurate in this respect, when latah crossed the Indian Ocean it also crossed the line of gender. Of course, the many Arabs who sojourned in Sumatra, Java and Malaya were men rather than women, so that if latah were to be acquired it was men rather than women who would be in a position to do so.

4: LATAH IN KELANTAN: AN OVERVIEW

1. The literature on latah is replete with observations about the occurrence and social correlates of latah – in general and among different types of persons including men and women, the old and the young, the marginal and the poor and the better off; that it is "common," "most common," "uncommon," "rare," "seldom met with," "easily observed," "hardly ever found," and so forth in different areas or among different types of persons. What is lacking,

however, is specific information on actual numbers of persons in particular villages or neighborhoods, let alone numbers in relation to gender, age, status and other possible significant social and cultural distinctions. The problem is not getting specific information, of which I obtained an enormous amount, for particular areas. It is rather having other specific information with which to compare my own.

2. My research efforts in Kelantan involved surveys of a total of 471 households. In the course of these surveys I encountered and briefly interviewed a total of ninety-five persons who were identified by themselves and others as being more or less latah. I also found and interviewed seventy-one latah persons at length, although some of these had also been encountered in the surveys. These longer interviews included eighteen Malay men, twenty-seven Malay women, one rural Chinese man, ten rural Chinese women, one Thai man, ten Thai women, and three Cambodian Cham women. My total data set of latah persons in Kelantan thus includes twenty-four Malay men, seventy-one Malay women, three rural Chinese men, nineteen rural Chinese women, two Kelantanese Thai men, forty Kelantanese Thai women, and four Cham women. In addition to these longer and shorter interviews I also worked with a number of acquaintances, some of whom I had known for long periods of time. Several of these people were more or less latah and all were familiar with latah and knew many latah persons.

3. The exception are a dozen Muslim Cambodian Cham families who came to Kelantan as refugees after the fall of Phnom Penh. While some of these families – almost all of whom have turned to small-scale trade – live in shop-houses along Atas Paloh Street, others live in raft-houses tied up along the riverbank that are reached by paths that wind through the squatter areas.

4. The distinction may be in the process of breaking down as Village and Town Chinese children attend the same schools, as more Village Chinese work in town, as more Town Chinese buy Rural Chinese land and intermarry with them and as ethnic distinctions between Malays and the other communities have been emphasized. The former type includes a number of speech groups, though Hokkien speakers predominate.

5. As readers may note, the various experiences associated by some latah persons with the beginning of latah are reminiscent of traumatic incidents described by Breuer and Freud as underlying hysteria (Laderman 1991: 43). The specific precipitating events and subsequent phobias they recount include snakes, thunderstorms and startle or severe fright involving the sudden appearance of other persons (Breuer and Freud 1957[1895]: 4–5, 24, 38, 62, 87).

While there may be important cross-cultural commonalities at work here, certain differences should also be noted. Breuer and Freud say that the original underlying traumatic cause of hysteria in their patients is repressed into the unconscious and only revealed under hypnosis or after lengthy therapy. They also note that once the original cause of some hysterical symptom was finally revealed to the patient the symptom went away.

Neither of these findings seems to apply to latah, either as reported by earlier observers or as I found it. The incidents to which some latah persons attributed their condition are consciously apparent to them, not locked away in the unconscious. Further, and quite obviously in such instances, awareness of the original precipitating trauma of latah has not brought its disappearance. It is true that not all latah persons reported an initial incident, and it is also possible that the incidents that were described were not the real ones, which could only be gotten at through techniques of analysis, which I did not employ. In this regard it may be noted that while Freudian interpretations of latah have been offered by various observers over the years, there is no evidence that any of them have been based on the sort of analytical case histories used by Freud and other psychoanalysts to establish their conclusions.

6. There is a well-known Malay proverb (*jangan disangka keli*), the literal meaning of which is "do not mistake a catfish for a serpent."

7. The *bidandari* are apparently well known throughout the country. The term itself is an interesting synthesis of "bidan" and the originally Sanskritic "bidadari," whereby the celestial dancing girls of Indo-Malay mythology have become celestial midwives who are spiritual guardians of earthly midwives (Laderman 1983: 132).

5: LATAH AND MALAY CULTURE

1. The latah pattern would appear to be mainly beyond the realm of the secondary-behavior part of Landis and Hunt's startle model. They note only one possibility which suggests that latah behavior might be considered an integral part of the secondary pattern. This concerns reactions ". . . in which the primary response either persists while the individual remains immobile, and which are apparently due to a sort of tonic preservation of the response, or in which the primary response is continued and heightened into a secondary behavior which appears to be voluntary in nature" (Landis and Hunt 1939: 139–140). Unfortunately, they do not discuss either latah, of which they do not appear to be aware, or other such patterns in this respect; nor do they otherwise deal with such "untypical prolonged secondary reactions."

2. If it is indeed the case that repeated exposure of latah persons to provocation actually facilitates the reaction this would be further evidence of the difference between latah and basic neurophysiological startle.

3. Clifford Geertz (1960: 312–313) reports that lynchings were commonly attributed to startle by the Javanese at the time of his fieldwork.

4. Carol Laderman (1983: 94–95) reports that in rural Trengganu Malays believe that a pregnant woman who is startled or disgusted may pass on the consequences to her child as an abnormality. The mother of a child who spits up excessively may recall being startled by seeing a cat vomiting while she was pregnant.

5. It is not possible to know for certain the extent to which this occurrence can be generalized to a larger area. At one point after I became aware of the number of *bidan* in Pasir Mas who were latah I sought out the government midwives at the local clinic, told them what I had found, and asked if latah was as common among *bidan kampung* in other areas as it was in the one in which my attention was concentrated. They knew that the *bidan* I was talking about were latah but said that of those in other areas, some were latah and some were not. My own further inquiries in other areas suggest that latah is common among village midwives in general in rural Kelantan, though not necessarily as much so as it happens to be in Belukar and surrounding villages.

6. Moreover, among Malays such states were traditionally learned early. They are (or were) manifest in the form of certain children's games noted by colonial scholars in earlier periods. One of those described by R. J. Wilkinson (1910: 14–15) was *main hantu musang* (the polecat spirit game). One child was put into a trance by the other children. Then, possessed by the *musang*, this child would proceed to climb trees and leap from branch to branch like a polecat. Adults were said to disapprove of the game, but while Murphy suggests that this was because they disapproved of children playing with trance it may have also been because they feared for the safety of the child.

7. Many scholars now agree that trance states have an important neurobiological dimension. The literature on trance states contains a discussion of a number of processes of relevance to latah. Such states are produced by a wide variety of agents and circumstances and range from highly positive, pleasant, and rejuvenating experiences to very negative ones of panic and terror. Several decades ago Arnold Ludwig (1966) argued that altered states of consciousness share various characteristics including a disturbed sense of time, changes in thinking, and in emotional expression and body image, perceptual distortions and hypersuggestibility. He focuses especially on the dissolution of the normal subjective distinction of the self and the external environment, and on hyper-suggestibility as a reflection of this dissolution. It has also been suggested that such trance states in general involve a shift from left-brain (which is associated with the production of speech, with linear, analytical thought, and with the assessment of the passage of time) to right-brain dominance. The right brain controls spatial and tonal perception and includes the recognition of patterns. The repetitive mimicry that often forms a part of latah suggests right-brain modalities and the temporary absence of left-brain analytical awareness of the distinction between self and other, and of the passage of time (Lex 1979: 125–126; Mandell 1980: 414–415).

Trance states also involve the autonomic nervous system, which includes the sympathetic and the parasympathetic nervous subsystems. Fear and anger and, one may presume, startle excite the sympathetic nervous system beyond its normal level of activity. Blood pressure rises, heartbeat increases, and blood moves to the muscles. Altered states of consciousness are associated with the parasympathetic nervous system or "rebound," the release of epinephrine and the neutralization of the sympathetic activity. Trance states can occur with the continuation of rebound effects and the control of the cortical and subcortical centers of the autonomic nervous system.

It is also likely that shock, or startle, is among the agents which can bring about the decrease in control over the subcortical centers that facilitate trance states (Lex 1979: 134). If so, it constitutes what has been called a "driver," that is an agent which can alter the body's biochemical milieu. More than some other drivers, startle is associated with anxiety, which can lead to mixed neural discharges and result in dysphasia, a characteristic of latah. The initial startle or trauma that has frequently been held to be a precipitating factor in latah may also have a neurophysiological dimension. A "kindling" pattern is said to involve a permanent or long-lasting reduction in the threshold of neural excitability stemming from an initial trauma which affects the central nervous system (Mandell 1980: 396–399; Winkelman 1986: 184–185).

8. There is thus other evidence that Malayan peoples in Southeast Asia hold such views of the person, at least implicitly and in some instances explicitly. Such views are apparent, for example, in accounts of cultural efforts to create barriers to protect the inner self from external disruption – as in the Balinese cultivation of "awayness" in the context of business and crowds, as famously noted by Margaret Mead (Bateson and Mead 1942: 4): "In the most rapt of crowds, when the clowns are performing some fascinating new version of an absolutely reliable joke, one can still see face after face which contains no response to the outside world"; see also Clifford Geertz on the Javanese (1960: 249–260). In Kelantan the various ritual practices and magical beliefs described earlier also show evidence of such concerns. The strong interest in invulnerability (*kebal*) magic and in *silat* have been noted. The special ritual significance of spiritually endowed (*bertuah*) weapons (above all the *keris*) lies in the fact that they both provide protection for the self, with which they are closely identified, and facilitate the penetration of the selves by others – as in sexual conquest and in deadly combat.

9. His point is that although Malay society is not simply or even primarily preliterate, large segments of the population remain "radically oral." In such a tradition, learning tends to be by rote and imitation, discourse tends to be repetitious, and the experience of theater and recitation based on oral transmission lends itself to movement into alternative states of consciousness (Sweeney 1987: 196–197). With regard to the concept of the person:

> Only when the knower is separated from the known [through written, above all print-based learning] can "the self" become an object of the knower. It is understandable, therefore, that many members of Malay society are little given to self-analysis: the individual is so much a part of his situation that he is unable to extricate the center of that situation – himself – for the purpose of introspective examination of that self. (Sweeney 1987: 159)

10. In the mid-1960s when seances were held with some frequency around Pasir Mas, I knew of one woman as well as many men who were shamans. In the past women who played in traveling *Mak Yong* theatrical troupes may have also performed as shamans in *main peteri* seances. But even so the number or proportion of female shamans was not likely ever large.

11. It is true that trance or semi-trance at least may play some role in Islamic religious ceremonies which remain very popular in Kelantan. Groups of men gather at funerals and on holy days to *meratek*, that is to recite in unison over and over the phrase "There is no God but God" while swaying from side to side. The purpose of such chanting is generally not held to achieve a state of ecstasy but to glorify Allah and to earn merit (*pahala*) accordingly. Such as they are, these opportunities are commonly available to Malay men but not Malay women – who do, however, hear them going on.

12. Such attacks have been extensively studied and discussed by Western-trained Malaysian psychiatrists, psychologists, and social scientists and described in terms of social, cultural, psychological, and sexual tension and conflict. However, such incidents have usually been successfully resolved not by Western modes of therapy but by traditional Malay techniques. When an attack occurs a *bomoh* is called who will calm the affected students or workers with ritual

utterances and eventually exorcise the offending spirits and perform cleansing and "release" (*lepas*) rituals. As in more distinctively traditional instances of individual spirit possession, the problem may be diagnosed as either sorcery or the attack of some local spirit or spirits (*hantu*) that have been offended. Very often the latter are found to be the spirits of soldiers killed during the Second World War and buried in unmarked graves and subsequently disturbed by the school or factory erected on or near their remains.

13. Clive Kessler (1977), who did fieldwork in the Jelawat area between 1967 and 1969, provides the most extensive information for this period. He reports attending a hundred seances, and while many of these probably involved the same group, the individuals for whom the seances were held would have been different.

6: SYMBOLIC MEANINGS AND SOCIAL USES

1. Therefore my own expectation is quite at variance with the hypothesis that an American could easily develop an imitative form of "latah" under certain conditions (Simons 1980: 200).

2. It has been said by Kapferer regarding the Sinhalese villagers and working classes in criticism of Lewis's argument that even though women are at a severe disadvantage to the point that they may be freely beaten by husbands, they see nothing to protest in that their status is "culturally constituted." While in some respects the same point might be made regarding Malay women in Kelantan, here women are quite conscious that their problems have to do with the marrying and divorcing inclinations of men. The possibility of a man wanting to *berbini muda* (marry a young wife) is a frequent topic of conversation. While living by myself in Pasir Mas I was frequently questioned about my marital and family status, and I was sometimes further asked by Malay women if my wife minded that I was there alone, and if I ever considered getting married while I was away. The latter question was meant to tease but seemed to reflect the common anxiety that husbands who are away are liable to take up with other women, perhaps not of their own inclination but because they have been trapped by love magic.

3. In Kelantan Malay women are well known for their business acumen and their involvement in market trade. However this frequently reflects difficult economic circumstances. Women without property or other means of support can become involved in petty market trade with little capital. Most women who trade in the market are married but have husbands who work as laborers or trishaw drivers, or are farmers with little or no land. While Malay women may be freer than men to express themselves in some respects, they are at a disadvantage in other ways. Divorce was and is very common and it generally is to the detriment of women. It is true that Malay women are independent and may precipitate an end to an unsatisfactory marriage, and that divorced women as such are not stigmatized and generally remarry. None the less women are put at a considerable disadvantage in matrimonial arrangements. Older women, whether divorced or widowed, cannot remarry as readily as younger women. In particular, there is a marked difference in the marriage status or prospects of middle-aged and older men and women. Unless a man is destitute or physically or mentally infirm he can remarry. Women are not in this position. Older men

not uncommonly marry women who are younger than themselves (sometimes much younger) but the opposite is rare and occasions speculation about sorcery. The tendency for husbands to be older than wives also means that women are more likely to become widows than men widowers. In my surveys and censuses I frequently encountered older women living by themselves but hardly ever found men in this position. An old man, even if single, is more apt to own a house and land and can thus have a married child and his or her family living with him. An older single woman may be a member of the household of a child or grandchild but even if a family has the means such a woman will often be maintained in a small house on her own.

4. The religious life of the rural community provides somewhat more limited opportunities for the participation of women than men. In contrast to their involvement in more distinctly customary ceremonial activities, the involvement of women in formal Islamic matters is restricted or precluded. Women like men may go to local prayer-houses for daily prayers, frequently teach the Koran to local children, and are involved in the preparations for religious feasts of their own and neighboring households. Women as well as men attend weddings as guests and pay visits to the houses of friends, neighbors, relatives, and important persons on the great holidays of the new year (*Hari Raya*) and the annual sacrifice (*Hari Raya Haji* [or *Korban*]). However they do not attend Friday prayers at the mosque or participate in most of the other formal rituals and feasts held throughout the year.

5. In Belukar both of the village midwives (*bidan kampung*) are latah, as is Mak Daud the retired shaman. While traditional *bidan* are affected by some of the same currents of change affecting Malay villagers in general they are also affected by more specific ones relating to their profession. The Malaysian government has determined as a matter of national policy that the practice of village midwifery as it traditionally exists will cease, that no new village midwives will be licenced to practice, and that women will be delivered either in clinics or hospitals, or by government midwives at home. In the mid-1980s the transition was still in progress and it remains to be seen whether *bidan kampung* in Kelantan or elsewhere will actually be entirely replaced by *bidan kerajaan*. Licenced *bidan kampung* are to continue to practice but under the supervision of government midwives. Carol Laderman who studied Malay midwives in Trengganu in detail describes the situation as one of superficial harmony masking tension and animosity. Wazir Jahan Karim (1984) reports much the same thing in rural Kedah but also notes common recourse to sorcery.

7: LATAH IN BORNEO

1. Previously a part of the old Malay Brunei Sultanate, Sarawak became an independent country in 1841 under the rule of the English adventurer James Brooke. The Brooke Dynasty effectively ended in 1941 with the arrival of the Japanese. Following the defeat of the latter and the formal abdication by the last Brooke raja, it became a British colony in 1946 and remained so until becoming a part of Malaysia in 1963.

2. Formerly the term was used in a much more restricted manner to mean the two native groups. These were Land (or sometimes "Hill") Dayaks, on the one

hand, and Sea Dayaks, on the other. Yet other groups such as the Melanau, the Kenyah, and the Kayan, located in regions subsequently incorporated into Sarawak, were known by more specific terms. Moreover, of the two Dayak populations recognized in such colonial usage, only the Sea Dayak (now known as the Iban) comprised a single ethnolinguistic group; the Land Dayak (now known as Bidayuh) grouping included a number of separate ones.

3. Apart from the Malays, those groups which have latah are generally ones in which traditional hereditary distinctions in status are absent. Latah does not appear to be found among most of the hierarchical up-river societies of central Sarawak – the Sekapan, the Kenyah, and the Kayan – among whom I was able to make limited inquiries. It does occur among some of the coastal Melanau, which are traditionally stratified, but those which have it – that is, the Muslims – are no more hierarchical than are the pagan or the Christian communities.

   This is not to say that latah has been clearly favored by the egalitarian Dayak groups and rejected by the stratified ones. With the exception of the Melanau the hierarchically ordered Central Bornean societies in Sarawak are located in the upper reaches of the Rajang, Baram, and other rivers where there are few or no Malays from whom they also might have gotten latah. It is rather that a traditional pattern of hereditary stratification has probably been irrelevant.

4. It is true that Muslim Melanau (as well as the Malays, all of whom are Muslim) have latah while Christian and pagan Melanau apparently do not. This suggests a possible link between Islam and latah, in this region at least. Therefore, while it is possible that certain aspects of Islam – relating perhaps to the position of women – might favor latah, this is at most a secondary factor. Otherwise, the link with Islam in the case of the Melanau probably has little to do with Malayan Islamic culture in itself.

5. The most widespread of these is *gigiren*, reported earlier by van Loon (1924) as the term for latah among Bornean Malays, recently by Maxwell (1990) for the Kadayan of Brunei and, in the reflexive form of *gagiren* or *giren*, for the Ngaju of South Kalimantan (Schiller 1987, pers. commun.). Since yet another evident version of this term also occurs outside of Borneo (as *gigian* in Bali [Wikan 1989: 45]), it may have an external origin, possibly Javanese (Maxwell 1990: 10). Several other terms for latah, however, are evidently locally Bornean, including *obingsalah* ("to be mistaken") in the case of the Rungus Dusun (Doolittle 1991: 124) and *bibiran* ("lipping") and *kakajubat* ("pig's snout") among the Timogun Murut (Brewis 1992: 11). It is likely that additional such instances remain to be noted from other areas of Borneo as well. In searching for latah I both described the pattern and asked about the term. I also made inquiries among scholars familiar with other regions and groups in Sarawak, none of which revealed instances of which I was not already aware.

6. I interviewed a total of eight Muslim Melanau latah women and learned of several others. On the other hand, during my inquiries in all of the Melanau villages of Batang Oya, Sungai Kut, and Batang Igan above the juncture of Sungai Kut, I did not turn up any cases or any knowledge of latah among either Christian or traditional Melanau. This seemed unlikely at first since Muslim Melanau generally knew about latah and since they are not isolated from the non-Muslims, some of whom are neighbors, at least in the Dalat area.

7. The psychiatric survey of latah among Malay and Iban populations in Sarawak

in the late 1960s is one of the few studies which has ever attempted actually to determine the presence or absence of mental abnormality as defined in Western psychiatric terms. In it T. L. Chiu, J. E. Tong, and K. E. Schmidt distinguished latah persons who displayed symptoms of identifiable clinical dysfunction from those who did not. They located a total of seventeen latah persons in their Iban population (not well defined) and a somewhat larger number in their Malay one and supposed that in both groups many other milder or more ambiguous instances had escaped their attention. Of the seventeen identified Iban latah persons, they decided that three showed recognizable symptoms of one or another standard psychiatric disorder, in all instances a neurosis rather than a psychosis. Even excluding those other more ambiguous instances not included in their survey, most latah persons were thus found not to be mentally ill. They do note that the initial experiences reported by the latah persons interviewed were often associated with anger, sadness or depression but do not conclude that latah is clearly an expression of such emotional states, or suggest why it would be an appropriate cultural mode for their expression. They reached the conclusion that the development of latah in individuals is related to mild depression but the pattern itself "... causes no great distress for the majority of cases" (Chiu, Tong, and Schmidt 1972: 162).

8. According to the earlier Chiu, Tong, and Schmidt (1972) report on latah in Sarawak such dreams were more explicitly sexual than those recounted to me. These dreams, in which male sexual organs figured prominently, are very similar to the Javanese ones noted by van Loon in the 1920s. Since the more recent accounts of latah in Java do not mention such dreams it is possible that in all three places (Malaya, Borneo, and Java) there has been a pattern of change.

9. See the collection on spirit possession, trance, and mediumship (Winzeler 1993a).

10. Spirits in Borneo are often highly charged with sexual energy. This is evident in the many carvings which show male spirits with large, erect penises and female spirits with swollen or gaping vaginas. As with humans, the sexual energy of spirits has both essential and dangerous associations; with the fertility of crops, especially rice, as well as with humans, on the one hand, and with the malevolent seduction or rape of persons, on the other.

8: LATAH AND THE IBAN

1. In 1989 a young Iban man in Kuching told me of an instance of latah near Song.
2. Writing of the Saribas area in general Freeman notes that at the time of his research in 1951,

... Malay influence which had begun two or more centuries earlier was omnipresent. For example, the thirteen *bilek*-families of Plandok, a long-house with a total population of seventy-nine, had working on their rubber plantations no fewer than fifty-two Malay share-croppers, as well as one Chinese. Their palatial long-house, of milled timber and with windows of coloured glass, had been built, I was told, by Malay and Chinese carpenters. The most popular nocturnal activity of the younger Dayak people of the region was a form of Malay dancing called *betanda*, which was performed in long-houses, with numerous Malays participating, to songs composed in the Malay language and intoned by professional Malay singers. As a result of this intermingling with Malays, virtually all of the Saribas Dayaks had an acquaintance with, and many an expert knowledge of, the Malay language; and, indeed, in not a few instances Malay terms had replaced Iban words in everyday usage. (Freeman 1981: 7)

3. More recently other scholars have suggested that Freeman has put all of this a bit too strongly in an effort to apply an orthodox Freudian explanation but no one has questioned the specific beliefs and practices that he and others have described. One line of criticism is that the male ethnographer did not give adequate attention to the activities of women, to the possibility that they had interests and sources of satisfaction and status quite apart from those of the men – especially weaving, the "woman's warpath," which was difficult, time consuming, symbolically rich, and ritually elaborated (Mashman 1991). Others have supposed that Freeman was led to overemphasize sexual tension and jealousy. In making this point Julian Davison and Vinson Sutlive (1991: 164 and *passim*) note that contemporary Iban regard the sexual banter at headhunting festivals as lighthearted fun and that men willingly also play the part of women on such occasions – gathering firewood, cooking, and so on.

However, while there is a certain amount of information available on Iban social relations in the older literature, most present-day scholars have known the Iban under conditions quite different from those obtaining in Baleh, circa 1950.

4. Ceremonial inter-sexual joking is apparently common among Dayak peoples. Hose and McDougall (1912: 114) note this regarding "Klemantans" and provide a photo of two women dressed up as men. See also Metcalf (1982: 125–132) for an account of the Berawan headhunting and mortuary celebrations involving sexual joking and licence.

9: EXPLAINING LATAH: PARADIGM AND PARADOX, SYNDROME AND RITUAL, NATURE AND CULTURE

1. Simons (1987) suggests that latah would be medicalized if a cure were offered. He reports that rural Malays in Melaka were receptive to his query about taking medicine (if it existed) for latah. I encountered some inclination on the part of urbane Western-educated Malays to suppose that latah persons might benefit from psychotherapy. However, most Western-trained Malaysian medical professionals I met who knew about latah seemed to regard it more as a local cultural pattern than a medical disorder, and some did not think that it was much of a problem in any case. Malay and some non-Malay medical personnel at hospitals in Kuala Lumpur and Kota Baru were familiar with latah. But the latah persons whom they knew were often individuals who worked at the hospital rather than patients. One doctor told me that "Oh yes you see latah. Some of the women who work here are latah, even a few of the nurses. You see it occasionally when one is startled going through a door and someone else is coming the other way."

2. Excessive startle has also been found in some children with cerebral palsy or lipidosis. Further, exaggerated startling is also a feature of magnesium deficiency and tetanus, and it appears in certain degenerative brain disorders, such as Creutzfeldt-Jacob disease and it may also develop as part of various illnesses

which evoke chronic tension. On the other hand, startling tends to be reduced in intensity in patients with epileptic disorders (Kunkle 1967: 356–357).

3. In an early work on schizophrenia Kraeplin (1919: 39) held that both echolalia and echopraxia were forms of "command automatism" which also suggests similarities with the other well-known latah characteristic of the involuntary following of orders. In a later paper several observers (Carluccio, Sours, and Kolb 1964) described two instances in which the behavior of mental patients diagnosed as schizophrenic included extensive verbal mockery of others. It was assumed in these instances that such behavior was conscious and deliberate, and therefore a form of aggression. In other instances, however, echo reactions as well as obscenity have also been described as occurring in cases of schizophrenia in which conscious volition was in doubt. These included cases in which there was extensive hallucination, which was linked to alcohol psychosis and epileptic seizures. Further, in some of these cases echo reactions were associated with grasping and sucking reactions which suggested a general disintegration of personality and a reversion to an infantile or primitive level of mental functioning, or a loss of cerebral dominance (Schneider 1938).

4. Echo reactions and coprolalia have thus also been observed to occur in patients with brain damage of one form or another, some of which involved *aphasia* or a loss of speech. In some of the latter cases it has been suggested that verbal echoing is an alternative to genuine, rational speech (Brain 1965: 57). Beyond the specific link of some forms of aphasia and echolalia, echoing behavior has been associated with damage to the frontal lobe of the brain, as well as with mid-brain lesions. The specific causal links involved in these instances appear to remain in doubt.

Bibliography

Aberle, David F. 1952 "Arctic Hysteria" and Latah in Mongolia. *Transactions of the New York Academy of Sciences, Series 2* vol. xiv (7) 7: 291–297.

Abraham, J. J. 1911 *The Surgeon's Log: Being Impressions of the Far East*. New York: E. P. Dutton & Company.

1912 Latah and Amok. *British Medical Journal* Jan. 24: 438–439.

Ackerman, S. E. and R. L. M. Lee 1981 Communication and Cognitive Pluralism in a Spirit Possession Event in Malaysia. *American Ethnologist* 8(4): 789–799.

Adam, Tassilo 1946 Latah, a Peculiar Malay Disease. *Knickerbocker Weekly*, March 18: 21–23.

Alatas, Syed Hussain 1977 *The Myth of the Lazy Native*. London: Frank Cass.

Allbutt, C. and H. D. Rolleston 1910 *A System of Medicine*, Vol. II, part ii. London: MacMillan and Co., Ltd.

American Psychiatric Association 1987 *Diagnostic and Statistical Manual of Mental Disorders*, 3rd edn. – revised. Washington D.C.

Arieti, S. 1974 *American Handbook of Psychiatry*, 2nd edn. Vol. III, Adult Clinical Psychiatry. New York: Basic Books.

Ballard, E. F. 1912 Comment on Amok and Latah. *British Medical Journal* March 16: 652.

Barnouw, V. 1985 *Culture and Personality*, 4th edn. Homewood, Illinois: The Dorsey Press.

Basso, Keith 1979 *Portraits of The Whiteman: Linguistic Play and Cultural Symbols Among the Western Apache*. Cambridge: Cambridge University Press.

Bastian, Adolph 1867 *Reisen in Siam im Jahre 1863*. Jena: H. Costenoble

Bateson, Gregory and Margaret Mead 1942 *Balinese Character: A Photographic Analysis*. New York: New York Academy of Sciences.

Beard, G. M. 1880 Experiments with the "Jumpers" or "Jumping Frenchmen" of Maine. *The Journal of Nervous and Mental Disease* 7: 487–490.

Belo, Jane 1960 *Trance in Bali*. New York: Columbia University Press.

Bordier, A. 1884 *La Géographie Médicale*. Paris: C. Reinwald, Libraire-Editeur.

Bourguignon, E. 1979 *Psychological Anthropology: An Introduction to Human Nature and Cultural Differences*. New York: Holt, Rinehart and Winston.

Brain, Lord W. R. 1965 *Speech Disorders: Aphasia, Apraxia and Agnosia*. Washington: Butterworths.

Bramwell, J. M. 1903 *Hypnotism, Its History, Theory and Practice*. London: Grant Richards.

Brero, P. C. Z. van 1895 Latah. *Journal of Mental Sciences* 41(174): 537–538.

1896 Eineges uber die Geisteskrankheite der Bevolkerung des Malayischen Archipels. *Allgemeine Zeitschrift für Psychiatrie und psychisch-gerichtliche Medicin* 53: 25–33.

Breuer, Josef and Sigmund Freud 1957 *Studies on Hysteria*. Translated from the German and edited by James Strachy, in collaboration with Anna Freud. New York: Basic Books Inc. [Original, 1895].

Brewis, Keilo A. 1992 Self as the Mirror of the Cosmos: A Timogun Perspective. Paper presented at the Borneo Research Council Second Biennial International Conference, Kota Kinabalu, Sabah, Malaysia, July 13–17.

Buckingham, B. H., George C. Foulk, and Walter McLean 1883 *Observations upon the Korean Coast, Japanese-Korean Ports, and Siberia, Made during a Journey from The Asiatic Stations To The United States through Siberia and Europe, June 3 to September 8, 1882*. Office of Naval Intelligence, Navy Department. Washington: Government Printing Office.

Burg, C. L. van der 1887 *De Geneesheer in Nederlandsch-Indie* ii: 119.

1895 Uber das sogenannt latah. *Allgemeine Zeitschrift für Psychiatrie und psychisch-gerichtliche Medicin* 51: 939–948.

Carluccio, Charles, John A. Sours, and Lawrence C. Kolb 1964 Psychodynamics of Echo-Reactions. *Archives of General Psychiatry* 10: 623–629.

Castellani, Aldo and A. J. Chalmers 1919 *Manual of Tropical Medicine*, 3rd edn. London: Bailliere, Tindall and Cox.

Caudill, W. and Tsung-Yi Lin 1969 *Mental Health Research in Asia and The Pacific*. Honolulu: East–West Center Press.

Chapel, James L. 1970 Latah, Myriachit, and Jumpers Revisited. *New York State Journal of Medicine* September 1: 2201–2204.

Chiu, T. L., J. E. Tong, and K. E. Schmidt 1972 A clinical and survey study of latah in Sarawak, Malaysia. *Psychological Medicine* 2: 155–165.

Christian, H. A. 1944 *Osler's Principles and Practice of Medicine*, 15th edn. New York.

Clifford, Hugh 1898 Some Notes and Theories Concerning Latah. In *Studies in Brown Humanity*. Edited by Hugh Clifford, pp. 186–201. London: Grant Richards.

Collinder, Bjorn 1949 *The Lapps*. Princeton: Princeton University Press.

Connor, Linda 1982 The Unbounded Self: Balinese Therapy in Theory and Practice. In *Cultural Conceptions of Mental Health and Therapy*. Edited by A. J. Marsella and G. M. White, pp. 251–267. Boston: D. Reidel.

Cuisinier, Jeanne 1936 *Danses magiques de Kelantan*. Travaux et Mémoire de l'Institut d'Ethnologie, Paris: *Université de Paris*, XXII.

Czaplicka, M. A. 1969 *Aboriginal Siberia: A Study in Social Anthropology*. Oxford: The Clarendon Press. [Original, 1914].

Darwin, Charles 1845 *Naturalist's Voyage Around the World*. New York: Appleton and Company. [Original, 1839].

Davison, Julian and Vinson H. Sutlive 1991 The Children of *Nising*: Images of Headhunting and Male Sexuality in Iban Ritual and Oral Literature. In *Female and Male in Borneo: Contributions and Challenges to Gender Studies*. Edited by Vinson H. Sutlive, pp. 153–230. Borneo Research Council Monograph Series, Vol. 1.

Dentan, R. K. 1968 Semai Response to Mental Aberration. *Bijdragen tot de Taal-,*

Land- en Volkenkunde 124: 135–158.

Doolittle, Amity Appell 1991 *Latah* Behavior by Females Among the Rungus of Sabah. In *Female And Male in Borneo*. Edited by Vinson H. Sutlive, pp. 121–152. Borneo Research Council Monograph Series, Vol. 1.

Douglas, Mary 1968 The Social Control of Cognition: Some Factors in Joke Perception. *Man* (New Series) 3(2): 361–376.

   1975 *Implicit Meanings: Essays in Anthropology*. London: Routledge and Kegan Paul.

Drush, Jacques 1984 Latah: Un Probléme Ethnopsychiatrique. *Perspectives Psychiatriques* 5(99): 430–439.

Ekman, Paul, Wallace V. Friesen, and Ronald Simons 1985 Is the Startle Reaction an Emotion? *Journal of Personality and Social Psychology* 49(5): 1416–1426.

Ellis, W. Gilmore 1897 Latah. A Mental Malady of the Malays. *The Journal of Mental Science* 43(180): 32–40.

Endicott, Kirk Michael 1970 *An Analysis of Malay Magic*. Oxford: Clarendon Press.

Favre, L'Abbé P. 1875 *Dictionnaire Malais–Français*. (2 vols.) Paris: Vienne.

Firth, Sir Raymond 1967 Ritual and Drama in Malay Spirit Mediumship. *Comparative Studies in Society and History* 9(2): 190–207.

   1974 Faith and Skepticism in Kelantan Village Magic. In *Kelantan: Essays in Religion, Society and Politics in a Malay State*. Edited by William Roff, pp. 190–224. Kuala Lumpur: Oxford University Press.

Fitzgerald, R. D. 1923 A Thesis on Two Tropical Neuroses (Amok and Latah) Peculiar to Malaya. *Transactions of the Fifth Congress of the Far-Eastern Association of Tropical Medicine* 148–161. Singapore.

Fletcher, W. 1908 Latah and Crime. *The Lancet* 2: 254–255.

   1938 Latah and Amok. *British Encyclopaedia of Medical Practice* VII: 641–650. London: Butterworth.

Forbes, H. O. 1885 *A Naturalist's Wanderings in the Eastern Archipelago*. New York: Harper and Brothers.

Foster, George M. and Barbara Gallatin Anderson 1978 *Medical Anthropology*. New York: Alfred A. Knopf.

Foulks, Edward F. 1972 *The Arctic Hysterias of the North Alaskan Eskimo*. Anthropological Studies of the American Anthropological Association No. 10.

Freeman, Derek 1967 Shaman and Incubus. *The Psychoanalytic Study of Society* 4: 315–343.

   1968 Thunder, Blood and the Nicknaming of God's Creatures. *The Psychoanalytical Quarterly* 37: 353–399.

   1970 *Report on the Iban*. London: The Athlone Press. [Original, 1955].

   1981 *Some Reflections on Iban Society*. An Occasional Paper of the Department of Anthropology, Research School of Pacific Studies, The Australian National University, Canberra.

Friedhoff, A. J. and T. N. Chase (eds.) 1982 *Gilles de la Tourette Syndrome*. New York: Raven Press.

Friedmann, C. T. H. and R. A. Faguet 1982 *Extraordinary Disorders of Human Behavior*. New York: Plenum Press.

Gajdusek, D. Carleton 1970 Physiological and Psychological Characteristics of

Stone Age Man. *Engineering and Science* 33: 26–33, 56–62.

Galloway, D. J. 1913 Latah. In *Noctes Orientales: Being a Selection of Essays Read Before the Straits Philosophical Society Between the Years 1893 and 1910*, pp. 115–126. Singapore: Kelly and Walsh Ltd.

1922 A Contribution to the Study of "Latah." *Journal of the Straits Branch of the Royal Asiatic Society* 85: 140–150.

Geertz, Clifford 1960 *The Religion of Java*. Glencoe: The Free Press.

1973 Deep Play: Notes on the Balinese Cockfight. In *The Interpretation of Cultures*, pp. 412–453. New York: Basic Books. [Original, 1960].

Geertz, Hildred 1959 The Vocabulary of Emotion: A Study of Javanese Socialization Processes. *Psychiatry* 22(3): 225–237.

1961 *The Javanese Family: A Study of Kinship and Emotion*. New York: The Free Press of Glencoe, Inc.

1968 Latah in Java: a Theoretical Paradox. *Indonesia* 5: 93–104.

Gerrard, P. N. 1904 Hypnotism and Latah. *Dublin Journal of Medical Science* 118: 13–17.

Gilmour, Andrew 1902 "Latah" Among South African Natives. *Scottish Medical Journal* 10: 18–19.

Gimlette, John D. 1897 Remarks on the Etiology, Symptoms and Treatment of Latah, With a Report of Two Cases. *The British Medical Journal* August 21: 455–457.

1939 *A Dictionary of Malayan Medicine*. Edited and Completed by H. W. Thomson. London: Oxford University Press.

1971 *Malay Poisons and Charm Cures*. Singapore: Oxford University Press. [Original, 1915].

Goetz, C. G. and H. L. Klawans 1982 Gilles de la Tourette on Tourette Syndrome. In *Gilles de la Tourette Syndrome*. Edited by A. J. Friedhoff and T. N. Chase, pp. 1–16. New York: Raven Press.

Gomes, The Reverend Edwin H. 1917 *The Sea Dayaks of Borneo*, 3rd edn. London: Society for the Propagation of the Gospel in Foreign Parts.

Gonda, J. 1973 *Sanskrit in Indonesia*, 2nd edn. New Delhi: International Academy of Indian Culture.

Gullick, John 1987 *Malay Society in the Nineteenth Century: The Beginnings of Change*. Singapore: Oxford University Press.

Hahn, Robert A. 1985 Culture-Bound Syndromes Unbound. *Social Science and Medicine* 21(2): 165–171.

Hammond, William A. 1884 Miryachit, A Newly Described Disease of the Nervous System. *New York Medical Journal* 39(Feb. 16): 191–192.

Harrison, Tom 1970 *The Malays of South-West Sarawak before Malaysia: A Socio-Ecological Survey*. East Lansing: Michigan State University Press.

Heider, Karl G. 1991 *Landscapes of Emotion: Mapping Three Cultures of Emotion in Indonesia*. Cambridge: Cambridge University Press.

Helman, Cecil G. 1990 *Culture, Health and Illness*, 2nd edn. London: Wright.

Heppell, Michael 1975 Iban Social Control: The Infant and the Adult. Unpublished Ph.D. thesis, Australian National University.

Hill, Robert F. and J. Dennis Fortenberry 1992 Adolescence as a Culture-Bound Syndrome. *Social Science and Medicine* 35(1): 73–80.

Honigman, John 1967 *Personality in Culture*. New York: Harper and Row,

Publishers.

Hose, Charles and William McDougall 1912 *The Pagan Tribes of Borneo*, Volume I. London: Frank Cass and Co. Ltd.

Howell, William 1963a Dayak Marriage Ceremonies. In *The Sea Dayaks and Other Races of Sarawak*. Edited by Anthony Richards, pp. 48–50. Kuching: Borneo Literature Bureau. [Original, 1908].

1963b Pregnancy and Childbirth (Restrictions). In *The Sea Dayaks and Other Races of Sarawak*. Edited by Anthony Richards, pp. 50–56. Kuching: Borneo Literature Bureau. [Original, 1910].

Hufford, David J. 1982 *The Terror that Comes in the Night: An Experience-Centered Study of Supernatural Assault Traditions*. Philadelphia: The University of Pennsylvania Press.

Hughes, Charles C. 1985a Culture-Bound or Construct-Bound? The Syndromes and DSM-III. In *The Culture Bound Syndromes*. Edited by R. Simons and C. Hughes, pp. 3–24. Dordrecht: D. Reidel.

1885b Glossary of "Culture-Bound" or Psychiatric Syndromes. In *The Culture Bound Syndromes*. Edited by R. Simons and C. Hughes, pp. 475–505. Dordrecht: D. Reidel.

Inden, Ronald 1990 *Imagining India*. Oxford: Basil Blackwell Ltd.

Infurna, Guiseppe 1928 Un Piccolo Focolo di *Latah* in Eritrea. *Archivio Italiano di Scienzi Medichi Coloniali* 9: 560–562.

Jay, Robert R. 1969 *Javanese Villagers: Social Relations in Rural Modjokuto*. Cambridge: The MIT Press.

Jenner, J. A. 1990 Latah as Coping: A Case Study Offering a New Paradox to Solve the Old One. *The International Journal of Social Psychiatry* 36(3): 194–199.

Jensen, Erik. 1974 *The Iban and Their Religion*. Oxford: Clarendon Press.

Jilek, Wolfgang G. and Louise Jilek Aall 1985 The Metamorphosis of the "Culture-Bound" Syndromes. *Social Science and Medicine* 21(2): 205–210.

Jocalson, Waldemar 1908 *The Koryak*. Memoirs of The American Museum of Natural History, Vol. VI, part ii. New York.

1910 *The Yukaghir and the Yukaghirized Tungus*. Memoirs of The American Museum of Natural History, Vol. XIII, part i. New York.

Kapferer, Bruce 1983 *A Celebration of Demons: Exorcism and the Aesthetics of Healing in Sri Lanka*. Bloomington: Indiana University Press.

Karp, Ivan 1985 Deconstructing Culture-Bound Syndromes. *Social Science and Medicine* 21(2): 221–228.

Kedit, Peter 1987 Iban Bejalai. Unpublished Ph.D. thesis, Sydney University.

1991 "Meanwhile, Backhome . . .": *Bejalai* and Their Effects on Iban Men and Women. In *Female and Male in Borneo: Contributions and Challenges to Gender Studies*, Edited by Vinson H. Sutlive, pp. 295–316. Borneo Research Council Monograph Series, Vol. 1.

Kenny, Michael G. 1978 *Latah*: The Symbolism of a Putative Mental Disorder. *Culture, Medicine and Psychiatry* 2: 209–231.

1983 Paradox Lost: The Latah Problem Revisited. *The Journal of Nervous and Mental Disease* 171(3): 159–167.

1990 Latah, the Logic of Fear. In *The Emotions of Culture: A Malay Perspective*. Edited by Wazir Jahan Karim, pp. 123–141. Singapore: Oxford University Press.

Kessler, Clive S. 1977 Conflict and Sovereignty in Kelantanese Malay Spirit Seances. In *Case Studies in Spirit Possession*. Edited by Vincent Crapanzano and Vivian Garrison, pp. 295–331. New York: John Wiley and Sons.

Kluckhohn, Clyde, Henry A. Murray, and David M. Schneider (eds.) 1953 *Personality in Nature, Society and Culture*. New York: Alfred A. Knopf.

Kraeplin, E. 1919 *Dementia Praecox and the Paraphrenias*. Edinburgh: Livingston.

Kumasaka, Y. 1964 A Culturally-determined Mental Reaction Among the Ainu. *Psychiatric Quarterly* 38: 733–739.

Kunkle, Charles E. 1967 The "Jumpers" of Maine: A Reappraisal. *Archives of Internal Medicine* 119: 355–358.

Laderman, Carol 1983 *Wives and Midwives: Childbirth and Nutrition in Rural Malaysia*. Berkeley: University of California Press.

1991 *Taming the Wind of Desire: Psychology, Medicine and Aesthetics in Malay Shamanistic Performance*. Berkeley: University of California Press.

Landis, Carney and William A. Hunt 1939 *The Startle Pattern*. New York: Farrar and Rinehart Inc.

Landy, David (ed.) 1977 *Culture, Disease and Healing: Studies in Medical Anthropology*. New York: Macmillan.

Langen, C. D. de and A. Lichtenstein 1936 *A Clinical Textbook of Tropical Medicine*. Batavia: G. Kolff & Company.

Leach, E. R. 1950 *Social Science Research in Sarawak*. London: His Majesty's Stationery Office.

Lebar, Frank M. (editor and compiler) 1972 *Ethnic Groups of Insular Southeast Asia*, Vol. I: Indonesia, Andaman Islands, and Madagascar. New Haven: Human Relations Area Files Press.

Lebra, W. P. 1976 *Culture-Bound Syndromes, Ethnopsychiatry and Alternate Therapies*. Mental Health Research in Asia and the Pacific, Vol. 4. Honolulu: The University Press of Hawaii.

Lee, Raymond L. M. 1981 Structure and Anti-Structure in the Culture-Bound Syndromes: The Malay Case. *Culture, Medicine and Psychiatry* 5: 233–248.

Lee, Raymond L. M. and Susan Ackerman 1978 Mass Hysteria and Spirit Possession in Urban Malaysia: A Case Study. *Journal of Sociology and Psychology* 1: 24–34.

1980 The Sociocultural Dynamics of Mass Hysteria: A Case Study of Social Conflict in West Malaysia. *Psychiatry* 43: 78–88.

Leent, F. J. van 1867 Contributions à la géographie médicale. *Archives de Médecine Navale* 8: 172–173.

1868 *Geneeskundig-topographische opmerkingen betroffenden Batavia, hare neede en het eiland Onnust*. The Hague.

Lévi-Strauss, Claude 1969 *The Elementary Structures of Kinship*. London: Eyre and Spottiswoode.

Levine, Robert A. 1973 *Culture, Behavior and Personality*. Chicago: Aldine Publishing Co.

Lewis, I. M. 1986 *Religion in Context: Cults and Charisma*. Cambridge: Cambridge University Press.

1989 *Ecstatic Religion: A Study of Shamanism and Spirit Possession*, 2nd edn. London: Routledge.

1990 Forward. In *Emotions of Culture: A Malay Perspective*. Edited by Wazir

Jahan Karim, pp. v–vi. Singapore: Oxford University Press.

Lex, Barbara 1979 The Neurobiology of Ritual Trance. In *The Spectrum of Ritual: A Biogenetic Structural Analysis*. Edited by Eugene G. d'Aquili, Charles D. Laughlin, Jr., and John McManus, pp. 117–151. New York: Columbia University Press.

Linton, Ralph 1956 *Culture and Mental Disorders*. Springfield: Charles Thomas.

Littlewood, Roland and Maurice Lipsedge 1985 Culture-Bound Syndromes. In *Recent Advances in Psychiatry – 5*. Edited by K. Granville-Grossman, pp. 105–142. Edinburgh: Churchill-Livingstone.

1987 The Butterfly and the Serpent: Culture, Psychopathology and Biomedicine. *Culture, Medicine and Psychiatry* 11: 289–335.

Lock, Margaret 1992 The Fragile Japanese Family: Narratives about Individualism and the Postmodern State. In *Paths to Asian Medical Knowledge*. Edited by Charles Leslie and Allan Young, pp. 98–125. Berkeley: University of California Press.

Logan, J. R. 1849 Five Days in Naning. *Journal of the Indian Archipelago and Eastern Asia* 3: 24–41.

Loon, F. G. H. van 1924 Latah, a Psycho-neurosis of the Malay Races. *Mededeelingen van den Burgerlijken Geneeskundigen Dienst in Nederlandsch-Indië* 305–320.

1927 Amok and Lattah. *Journal of Abnormal and Social Psychology* 21(4): 434–444.

Low, Hugh 1848 *Sarawak; Its Inhabitants and Productions: Being Notes During a Residence in That Country with His Excellency Mr. Brooke*. London: Richard Bently.

Ludwig, Arnold M. 1966 Altered States of Consciousness. *Archives of General Psychiatry* 15: 225–234.

McElroy, Ann and Patricia Townsend 1989 *Medical Anthropology in Ecological Perspective*, 2nd edn. Boulder: Westview Press.

Maier, Hendrik M. J. 1988 *In the Center of Authority: The Malay Hikayat Merong Mahawangsa*. Studies on Southeast Asia, Southeast Asia Program, Cornell University, Ithaca.

Mandell, Arnold J. 1980 Toward a Psychobiology of Transcendence: God in the Brain. In *The Psychobiology of Consciousness*. Edited by Julian M. Davidson and Richard J. Davidson, pp. 379–464. New York: Plenum Press.

Manson, Patrick 1910 Latah. In *A System of Medicine*, Vol. II, part ii. Edited by C. Allbutt and H. D. Rolleston, pp. 767–771. London: MacMillan and Co., Ltd.

1950 *Manson's Tropical Diseases*, 13th edn. Phillip H. Manson-Bahr (ed.). Baltimore: Williams and Wilkins.

Marano, Lou 1982 *Windigo* Psychosis: The Anatomy of an Etic–Emic Confusion. *Current Anthropology* 23: 385–412.

Marsden, W. 1783 *The History of Sumatra*. London: Thomas Payne and Son.

1984 *A Dictionary and Grammar of the Malayan Language*. (2 vols.) Kuala Lumpur: Oxford University Press. [Original, 1812].

Mashman, Valerie 1991 Warriors and Weavers: A Study of Gender Relations Among the Ibanic People. In *Female and Male in Borneo: Contributions and Challenges to Gender Studies*. Edited by Vinson H. Sutlive, pp. 231–270. Borneo Research Council Monograph Series, Vol. 1.

Maxwell, Allen R. 1990 Ethnographic and linguistic notes on *Gigiran* (*Latah*), the Kadayan hyperstartle reaction. *The Sarawak Museum Journal* 41(62)[New Series]: 9–19.

Mead, Margaret and F. C. MacGregor 1951 *Growth and Culture: A Photographic Study of Balinese Childhood*. New York: Putnam.

Metcalf, Peter 1982 *A Borneo Journey into Death: Berawan Eschatology from its Rituals*. Philadelphia: University of Pennsylvania Press.

Meth, J. M. 1974 Latah. In *American Handbook of Psychiatry*, Vol. III. Edited by S. Arieti and E. B. Brody, pp. 727–729. New York: Basic Books.

Metzger, G. 1887 Sakit Latah. *Globus* 52: 381–383.

Moore, Lorna G., Peter van Arsdale, Jo Ann E. Glittenberg, and Robert A. Aldrich 1980 *The Biocultural Basis of Health: Expanding Views of Medical Anthropology*. Prospect Heights: Waveland Press, Inc.

Munro, Neil Gordon 1963 *Ainu Creed and Cult*. New York: Columbia University Press.

Murphy, H. B. M. 1972 History and the Evolution of Syndromes: The Striking Case of *Latah* and *Amok*. In *Psychopathology: Contributions from the Social, Behavioral, and Biological Sciences*. Edited by M. Hammer, K. Salzinger, and S. Sutton, pp. 33–55. New York: John Wiley and Sons.

1976 Notes for a Theory on *Latah*. In *Culture-Bound Syndromes, Ethnopsychiatry, and Alternate Therapies*. Edited by William P. Lebra, pp. 3–21. Honolulu: The University Press of Hawaii.

1982 *Comparative Psychiatry: The International and Intercultural Distribution of Mental Illness*. Berlin: Springer-Verlag.

1983 Commentary on "The Resolution of the Latah Paradox." *The Journal of Nervous and Mental Disease* 171(3): 176–177.

Musgrave, W. E. and A. G. Sison 1910 Mali-Mali, A Mimic Psychosis in the Philippine Islands. A Preliminary Report. *Philippine Journal of Science*, Section B, Medical Science 5: 335–339.

Natoli, Angelo 1937 Casi di "Lâtah" riscontrati fra indigeni a Bengasi. *Giornale Italiano Di Clinia Tropicale* 1(New Series): 20–24.

Neale, R. 1884 Miryachit or Lata. *The British Medical Journal* 1: 884.

O'Brien, H. A. 1883 Latah. *Journal of the Straits Branch of the Royal Asiatic Society* 11: 143–153.

1884 Latah. *Journal of the Straits Branch of the Royal Asiatic Society* 12: 283–284.

Ohnuki-Tierney, Emiko 1985 Shamans and *Imu*: Among Two Ainu Groups. In *The Culture Bound Syndromes*. Edited by Ronald Simons and Charles Hughes, pp. 91–110. Dordrecht: D. Reidel Publishing Company.

Ong, Aihwa 1987 *Spirits of Resistance and Capitalist Discipline: Factory Women in Malaysia*. Albany: State University of New York Press.

Opler, Marvin K. 1967 *Culture and Social Psychiatry*. New York: Atherton Press.

Ornstein, Robert E. 1977 *The Psychology of Consciousness*, 2nd edn. San Diego: Harcourt Brace Jovanovich.

Osler, William 1944 *The Principles and Practice of Medicine*, 15th edn. revised by H. A. Christian. New York.

Oxley, T. 1849 Malay Amoks. *Journal of the Indian Archipelago* 3: 532–533.

Peacock, James 1968 *Rites of Modernization: Symbolic and Social Aspects of Indonesian Proletarian Drama*. Chicago: The University of Chicago Press.

1978 *Muslim Puritans: Reformist Psychology in Southeast Asian Islam.* Berkeley: University of California Press.

Penso, Guiseppi 1934 Il "latah" nella Somalia Italiana. *Archivio Italiano di Scienze Mediche Coloniali* 15: 364–367.

Pfeiffer, W. 1968 New Research Findings Regarding Latah. *Transcultural Psychiatric Research* 5: 34–38.

1971 *Transkulturelle Psychiatrie: Ergebnisse und Probleme.* Stuttgart: George Thieme Verlag.

1982 Culture-Bound Syndromes. In *Culture and Psychopathology.* Edited by Ihsan Al-Issa, pp. 201–218. Baltimore: University Park Press.

Price, F. W. 1941 *Text-book of the Practice of Medicine, 6th edn.* London: Oxford University Press.

Prince, Raymond and Françoise Tcheng-Laroche 1987 Culture-Bound Syndromes and International Disease Classifications. *Culture, Medicine and Psychiatry* 11: 3–19.

Pringle, Robert. 1970 *Rajahs and Rebels: The Ibans of Sarawak under Brooke Rule, 1841–1941.* Ithaca: Cornell University Press.

Provencher, Ronald 1990 Covering Malay Humor Magazines: Satire and Parody of Malaysian Political Dilemmas. *Crossroads* 5(2): 1–25.

Provencher, Ronald and Jaafar Omar 1988 Malay Humor Magazines as a Resource for the Study of Modern Malay Culture. *Sari* 6: 87–99.

Rabinovitch, Reuben 1965 An Exaggerated Startle Reflex Resembling a Kicking Horse. *Canadian Medical Association Journal* 93(July 17): 130.

Radcliffe-Brown, A. R. 1977 *The Social Anthropology of Radcliffe-Brown.* Edited by Adam Kuper. London: Routledge and Kegan Paul Ltd.

Raffles, T. S. 1817 *The History of Java.* (2 vols.) London: Black, Parbury and Allen.

Rathbone, A. B. 1898 *Camping and Tramping in Malaya: Fifteen Years' Pioneering in the States of the Malay Peninsula.* London: Swan Sonnenschein and Co. Ltd.

Razha Rashid 1990 Martial Arts and the Malay Superman. In *Emotions of Culture: A Malay Perspective.* Edited by Wazir Jahan Karim, pp. 64–95. Singapore: Oxford University Press.

Repond, A. 1940 Le Lattah: une psycho-névrose exotique. *Annales Medico-Psychologiques* 98(4): 311–324.

Richards, Anthony 1963 *The Sea Dayaks and Other Races of Sarawak.* Kuching: Borneo Literature Bureau. [Original, 1909].

1988 *An Iban–English Dictionary.* Petaling Jaya: Oxford University Press.

Ridley, H. N. 1913 Latah. In *Noctes Orientales: Being a Selection of Essays Read Before the Straits Philosophical Society Between the Years 1893 and 1910,* 126–130. Singapore: Kelly and Walsh, Ltd. [Original, 1897].

Ritenbaugh, C. 1982 Obesity as a Culture-Bound Syndrome. *Culture, Medicine and Psychiatry* 6: 347–361.

Rousseau, Jérôme 1990 *Central Borneo: Ethnic Identity and Social Life in a Stratified Society.* Oxford: Clarendon Press.

Rubel, Arthur J., Carl W. O'Nell, and Rolando Collado-Ardón 1984 *Susto, a Folk Illness.* Berkeley: University of California Press.

St. John, Spenser 1862 *Life in the Forests of the Far East.* (2 vols.) London: Smith, Elder and Company.

Sandin, Benedict 1968 *The Sea Dayaks of Borneo.* East Lansing: Michigan State

University Press.

Sanib Said. 1985 *Malay Politics in Sarawak 1946–1966: The Search for Unity and Political Ascendancy.* Singapore: Oxford University Press.

Sarnelli, Tommaso 1934 Primi Casi di "Lâtah" Osservati nell'alto Yemen (Arabia S. O.). *Archivio Italiano di Scienze Mediche Coloniali* 15: 750–759.

Sather, Clifford 1978 The Malevolent *Koklir. Bijdragen tot de Taal-, Land- en Volkenkunde* 134: 310–355.

Scheube, B. 1903 The Latah Disease. In *The Diseases of Warm Countries: A Handbook for Medical Men.* Translated from the German by Pauline Falcke, pp. 514–515. London: John Bale and Sons and Danielson, Ltd.

Schneider, Daniel E. 1938 The Clinical Syndromes of Echolalia, Echopraxia, Grasping and Sucking: Their Significance in the Disorganization of the Personality. *The Journal of Nervous and Mental Disease* 88: 18–35, 200–216.

Schwartz, Theodore 1976 The Cargo Cult: A Melanesian Type-Response to Change. In *Responses to Change: Society, Culture and Personality.* Edited by George A. DeVos, pp. 157–206. New York: D. Van Nostrand and Company.

Setyonegoro, R. Kusumanto 1971 Latah in Java. *Proceedings of the World Federation for Mental Health Workshop: Mental Health Trends in Developing Society.* Edited by P. M. Yap and P. W. Ngui, pp. 91–95. Singapore.

Shapiro, Arthur K. and Elaine Shapiro 1982 Tourette Syndrome: History and Present Status. In *Gilles de la Tourette Syndrome.* Edited by Arnold J. Friedhoff and Thomas N. Chase, pp. 17–23. New York: Raven Press.

Shirokogoroff, S. M. 1935 *The Psychomental Complex of the Tungus.* London: Kegan Paul, Trench, Trubner and Company Ltd.

Siegel, James 1986 *Solo in the New Order: Language and Hierarchy in an Indonesian City.* Princeton: Princeton University Press.

Simons, Ronald C. 1980 The Resolution of the Latah Paradox. *The Journal of Nervous and Mental Disease* 168(4): 195–206.

1983a Latah II – Problems with a Purely Symbolic Interpretation. *The Journal of Nervous and Mental Disease* 171(3): 168–175.

1983b Latah III – How Compelling Is The Evidence for a Psychoanalytic Interpretation? *The Journal of Nervous and Mental Disease* 171(3): 178–181.

1983c Latah: A Culture-specific Elaboration of the Startle Reflex. (Film) Bloomington: Indiana University Audiovisual Center.

1987 A Feasible and Timely Enterprise: Commentary on "Culture-Bound Syndromes and International Disease Classifications" by Raymond Prince and Françoise Tcheng-Laroche. *Culture, Medicine and Psychiatry* 11: 21–28.

Simons, R. C. and C. C. Hughes 1985 *The Culture-Bound Syndromes: Folk Illnesses of Psychiatric and Anthropological Interest.* Dordrecht: D. Reidel Publishing Company.

Skeat, Walter William 1966 *Malay Magic: An Introduction to the Folklore and Popular Religion of the Malay Peninsula.* New York: Barnes and Noble. [Original, 1900].

Stevens, Harold 1964 Jumping Frenchmen of Maine. *Transactions of the American Neurological Association* 89: 65–67.

1965 Jumping Frenchmen of Maine (*Myriachit*). *Archives of Neurology* 12: 311–314.

Still, R. M. Lloyd 1940 Remarks on the Aetiology and Symptoms of *Young-Dah-*

Hte with a Report on Four Cases and Its Medico-Legal Significance. *The Indian Medical Gazette* Feb.: 88–91.

Strange, Heather 1987 Rural Malay Aged in Contrasting Developmental Contexts. In *Aging and Cultural Diversity: New Directions and Annotated Bibliography.* Edited by Heather Strange and Michele Teitelbaum, pp. 14–38. Massachusetts: Bergin and Garvey Publishers, Inc.

Strong, Richard P. 1944 *Stitt's Diagnosis, Prevention and Treatment of Tropical Diseases,* 7th edn. Philadelphia: The Blakiston Company.

Sutlive, Vinson H. 1978 *The Iban of Sarawak.* Arlington Heights: AHM Publishing Corporation.

1991a (ed.) *Female and Male in Borneo: Contributions and Challenges to Gender Studies.* Borneo Research Council Monograph Series, Vol. I.

1991b Keling and Kumang in Town: Urban Migration and Differential Effects on Iban Women and Men. In *Female and Male in Borneo: Contributions and Challenges to Gender Studies.* Edited by Vinson H. Sutlive, pp. 489–515. Borneo Research Council Monograph Series, Vol. I.

Suwanalert, Sangun 1972 Psychiatric Study of Bahtsche (Latah). *Journal of the Psychiatric Association of Thailand* 17: 380–398.

1984 A Study of Latah in Thailand. Paper presented at the Third Pacific Congress of Psychiatry, Seoul, Korea.

Sweeney, Amin 1987 *A Full Hearing: Orality and Literacy in the Malay World.* Berkeley: The University of California Press

Swettenham, F. A. 1900 Lâtah. In *Malay Sketches.* Edited by Frank Swettenham, pp. 64–82. London: John Lane. [Original, 1896].

Tan, E. S. 1963 Epidemic Hysteria. *The Medical Journal of Malaya* 18(2): 72–76.

Teoh, Jin-Inn and Eng-Seong Tan 1976 An Outbreak of Epidemic Hysteria in West Malaysia. In *Culture-Bound Syndromes, Ethnopsychiatry and Alternate Therapies.* Edited by William Lebra, pp. 32–43. Honolulu: The University Press of Hawaii.

Thomson, J. T. 1984 *Glimpses into Life in Malayan Lands.* Singapore: Oxford University Press. [Original, 1864].

Thorne, Frederick C. 1944 Startle Neurosis. *American Journal of Psychiatry* 101: 105–109.

Tourette, Gilles de la 1884 Jumping, Latah, Myriachit. *Archives de Neurologie* 8: 68–74.

1885 Étude sur une affection nerveuse caracterisée par de l'incoordination motrice accompagnée de echolalie et de copralalie. *Archives de Neurologie* 9: 19–42.

Uchibori, Motomitsu 1984 Transformations of Iban Social Consciousness. In *History and Peasant Consciousness in South East Asia.* Edited by A. Turton and S. Tanabe, pp. 211–234. Senri Ethnological Studies no. 13, National Museum of Ethnology, Osaka.

Uchimura, Y. 1935 "Imu": A Malady of the Ainu. *The Lancet* (June 1): 1272–1273.

Wallace, Alfred Russel 1962 *The Malay Archipelago: The Land of the Orang-Utan and the Bird of Paradise.* New York: Dover Publications Inc. [Original, 1869].

Wallace, Anthony 1970 *Culture and Personality,* 2nd edn. New York: Random House.

Wazir Jahan Karim 1984 Malay Midwives and Witches. *Social Science and*

Medicine 18(2): 159–166.
1990 Prelude to Madness: The Language of Emotion in Courtship and Early Marriage. In *Emotions of Culture: A Malay Perspective*. Edited by Wazir Jahan Karim, pp. 21–63. Singapore: Oxford University Press.
Wikan, Unni 1989 Illness From Fright or Soul Loss: A North Balinese Culture-Bound Syndrome? *Culture Medicine and Psychiatry* 13: 25–50.
1990 *Managing Turbulent Hearts: A Balinese Formula for Living*. Chicago: University of Chicago Press.
Wilkinson, R. J. 1902 *A Malay English Dictionary*, Part II. Singapore: Kelly and Walsh.
1910 Malay Amusements. (Life and Customs, Part III), *Papers on Malay Subjects*. Edited by R. J. Wilkinson. Kuala Lumpur: F.M.S. Government Printer.
Winairz, W. and J. Wielawski 1936 Imu – a Psychoneurosis Occurring Among Ainus. *The Psychoanalytic Review* 23: 181–186.
Winkelman, Michael 1986 Trance States: A Theoretical Model and Cross-Cultural Analysis. *Ethos* 14(2): 174–203.
Winstedt, Sir Richard 1969 *Start From Alif: Count From One: An Autobiographical Mémoire*. Kuala Lumpur: Oxford University Press.
Winzeler, Robert L. 1984 The Study of Malayan Latah. *Indonesia* 37: 77–104.
1985 *Ethnic Relations in Kelantan: A Study of the Chinese and Thai as Ethnic Minorities in a Malay State*. Singapore: Oxford University Press.
1990a Amok: Historical, Psychological and Cultural Perspectives. In *Emotions of Culture: A Malay Perspective*. Edited by Wazir Jahan Karim, pp. 96–122. Singapore: Oxford University Press.
1990b Report on *latah* in central and southwestern Sarawak. *The Sarawak Museum Journal* 41 (62)[New Series]: 1–8.
1990c Malayan *Amok* and *Latah* as "History Bound" Syndromes. In *The Underside of Malaysian History: Pullers, Prostitutes, Plantation Workers....* Edited by Peter J. Rimmer and Lisa M. Allen, pp. 214–229. Singapore: Singapore University Press.
1991 *Latah* in Sarawak, with Special Reference to the Iban. In *Female and Male in Borneo: Contributions and Challenges to Gender Studies*. Edited by Vinson H. Sutlive, pp. 317–333. Borneo Research Council Monograph Series, Vol. I.
1993a *The Seen and the Unseen: Shamanism, Mediumship and Possession in Borneo*. Borneo Research Council Monograph Series, Vol. II.
1993b Shaman, Priest and Spirit Medium: Religious Specialists, Tradition and Innovation in Borneo. In *The Seen and the Unseen: Shamanism, Mediumship and Possession in Borneo*. Edited by Robert L. Winzeler, pp. ix–xxxi. Borneo Research Council Monograph Series, Vol. II.
Wulfften Palthe, P. M. van 1933 Psychiatry and Neurology in the Tropics. *The Malayan Medical Journal* 8: 133–139.
1936 Psychiatry and Neurology in the Tropics. In *A Clinical Textbook of Tropical Medicine*. Edited by C. D. de Langen and A. Lichtenstein, pp. 525–538. Batavia: G. Kolff & Company.
Yap, P. M. 1952 The Latah Reaction: Its Pathodynamics and Nosological Position: *The Journal of Mental Science* 98: 515–564.
1960 The Possession Syndrome: A Comparison of Hong Kong and French

findings. *The Journal of Mental Science* 106: 114–137.

1966 The Culture-bound Reactive Syndromes. In *Mental Health Research in Asia and The Pacific*. Edited by William Caudill and Tsung-Yi Lin, pp. 35–53. Honolulu: East-West Center Press.

1967 Classification of the Culture-bound Reactive Syndromes. *Australian and New Zealand Journal of Psychiatry* 1: 172–179.

1974 *Comparative Psychiatry: A Theoretical Framework*. Edited by M. P. Lau and A. B. Stokes. Toronto: University of Toronto Press.

Zoetmulder, P. J., with the collaboration of S. O. Robson 1982 *Old Javanese–English Dictionary*. 'S-Gravenhage: Martinus Nijhoff.

Index

Abraham, J. J., 18
Ackerman, Susan, 89
age, 16, 22, 38, 40, 58, 60–2, 67, 69–70, 71,
 72, 76, 77, 95, 97, 98–9, 101, 103, 111,
 118, 119
Alatas, Syed Hussain, 3
altered state of consciousness, 7, 85–6,
 89–90, 114, 129, 148n7
amok, 3, 5, 12, 15, 16, 24, 27
animals, fright by and latah, 70–1, 79, 81,
 115
 see also snakes
Arctic Hysteria, 34, 42, 44, 45
attention-capture latah, 77, 93, 141n5
automatic obedience, 3, 21, 40–1, 47, 49–50,
 77, 131

Bali, Balinese, and latah, 40, 86, 97–8,
 149n8
Basso, Keith, 95
Bateson, Gregory, 40, 76, 86, 98
Beard, J. M., 41, 43, 49, 143n7
bidan, see midwife
Bidayuh, 110, 112–3, 116–7, 118, 121,
 151–2n2
biomedicine and latah, 133
Borneo, xvi, 7–8, 21, 32, 40, 109–26
 see also Dayak, Iban, Sarawak
Brero, P. C. Z. van, 15, 31, 144n12
Brewer, Josef, 146n5
Burg, C. L. van der, 15
Burma, Burmese "latah," 33, 38–9, 140

Chinese, 4, 12, 19, 60–2, 69, 72, 74, 82, 96,
 101, 111, 117, 120, 126, 137, 146n2n4,
 153n2
Chiu, T. L., 110, 153n7, 154n8
class distinctions and latah
 in Java, 23–4
 in Kelantan, 63–4
 see also poor, rich
Clifford, Hugh, 1–2, 12–4, 18, 20, 29, 30,
 31, 81, 141n1, 144n11

clowns and latah, 99–101, 125, 139, 149n8
 see also shamanism
Collinder, B., 42–3
colonial
 discourse and latah, 3–4, 14–5, 18–9,
 20–1, 26, 30, 38, 47–9, 84, 90, 129, 134,
 148n6, 152n2
 domination and latah, 3–4, 48, 110, 120,
 121
 society and latah, 23, 30–1, 129
 see also European, Orientalism
Connor, Linda, 87
culture-bound syndrome, 2, 4, 5–7, 8, 41,
 132–5, 141n5, 142n1
Czaplicka, M. A., 44, 45

Darwin, Charles, 37–8, 132
Dayaks, latah among, 8, 110–120, 124, 136,
 137, 151–2n2n3, 153n2
 see also Borneo, Iban, Sarawak
Dentan, Robert K., 9, 143n6
disease, "latah" as, vii, 3, 13, 25, 32, 43,
 45–6, 131–4, 144n11n12n13, 145n16,
 154n2
 "infectious disease" as a model for the
 development of latah, 25–6, 32
dissociation, 85–91, 92, 118, 129–32
Doolittle, Amity Appell, 114, 152n5
dreams and latah, 19, 20–2, 30, 71–2,
 79–80, 142n4n5, 153n8
 Dayak, 115–8, 136, 138
 Iban, 121–2, 123–4

echokinesis, 50, 134
 see also echopraxia
echolalia, 15, 44, 50, 134, 143n6, 155n3n4
echopraxia, 15, 134, 155n3
Ellis, W. G., 14, 15–6, 20, 21–2, 30, 33, 68,
 141n1
Endicott, Kirk, 79
European
 accounts of latah, 11–8, 19–20, 22, 25–8,
 31, 133–4

169